INTENTION AND WRONGDOING

According to the principle of double effect, there is a strict moral constraint against bringing about serious harm to the innocent intentionally, but it is permissible in a wider range of circumstances to act in a way that brings about harm as a foreseen but nonintended side effect. This idea plays an important role in just war theory and international law, and in the twentieth century Elizabeth Anscombe and Philippa Foot invoked it as a way of resisting consequentialism. However, many moral philosophers now regard the principle with hostility or suspicion. Challenging the philosophical orthodoxy, Joshua Stuchlik defends the principle of double effect, situating it within a moral framework of human solidarity and responding to philosophical objections to it. His study uncovers links between ethics, philosophy of action, and moral psychology, and will be of interest to anyone seeking to understand the moral relevance of intention.

JOSHUA STUCHLIK is Associate Professor of Philosophy at the University of St. Thomas, Minnesota. He works on ethics, the philosophy of action, and epistemology, and has published articles in journals including *Philosophical Studies*, *Synthese*, and the *Journal of Moral Philosophy*.

INTENTION AND WRONGDOING

In Defense of Double Effect

JOSHUA STUCHLIK

University of St. Thomas

Shaftesbury Road, Cambridge CB2 8EA, United Kingdom

One Liberty Plaza, 20th Floor, New York, NY 10006, USA

477 Williamstown Road, Port Melbourne, VIC 3207, Australia

314–321, 3rd Floor, Plot 3, Splendor Forum, Jasola District Centre, New Delhi – 110025, India

103 Penang Road, #05–06/07, Visioncrest Commercial, Singapore 238467

Cambridge University Press is part of Cambridge University Press & Assessment, a department of the University of Cambridge.

We share the University's mission to contribute to society through the pursuit of education, learning and research at the highest international levels of excellence.

www.cambridge.org
Information on this title: www.cambridge.org/9781009015738

DOI: 10.1017/9781009034210

First published 2022
First paperback edition 2023

A catalogue record for this publication is available from the British Library

ISBN 978-1-316-51652-2 Hardback
ISBN 978-1-009-01573-8 Paperback

To Cara, Ethan, and Charlotte

Contents

Preface

The Principle of Double Effect (PDE) is an important and controversial ethical principle. It says that there is a strict constraint against bringing about serious harm to the innocent intentionally, either as an end or as a means, but it is sometimes morally permissible to bring about harm as a nonintended side effect. For example, many people believe that in fighting a just war, it is sometimes permissible to cause harm to noncombatants as a side effect of destroying military targets, though it is wrong deliberately to attack noncombatants in order to help procure victory. The PDE plays an important role in just war theory and international humanitarian law, and in the twentieth century, Elizabeth Anscombe and Philippa Foot invoked it as a way of resisting consequentialism. However, many moral philosophers regard the principle with hostility or suspicion. In the face of the emerging philosophical orthodoxy, this book aims to provide a comprehensive defense of the PDE. I situate the principle within a region of morality structured around the concept of human solidarity, and I respond to the major objections that have been raised to it.

Intention and Wrongdoing makes three contributions to the philosophical literature. First, it extends the recent revival of interest in Anscombe and Foot into an area where their contributions have not been thoroughly explored. Most of the recent work on Anscombe has focused on her seminal monograph, *Intention*. Yet, one of the main reasons Anscombe wanted to get clear about the notions of intention and intentional action was her belief that these concepts have a central place in normative ethics. And while Foot's theory of moral goodness as a form of natural goodness has been widely studied, her ideas about how specific nonconsequentialist features of commonsense morality should be ethically grounded have received less attention.

Second, the book illustrates the significance of the philosophy of action for normative ethics. I elucidate an Anscombian account of intentional action and practical reasoning, and I argue that this account can be used to respond to objections to the PDE, such as the complaint that it is difficult to see why an agent's intentions in acting should make a difference to the moral status of her bodily actions and the objection that the PDE requires deliberating agents to focus their attention on their own intentions rather than on features of their environment. I also argue that other objections to the PDE can be met by drawing on Robert Audi's notion of *conduct*, where an agent's conduct does not consist merely in her instantiating an act-type but is three-dimensional: it is an agent's *doing something* in a certain *manner* and for a certain *reason* (or set of reasons) or with a certain *intention* (or intentions).

Finally, my book makes a contribution to the growing literature at the intersection of philosophy and cognitive science. One of the leading theoretical frameworks of contemporary moral psychology is Joshua Greene's dual-process theory of moral judgment. Greene claims that moral psychology has implications for normative ethics; in particular, he believes that empirical findings cast suspicion on deontological moral philosophy. I argue, however, that my rationale for the PDE provides a way of overcoming Greene's deontological debunking argument in relation to the constraint against intentional harm.

Although this book makes use of technical concepts and distinctions, I have tried to present these in clear and accessible prose. My hope is that the book will be valuable not only to moral philosophers but also to just war theorists, bioethicists, scholars interested in the ethical foundations of domestic and international law, and moral psychologists.

Acknowledgments

I have been interested in the Principle of Double Effect for over a decade. This book has profited from many discussions about moral philosophy and action theory with friends and colleagues. I have benefited from conversations with Kieran Setiya, John McDowell, John Schwenkler, Patrick Lee, Jennifer Frey, Romemarie West, Christopher Toner, Peter Distelzweig, William Junker, Matthews Grant, Stephen Brock, Robert Audi, Paul Blashko, Nicholas Teh, Therese Scarpelli Cory, Daniel Sportiello, and David Solomon. My understanding of the circumstances surrounding the atomic bombings of Hiroshima and Nagasaki was enhanced by a conversation with Bill Miscamble. I received helpful feedback on material from Chapters 3 and 5 from audiences at presentations at the Seminaro Interuniversitario de Ciencia Cognitiva at the University of Seville (2014), the Rocky Mountain Ethics Congress at the University of Colorado–Boulder (2015), and the Mountain-Plains Philosophy Conference at the University of Colorado–Denver (2018), and from participants at a seminar presentation at the University of Notre Dame (2020). I also thank two referees from Cambridge University Press for their comments on the manuscript.

I wrote the majority of this book during the 2019–2020 academic year while on a fellowship at the Institute for Advanced Study at Notre Dame (NDIAS). I give my heartfelt thanks to the institute's director, Meghan Sullivan, former associate director Donald Stelluto, Events and Academic Support program manager Carolyn Sherman, and the other members of the NDIAS staff who, despite the onset of the global coronavirus pandemic in early 2020, made my time at Notre Dame not only academically fruitful but intellectually stimulating and joyful. I am also grateful to my home institution, the University of St. Thomas (MN), for a Distinguished Early Career Grant, which enabled me to complete this project.

My biggest debt of gratitude is to my family. To my parents, Mark and Roberta Stuchlik – thank you for your love, support, and encouragement over the years in my pursuit of a career in academic philosophy. Most importantly of all, to my wife, Cara – thank you for being my most precious friend and constant companion – and to our children, Ethan and Charlotte – thank you for the abundance of curiosity, joy, and exuberance you bring into our lives each day.

Introduction

In 1956, Oxford University offered an honorary degree to former US President Harry S. Truman. Elizabeth Anscombe, at the time a research fellow at Somerville College, organized a motion to deny Truman the degree on the ground that he had authorized the atomic bombings of Hiroshima and Nagasaki. The bombing of Hiroshima killed approximately 80,000 people, most of them civilians, and it wounded a similar number. In Nagasaki, the bomb killed about 45,000 people, again mainly civilians, and left a similar number wounded. In both cases, many of the injured died in the ensuing weeks and months due to the effects of radiation exposure (Miscamble 2011, 93–4). Anscombe's motion was decisively quashed. Indeed, it received only four votes: her own; that of her husband, Peter Geach; the vote of her friend, Philippa Foot; and that of Foot's husband (Solomon 2019, 226).

The following year Anscombe published a short pamphlet, *Mr. Truman's Degree*, in which she explains her objections to honoring President Truman. She argues that the atomic bombings were wrong on the ground that they were aimed at killing large numbers of civilians as a means to forcing the Japanese to surrender. Furthermore, she contends that the war could have been brought to a swift conclusion even without the use of atomic weapons. She claims that the United States knew the Japanese were desirous of negotiating peace and suggests that their leaders would have been willing to end the war on the condition that the Allies guarantee the retention of the Emperor. This was disregarded by the Allies, however, because of their fixation on the doctrine of "unconditional surrender" – that is, on the vague and sweeping terms of the Potsdam Declaration. In light of this, to award Truman an honorary degree is to "share in the guilt of a bad action by praise and flattery" (1981b, 70).

Recent historical scholarship casts doubt on some of Anscombe's claims. We now know that the military leaders who controlled the Japanese government were not on the verge of surrendering. They were rather preparing to fight a decisive battle for the homeland (*Ketsu-Go*), believing they could inflict so much punishment on the American invaders that they would lose heart and agree to more favorable peace terms (Frank 1999; Miscamble 2011). The US military knew that the Japanese had correctly surmised where American forces were planning to land on Kyushu and had moved massive numbers of troops to the island. Moreover, the United States was also aware that altering the terms of the Potsdam Declaration to include the retention of the Imperial institution would likely not lead to a quick end to the war. While it is true that the inner cabinet of the Japanese government had reached out to the Soviet Union in the summer of 1945 to mediate a negotiated peace, Foreign Minister Shigenori Togo explicitly rejected the recommendation of just such terms by the Japanese ambassador to the USSR, and their communication was intercepted by American radio intelligence (Frank 1999, 229–30). What the Japanese leaders wanted was to retain the militaristic order that had launched the war of aggression in the Pacific, and this was totally unacceptable to the Allies.

Nonetheless, correcting these parts of Anscombe's argument leaves unscathed her principal objection to honoring Truman, which is that in authorizing the atomic bombings, he had authorized the intentional killing of thousands of innocent people.

Anscombe connects the atomic bombings with a strategy of aerial bombardment, which during the war was referred to under the euphemism "area bombing." Her pamphlet begins with a sketch of the sequence of events that led from initial assurances by the parties to the hostilities that civilians would not be targeted for attack to the use of nuclear weapons against the population of entire cities. She identifies as "the great change" (on the Allied part) the change of Royal Air Force policy in early 1942 to concentrate on area bombing.[1] In an article written during the height of the war, John C. Ford proposed that it would be more accurate to call this sort of bombing *obliteration bombing*. Obliteration bombing contrasts with precision bombing, which aims at destroying or damaging definite, limited

[1] The British government flirted with area bombing prior to 1942, but the explicit change in policy can be dated to the directive issued to Bomber Command on February 14 of that year, stating that attacks were henceforth to be "focused on the morale of the enemy civil population and in particular on the industrial workers." This was further clarified the following day by a communication from the Chief of the Air Staff: "Ref the new bombing directive: I suppose it is clear that the aiming points are to be the built-up areas, not, for instance, the dockyards or air factories" (qtd. in Garrett 2007, 170–1). For some recent accounts of the Allies' approach to the bombing of Germany, see Grayling (2006), Garrett (2007, 2014), and Lackey (2014).

military targets. In obliteration bombing, the target is not a well-defined military object but a large built-up area, such as a whole city or a very large section of a city, often including its residential districts (J. Ford 1944, 261). Obliteration bombing has a dual purpose: It is intended to destroy the industrial and economic system that enables the adversary to continue fighting, but even more importantly, it aims to break the morale of the adversary's population. The means it uses to try and accomplish this latter objective is to terrorize civilians by causing widespread death and injury, destroying their homes and property, and shattering the whole fabric of their civic life. Utilizing this strategy of aerial warfare, the Royal Air Force destroyed 80 percent of all major German cities, including Cologne, Hamburg, and Dresden, killing more than 500,000 civilians, injuring another million, and destroying approximately three million residences (Garrett 2007, 178–80). In the Pacific theater, the US Army Air Force carried out obliteration bombings of large- and medium-sized Japanese cities, resulting in approximately 330,000 dead and another 472,000 wounded (Frank 1999, 334).[2]

Anscombe saw that the atomic bombings proceeded according to the same logic as obliteration bombing with conventional weapons. In both cases, the purpose of the attacks was not simply to destroy the adversary's military capacities but also to affect their morale by inflicting harm on the civilian population. The main difference is that the atomic bombings were aimed not only at undermining the morale of the general populace but also at breaking the will of the Japanese leadership to continue fighting by impressing upon them that the United States had the ability to create weapons with the capacity to instantly destroy entire cities and the willingness to employ them until they capitulated. One of Truman's key advisors, Army Chief of Staff General George C. Marshall, summed up the strategy when he explained, "What they [the Japanese] needed was shock action, and they got it" (qtd. in Bland 1991, 424–5).

In defense of Truman's decision to authorize the bombings, it has been argued that they were necessary to end the war without invading the Japanese home islands. A land invasion would have led to a much higher number of Allied and Japanese casualties. It would have also increased the duration of the war and prolonged the suffering of people in Southeast

[2] Germany also engaged in attacks on civilians, such as the bombings of Warsaw, Rotterdam, Stalingrad, and the Blitz on Britain. Grayling estimates the Blitz killed around 30,000 British and injured an additional 50,000 (2006, 37). Although Germany engaged in obliteration bombing on a smaller scale than the Allies, Garrett notes that it can easily be argued that this was due more to limitations of operational capacity than humanitarian concern (2007, 180).

Asia under the brutal rule of the Japanese Empire.[3] Truman was not presented with any good options, and a utilitarian argument can be mounted that in authorizing the bombings, he was choosing the lesser of two evils (Miscamble 2011).[4]

Anscombe is fully aware of the utilitarian argument. She acknowledges that given the objective of unconditional surrender, the atomic bombings "pretty certainly saved a huge number of lives" (1981b, 65). However, in her analysis, it is not the case that the only morally relevant fact about human actions is the goodness of the outcomes they produce. Again, her principal objection to the atomic bombings is that in carrying them out, it was decided to kill a massive number of innocent civilians in order to procure victory. But intentionally killing innocent people, even as a means to a good end, is murder, and as such is seriously wrong:[5]

> Choosing to kill the innocent as a means to your ends is always murder. Naturally, killing the innocent as an end in itself is murder too; but that is no more than a possible future development for us: in our part of the globe it is a practice that has so far been confined to the Nazis. (Anscombe 1981b, 66)

A legitimate question can be raised about who counts as innocent during times of war. Anscombe argues that in this context, "innocence" does not refer to the lack of personal culpability but rather means "not harming": The innocent are those people who are not fighting or engaged in supplying those who are fighting with the material means of doing so (Anscombe 1981b, 67). She acknowledges that this criterion creates gray areas, but there are also clear cases: children, the sick and the elderly, and the multitude of people who are not engaged in the business of war but are simply "maintaining the life of the country" (1981e, 60). Many people

[3] Newman estimates that some quarter of a million people, mostly Asian, would have died each month the war continued beyond the summer of 1945 (1995, 139).

[4] Truman's Secretary of War Henry L. Stimson sought to justify the atomic bombings in utilitarian terms. Shortly after the war he wrote, "[T]he decision to use the atomic bomb was a decision that brought death to over a hundred thousand Japanese. No explanation can change that fact and I do not wish to gloss over it. But this deliberate, premeditated destruction was our least abhorrent choice" (1947, 107).

[5] Had Truman decided against utilizing atomic weapons, the obliteration bombing of Japanese cities by conventional weapons would almost certainly have continued. But I take it that Anscombe's position would be that it would have been possible for the Allies to finish the war without intentionally killing noncombatants and that this is what they should have done.

who were clearly innocent by this criterion were among those killed in the atomic bombings.[6]

To choose to kill the innocent as an end or as a means is always murder. Anscombe emphasizes that this statement is formulated precisely, for "killing the innocent, even if you know as a matter of statistical certainty that the things you do involve it, is not necessarily murder" (1981b, 66). She goes on to provide some illustrations that involve what is often referred to as "collateral damage":

> I mean that if you attack a lot of military targets, such as munitions factories and naval dockyards, as carefully as you can, you will be certain to kill a number of innocent people; but that is not murder. On the other hand, unscrupulousness in considering the possibilities turns it into murder.

Anscombe's critique of the atomic bombings therefore relies on a distinction between effects of a course of action that are intended and those that are not, even if they are foreseen to follow from it with certainty: Intentionally causing the death of the innocent is always murder; causing deaths that are foreseen but not intended *may* be murderous too, but it is not always so.

The claim that there is a morally significant difference between intention and simple foresight is characteristic of the Principle of Double Effect (PDE), which is the subject of this book. According to the PDE, there is a strict moral constraint against bringing about serious harm to the innocent intentionally, but it is permissible in a wider range of circumstances to bring about harm as a foreseen but nonintended side effect of one's actions. Jeff McMahan calls the PDE one of the pillars of traditional nonconsequentialism (2009, 352). Yet, many recent moral philosophers have rejected the principle, with critics denouncing it in unusually vehement terms. It has been called "an obscure, ambiguous, and controversial

[6] Ford provides a list of over one hundred classes of people he thinks certainly qualify as being innocent in war (1944, 283–4). Here is a sample:

> farmers, fishermen, foresters, lumberjacks, dressmakers, bakers, painters, paper hangers, piano tuners, plasterers, cobblers, tailors, upholsterers, furniture makers, glove makers, hat makers, suit makers, fish canners, fruit and vegetable canners, slaughterers and packers, sugar refiners, teamsters, clerks in stores, decorators, window dressers, deliverymen, inspectors, insurance agents, salesmen and saleswomen, undertakers, sculptors, reporters, architects, butchers, professors and school teachers, librarians, theater owners, priests and nuns, seminarians, physicians, social and welfare workers, Red Cross workers, judges, photographers, barbers, hotel workers, janitors, sextons, maids, nurses, porters, accountants, hospital patients, prison inmates and prison guards, institutional inmates, children, and the elderly.

artifact of medieval theology" (Rich 2001, 142), "wildly implausible" (Norcross 1999, 115), "absurd" (Thomson 1999, 515) and "a muddle" (Thomson 1999, 510), and "a baseless ideology" (Steinhoff 2018b, 261). McMahan describes the contemporary state of affairs in particularly striking terms:

> Over the past two decades . . . a number of distinguished deontological and contractualist moral theorists have joined the attack [with consequentialists], as have many practitioners of "experimental philosophy," and their combined efforts have probably reduced Double Effect to a minority position among moral philosophers. Between 2000 and 2007, when I was one of the editors of *Ethics*, I reviewed a number of submissions by junior philosophers in which Double Effect was relegated to a footnote and dismissed as an exploded view that no reasonable person could take seriously. I saw that as evidence of a decisive shift in philosophical orthodoxy. (2009, 345)

My goal in this book is to push back against the emerging philosophical orthodoxy by providing a comprehensive defense of the PDE. I aim to develop a compelling rationale for the principle and to respond to the major philosophical objections that have been raised against it. If my arguments succeed, then double effect is in much better shape than its critics believe.

CHAPTER 1

The Principle of Double Effect

1.1 Introduction

Human conduct is characteristically goal-directed.[1] When we act, we intend to achieve certain goals, but our conduct also has many effects that we foresee but do not intend to bring about. A "double effect" is a foreseen but nonintended side effect of an intentional action. According to the Principle of Double Effect (PDE), the moral constraint against bringing about evil as a foreseen side effect is less stringent than the constraint against bringing about evil intentionally. More precisely,

> *PDE*: There is a strict moral constraint against bringing about serious evil (harm) to an innocent person intentionally, but it is permissible in a wider range of circumstances to act in a way that brings about serious evil incidentally, as a foreseen but nonintended side effect.[2]

Thus, if *PDE* is true, then there are circumstances in which it is morally permissible to act in a way that brings about evil incidentally, though it would not be permissible to bring about that same evil intentionally.

[1] I will often use the term "conduct" instead of the more generic term "action." I employ this term in the sense identified by Audi (2016), according to which an agent's conduct is her doing something of a certain *type* for a certain *reason* or set of reasons (or with a certain *intention* or set of intentions) and in a certain *manner*. Intentional action typically has all three of these dimensions, yet moral philosophers tend to restrict their focus to the first. Since according to double effect an agent's intentions are relevant to assessments of moral permissibility, it will be useful to have a term that helps us not lose sight of the intentional dimension of human action.

[2] The PDE is often traced to Thomas Aquinas's discussion of killing in self-defense by a private individual (*Summa theologiae* [*ST*] II-II 64.7). Various formulations of the principle have been articulated. Mine is indebted to Anscombe (2005a) (see note 14). *PDE* is concerned with the actual intentions of particular agents. In this respect, it differs from FitzPatrick's (2003) version of double effect. In order to defend the PDE from a certain objection, in Stuchlik (2012) I distinguished permissibility and liceity and argued that the agent's intentions are directly relevant to the latter rather than the former. I now believe that this was a mistake and there is a better way to respond to the objection (Section 6.4).

In Section 1.2, I explain the key terms in *PDE*, and in Section 1.3, I distinguish between an absolutist and nonabsolutist version of the principle. In Section 1.4, I introduce two further principles that help guide agents when they foresee that their conduct will cause evil as a side effect: the Principle of Proportionality (PP) and the Principle of Due Care (PDC). In Section 1.5, I describe how the PDE figures in just war theory and international humanitarian law. Finally, in Section 1.6, I outline the plan for the remainder of the book.

1.2 Terminology

1.2.1 Intentional, Incidental, and Accidental

I use "intention" and its cognates to identify an agent's aims, goals, or purposes. An agent *intends* to ϕ when it is her aim, goal, or purpose to ϕ, she ϕ-s *intentionally* when ϕ-ing is among her aims, goals, or purposes in acting, and she brings about an effect intentionally when it is her aim, goal, or purpose to bring it about. An agent's aims, goals, and purposes include both the end for the sake of which she acts and the means (if any) she takes in order to achieve her end. Just as a traveler to a distant location reaches her ultimate destination by way of passing through intermediate locations, so too a person typically achieves her ultimate goals through achieving more proximate goals, which constitute her means. An agent ϕ-s *incidentally* when ϕ-ing is not among her aims, goals, or purposes in acting, but she knows or is aware that she is ϕ-ing; she brings about an effect incidentally when it is not among her purposes, but she is aware (knows, foresees, expects) that it will result, or likely result, from her conduct. Finally, an agent ϕ-s *accidentally* or *unintentionally* when ϕ-ing is not among her aims, goals, or purposes in acting and she is unaware that she is ϕ-ing; she brings about an effect accidentally or unintentionally when it is not among her purposes and she is unaware that it will result, or likely result, from her conduct.

The term "intentional" (and "intentionally") also has a broader sense, on which it is the contrary of "unintentional" ("unintentionally"). Since to say that someone did something unintentionally implies that she did it by mistake or accident, in the broad sense an agent does or brings about intentionally whatever she is aware of doing or bringing about (Scanlon 2008, 10; Finnis 2011b, 184). The broader sense of "intentional" thus encompasses both the incidental and the intentional in the narrower sense

I distinguished in the previous paragraph.[3] When I speak of what an agent does or brings about intentionally, I will always be using "intentionally" in the narrow sense.[4]

PDE refers to intentional and incidental evils. It does not cover evils that the agent does not bring about or make happen but simply allows.[5] It is important to note, however, that while human beings typically bring things about or make things happen by actively intervening in the course of events, it is sometimes possible to bring about an effect by omitting to do something. The lead actor of a play can intentionally spoil a performance by failing to show up, and a person can intentionally bring about his own death by sitting on the beach and refusing to move until submerged by the incoming tide.[6] Roughly, an agent brings about a state of affairs by not doing something when (1) had the agent done the thing in question the state of affairs would not (or not likely) have obtained, and (2)

[3] Following Bentham, some authors say that an agent "directly intends" effects that he aims at bringing about and that he "obliquely intends" incidental effects that he foresees with certainty or near certainty. I find this terminology misleading, and I avoid it in this book.

[4] Knobe (2003) claims that people consider morally negative foreseen side effects to be intentional but morally positive or neutral side effects to be unintentional. He gave subjects a scenario in which the CEO of a company decides to implement a new program in the belief that it will both turn a profit and produce another effect *x*. It is also stipulated that the CEO does not care at all about *x* and does not implement the new program for the reason that it will cause *x*. Knobe found that when *x* was specified as "harming the environment," most subjects (81 percent) said the CEO harmed the environment intentionally, but when *x* was specified as "helping the environment," most participants (77 percent) denied that he helped the environment intentionally. The latter response, but not the former, corresponds with my narrow usage of "intentionally."

Why do most people affirm that the CEO harms the environment intentionally? Here is a hypothesis. Knobe also found that in the harm condition the CEO deserves a lot of blame for his action (M = 4.8 on a 0–6 scale). Guglielmo and Malle (2010) observe that in Knobe's experiment the subjects were forced to make a dichotomous choice between "intentionally" and "not intentionally." It is reasonable to think that subjects may believe the CEO deserves a higher degree of blame for implementing the program knowing its harmful effect than if he implemented it unaware of that effect. Given that is the case, it would be more appropriate to say he harms it "intentionally" rather than "not intentionally," since to say that he does not harm it intentionally might suggest he harms it by accident, whereas "intentional" has a broad sense that includes foreseen side effects. This hypothesis receives support from one of Guglielmo and Malle's experiments. They asked participants which of the following four descriptions most accurately describes the CEO's action in the harming condition: he harms the environment "willingly," "knowingly," "intentionally," or "purposefully." When given these finer-grained options, 86 percent said the CEO knowingly harms the environment and 12 percent said he does so willingly. By contrast, only 1 percent said he harms it intentionally and only 1 percent said he harms it purposefully. At the very least, Guglielmo and Malle's finding shows that people are able to distinguish effects that are brought about incidentally and those that are brought about intentionally in the narrow sense.

[5] Nagel (1986, 180) and Kagan (1991, 129) say that the PDE covers both evils that an agent brings about and ones that she allows. I think this version of the PDE is less plausible, and the rationale that I provide in Chapter 3 will be concerned specifically with evils that the agent brings about.

[6] The first of these examples is from Foot (2002, 26), and the second is due to Antonin Scalia (*Cruzan* v. *Director, Missouri Department of Health*, 497 US 261 (1990) at 296 [Scalia, J., concurring]).

the agent ought to have done the thing in question, where the expectation in question can but need not be a moral expectation (D'Arcy 1963, 48).

I will have more to say about the intentional/incidental distinction in Chapter 4. For now, we need only note that there is a conceptual distinction between intention and simple foresight, for there is a difference between knowing or expecting that one's conduct will bring about a certain effect and aiming at that effect as a goal. An instructor may foresee that holding a final exam will cause her students to feel anxiety but not hold it *in order to* make them anxious, a golfer may be aware that he will likely hit the ball into the water hazard without its being his *goal* or *purpose* to hit it into the water hazard, and Samson knew he would certainly cause his own death when he brought down the Temple of Dagon, but he brought it down not with the *aim* of killing himself but with the aim of killing his captors.

1.2.2 Evil or Harm

PDE also makes use of the concept of an evil. In this context, "evil" does not refer to moral evils, that is, wrongful actions and vicious character traits, but to "natural" evils or *harms*. There are various philosophical theories of harm, and there are significant areas of overlap among them about what sorts of things are harmful. They sometimes diverge, however, and these divergences can have ethical implications.[7] Defending a theory of evil/harm is a major undertaking in its own right, and I will not attempt to do so here. I will instead flag cases where it is controversial whether a certain state should be counted as a harm as they arise.

I do not think it would be inappropriate, however, to indicate my own preferred account of harm. According to this account, in at least many cases, a harm is a deprivation of a good.[8] Goods are things and conditions that contribute to, favor, or enhance an individual's good – her welfare or flourishing. We can distinguish between two classes of goods: instrumental goods and intrinsic or personal goods. Instrumental goods are not themselves components of a person's welfare but are objects and conditions that are effective means to it or that somehow enable it or aid it. On the other

7 The most important of these divergences concerns the question of whether death is always an evil or whether there are circumstances in which death is neutral or good. The correct answer to this question is especially significant for biomedical ethics.

8 Pain is a possible exception. It is often claimed that painful sensations are positive realities and their badness cannot plausibly be understood in terms of the deprivation of a good. For an argument that pain can be accommodated by the deprivation theory, see D. Alexander (2012, 100–8).

hand, personal goods are aspects or components of a person's welfare insofar as he or she is a human being, a living creature naturally equipped with rational and sensitive capacities and a body with its own boundaries and integrity. These goods, which include life, bodily integrity, and physical and psychological well-functioning, are desirable in their own right. The corresponding harms are ones that are involved in offenses against the person: killing, which deprives someone of life; maiming and wounding, which deprive someone of bodily and psychological well-functioning; battery, which trespasses against a person's bodily integrity; and rape, which trespasses against a person's sexual boundaries. Following Robert Adams, we might call these offenses *violations*, for they damage or destroy aspects of what a person *is* rather than merely damaging or destroying things that she has (1999, 108).

The sort of serious evils at issue for the PDE consist in deprivations of personal goods rather than instrumental goods.[9] A person is harmed when his property is stolen or damaged, but insofar as instrumental goods are for the sake of persons, they are subordinate to them. Because instrumental goods are subordinate to persons, it is not always morally objectionable to sacrifice them when doing so is necessary to protect personal goods, even if the sacrifice is intentional (Lyons 2013, 294).

1.3 Absolutist vs. Nonabsolutist Versions of the PDE

According to *PDE*, there is a strict constraint against intentionally harming the innocent. How strict? Double effect has traditionally been employed in an absolutist framework, according to which there is an exceptionless prohibition against intentionally killing and bringing about other harms to the innocent (that is, serious harms – I will henceforth usually leave "serious" implicit).[10] The function of the PDE in this framework is to block the inference from the impermissibility of intentional harm to the impermissibility of incidental harm: While intentional harm to the innocent is always wrong, it is sometimes permissible to bring about harm incidentally.

Some contemporary proponents of double effect prefer a nonabsolutist version of the principle.[11] On this view, the constraint against intentional

9 I take it that serious pain is also a serious harm, even if the badness of pain is not best explained in terms of the deprivation of a good.

10 Absolutist proponents of the PDE include Anscombe (e.g., 1981a, 1981b, 1981e, 2005a, 2005c), Boyle (1980), Finnis (1991), and Cavanaugh (2006).

11 See, e.g., Quinn (1993b), FitzPatrick (2003), and Wedgwood (2011a).

harm is more stringent than the constraint against incidental harm, but it is not the case that intentional harm is categorically prohibited. Instead, the prohibition against intentional harm is capable of being overridden by consequentialist considerations when a great enough good is at stake. While there is a presumption that intentionally harming innocent persons is wrong, the constraint has a threshold, and if that threshold is met or surpassed, then the constraint may be permissibly infringed.[12] There is a whole spectrum of possibilities about where the relevant threshold should be placed. At one end of the spectrum, intentional harm is permissible only when it is necessary to prevent a moral catastrophe, while at the other end, intentional harm is only marginally more difficult to justify than incidental harm.

My aim in this book is to defend a version of the PDE that is serviceable to just war theory. While not all just war theorists are moral absolutists, there is general agreement that the constraint against intentionally causing serious harm to the innocent is very robust – robust enough to condemn the bombings of Hiroshima and Nagasaki.[13] Therefore, in what follows, I will adopt a version of the PDE that includes at least a very strong presumption against intentional harm, leaving open the question of whether the constraint against intentional harm is absolute.

1.4 Incidental Harm

PDE does not say that it is always morally permissible to act in a way that brings about incidental harm: It says only that incidental harm is permissible in a wider range of circumstances than intentional harm. When is it morally permissible to bring about incidental harm? *PDE* does not answer this question.[14] Some proponents of double effect are more ambitious.

[12] In Ross's (1930) terminology, the constraint against intentional harm describes a prima facie moral duty, but abiding by it is not always our duty proper or duty all things considered.

[13] Walzer (2015, ch. 16) and Rawls (1999, 98–9) allow for a "supreme emergency exemption" to the prohibition on intentionally killing noncombatants, and Primoratz claims that the prohibition may permissibly be infringed if it is necessary to prevent a moral disaster (2013, 104ff.). By contrast, Coady (2008) adheres to the absolutist position.

[14] In her essay "Action, Intention and 'Double Effect'," Anscombe is critical of the PDE, understood as a complete theory of the morality of killing. There she defends a more modest principle, the "principle of side effects," which says that while one must not aim at death, causing it does not necessarily incur guilt (2005a, 220). *PDE* is similar to Anscombe's principle of side effects, except that it also covers other serious evils and it does not exclude the possibility that the constraint against intentional harm is defeasible.

They seek to provide a list of sufficient conditions for the permissibility of incidental harm.[15]

Consider, for instance, the following principle:

> *PDE-Sufficient*: It is morally permissible to bring about serious harm to the innocent in the pursuit of a good end if and only if:
>
> (1) The course of action is not wrong in itself.
> (2) The harm is not intended either as an end or as a means.
> (3) The expected harm is not disproportionate to the value of the end.

The principle at issue in condition (3) is the Principle of Proportionality:

> *Principle of Proportionality (PP)*: It is permissible to pursue a course of action that brings about incidental harm only if the harm is not disproportionate to the value of the end being pursued.

The PP enjoins agents to weigh the reasons for engaging in the conduct that is expected to have harmful incidental effects against the reason opposing it that is generated by those harmful effects. In order for the conduct to be permissible, the badness of the harmful effects must not outweigh the good that it is aimed at achieving.[16] Given that the goods and evils that are produced by a course of action often belong to heterogeneous types, the PP is not an algorithm that can be applied mechanically; it takes a degree of practical wisdom to employ it correctly.[17]

The PP enables us to judge that some actions that cause incidental harm are wrong. A bomber pilot who drops his bombs with the aim of destroying an enemy airfield acts wrongly if the airfield has only minor military significance and its destruction is accompanied by dozens of civilian casualties. But *PDE-Sufficient* is open to other counterexamples. A case by C. A. J. Coady illustrates one type:

> *Terrorists in a Crowd:* A group of clearly identified terrorists are moving in a crowd of people. They can be shot at while in the crowd, but the foreseen result of doing so will be that a few innocent people will also be injured or killed. The foreseen harm to civilians is not out of proportion to the value of incapacitating the terrorists – they are on their way to carrying out an attack that will kill and injure many others. However, we also know that the

[15] See, e.g., Gury (1874) and Mangan (1949).

[16] In situations of uncertainty, the principle can be applied using the Learned Hand formula: the gravity and extent of the harm, discounted by the probability of its occurring, should be weighed against the value of the agent's objective, discounted by the probability that the course of action under evaluation will achieve it.

[17] For an attempt to categorize the different sorts of considerations that are relevant for judging proportionality in the context of warfare, see Hurka (2005).

> terrorists are going to part company with the crowd at the next intersection, where we will have a clear shot at them without the risk of harming civilians (2008, 144).

It would be wrong for us to shoot into the crowd in order to incapacitate the terrorists – though by hypothesis the incidental harm we cause would not be disproportionate – for the reason that these harms could have been avoided at little risk to our objective of incapacitating the terrorists. This is captured by another principle, the Principle of Due Care:

> *Principle of Due Care (PDC)*: It is permissible to pursue a course of action that brings about incidental harm only if all reasonable steps are taken to avoid or minimize that harm.

The basic motivation behind the PP and PDC is clear: While certain circumstances may justify causing harm as a side effect, incidental harm should be neither excessive nor gratuitous (Coates 2016, 224).

It is not difficult to find further counterexamples to *PDE-Sufficient*, even when supplemented by the PDC. Here is just one. Suppose a country decides to utilize chemical weapons in an offensive. However, it has also signed a treaty that prohibits the use of chemical weapons. Even if we suppose that the use of chemical weapons is not inherently wrongful and the PP and PDC are both satisfied, the country still acts wrongly in using them, for it is wrong to utilize weapons that are prohibited by just laws or treaties.

The example of using prohibited weapons points to a more general truth, which is that even when a certain course of action satisfies the PP and PDC, an examination of the circumstances may turn up some other wrong-making factors. It is difficult or perhaps even impossible to specify all these factors in advance. Therefore, when it comes to the permissibility of incidental evil, the best we can say is the following:[18]

> *Incidental Harm*: Conduct that brings about incidental harm is morally permissible just in case it satisfies the PP and the PDC and it does not have any other wrong-making features.

Incidental Harm singles out the PP and PDC as two general considerations that are always relevant for judging the morality of incidental harm. These principles are often associated with double effect, and in my view, this is no accident. In Chapter 3, I will argue that the strict constraint against intentional harm, the PP, and the PDC are grounded in a single

[18] Cf. Masek (2018, 120).

underlying rationale. The final clause of *Incidental Harm* is a catchall, however, and I think that is as it should be. Although proponents of double effect believe it is possible to formulate some general moral principles, they also ought to allow, with Aristotle, that correct ethical judgment is often the result of perceiving the particulars of the situation.

1.5 The PDE in Just War Theory and International Law

1.5.1 Just War Theory

One of the central areas where the PDE is applied is the morality of warfare.[19] The principle plays an important role in the tradition of moral theorizing about war known as just war theory.[20] Indeed, Anscombe's objection to the use of atomic weapons against the civilian population of Japan is an application of just war principles.[21]

Just war theory can be situated in relation to the opposing philosophies of pacifism and realism. While pacifists assert that morality prohibits war and other forms of armed conflict, realists claim that war is not subject to moral constraints. Just war theory is a mean between these extremes. Like pacifists and unlike realists, just war theorists claim that war is subject to moral constraints, but unlike pacifists, they believe that it is possible for war to be morally justified. However, while just war theorists hold that it is possible for war to be justified, they also hold that there are strict limitations both on when it is morally acceptable to enter into war and on what may be done in the course of fighting a war.

19 The PDE is also regularly applied to problems in biomedical ethics (see, e.g., Gómez-Lobo and Keown 2015). Its most well-known bioethical application is to distinguish morally between euthanasia, which essentially involves intentionally bringing about the death of a patient, and cases of palliative care where a foreseen effect of administering pain-killing drugs is the hastening of the patient's death. There is additional controversy about this application, however, due to disagreement about whether death is a serious harm in the circumstances in which euthanasia is typically requested.

20 See Vitoria (2001), Suárez (1944), and Grotius (1949). Contemporary representatives of just war theory include Ramsey (1968), Johnson (1999), Hartle (2004), Coady (2008), Orend (2013), Walzer (2015), and Coates (2016).

21 For Anscombe's criticism of the atomic bombings, see Introduction. At the outset of the Second World War, Anscombe and Norman Daniel published a pamphlet, *The Justice of the Present War Examined*, in which they assessed the British war against Germany using the principles of just war theory. They correctly predicted that the war would involve aerial attacks on noncombatants. The part of the pamphlet written by Anscombe is included in the third volume of her collected papers (1981c).

The major analytical distinction in just war theory is between *jus ad bellum* and *jus in bello*.[22] The purpose of *jus ad bellum* principles is to guide leaders on the question of when resort to war is morally justified. According to the principle of just cause, war is only justified when it is a response to a precedent injustice. In the paradigm case, we are defending ourselves from aggression that is objectively unjustified or we are coming to the aid of others who are the victims of unjustified aggression. In addition to having a just cause, war must be waged by a legitimate authority, with the intention of achieving just goals and securing a just peace, all reasonable means of resolving the injustice short of going to war must have been exhausted, the war must not be expected to cause more overall harm than good, and there must be a reasonable prospect of success. On the other hand, *jus in bello* principles govern the conduct of combatants who are engaged in hostilities. The reason for distinguishing *jus in bello* principles from *jus ad bellum* ones is the recognition that even if a political community is justified in entering into war, the *means* by which war is fought must also be morally assessed: Combatants can act wrongly by pursuing a just cause through wrongful means.

An important *jus in bello* principle is the principle of discrimination, which states that combatants must distinguish between legitimate and illegitimate objects of attack. While combatants fighting in a just war may target enemy combatants and objects that have a military function, they may not direct attacks at noncombatants. The principle of discrimination thus includes the Principle of Noncombatant Immunity (PNCI), which prohibits intentional attacks on noncombatants. As Michael Walzer puts it, "Noncombatants cannot be attacked at any time. They can never be the objects or the targets of military activity" (2015, 152). What justifies the PNCI? The classic just war argument is stated succinctly by Vitoria:

> The foundation of the just war is the injury inflicted upon one by the enemy ... but an innocent person has done you no harm. *Ergo*, etc. (2001, 315)

Vitoria's argument links the *in bello* PNCI to the *ad bellum* principle of just cause. The only justification for waging war is as a response to injustice. Therefore, in waging war, we are justified in directing violence only at the perpetrators of the injustice. But noncombatants are not

[22] The existence of an analytical distinction between *jus ad bellum* and *jus in bello* does not entail that the two parts of just war theory are independent of one another; how they are related is a disputed issue among just war theorists. Orend (2013) discusses an addition to just war theory, *jus post bellum*, which aims to provide moral guidance after war has been concluded.

engaged in perpetrating injustice, for they are not engaged in carrying out unjust actions or providing those who are with the material means for doing so. They are *in-nocent*: "not harming" or "not offending." Therefore, our justification for directing violence against the perpetrators of injustice does not extend to noncombatants.[23]

It is not the case, however, that all harm that befalls noncombatants during war is intentional. Sometimes noncombatants are harmed not because they are the targets or objects of attack, but because they are in the immediate vicinity of an attack on a legitimate military target. In such cases, just war theory permits incidental harm if it is in accord with the Principle of Proportionality, the Principle of Due Care, and any other moral considerations relevant to the situation. Thus, just war theory prohibits intentional harm to noncombatants but sometimes permits engaging in military operations that bring about incidental harm to noncombatants, and this combination of commitments is tantamount to the PDE.[24]

1.5.2 International Humanitarian Law

The PDE is also embodied in international humanitarian law, which forms a legal counterpart to the principles of *jus in bello*. The relevant document is the Additional Protocol I to the Geneva Conventions of 1977 (International Committee of the Red Cross 2010). Article 48 states that the "basic rule" for respecting civilians during armed conflict is that they shall not be made the object of military operations. The following articles then provide more detailed provisions. Among these, Article 51.2 prohibits intentional harm to civilians:

> The civilian population as such, as well as individual civilians, shall not be the object of attack. Acts or threats of violence the primary purpose of which is to spread terror among the civilian population are prohibited.

This is not exactly the same as the PNCI since it expressly applies to all civilians and the class of civilians is not completely coextensive with that of

[23] Who qualifies as a noncombatant? Coady argues that combatants include anyone who is involved in the "chain of agency" promoting or directing the injustice to which the war is a response (2008, 112). This includes soldiers, but it also includes persons who do not wear military uniforms, such as civilian contractors who support combat operations and political leaders who direct military forces. Nonetheless, the large majority of a warring nation's civilian population is not involved in this chain of agency. Even if they passively support the war, they are not, in Walzer's phrase, "engaged in the business of war" (2015, 43).

[24] Note, however, that some just war theorists allow that it is permissible to infringe the prohibition on intentionally harming noncombatants in situations of supreme emergency or moral disaster (see note 13).

noncombatants.[25] But insofar as the vast majority of civilians in any society are not combatants, it is clearly in the spirit of the PNCI.

The Protocol also provides guidance in regard to incidental harm to civilians. Here the foundational directive is, "In the conduct of military operations, constant care shall be taken to spare the civilian population, civilians, and civilian objects" (57.1). Parties to hostilities are therefore required to take all feasible precautions to verify that targets of attack are not civilians or civilian objects (57.2.a.i), to see to it that methods of attack are chosen with a view to avoiding or minimizing incidental loss of civilian life and damage to civilian objects (57.2.a.ii), and to refrain from launching any attack that may be expected to cause incidental harm to civilians and civilian objects that is excessive in relation to the anticipated military advantage (57.2.a.iii). International law therefore does not completely forbid incidental harm to civilians but mandates that operations expected to cause incidental harm accord with the PP and PDC.

1.6 Plan of the Book

The plan for the remainder of the book is as follows. In Chapter 2, I discuss the extent to which the PDE is supported by intuitions about cases. While the PDE enjoys considerable intuitive support, I argue that its proponents face the *grounding challenge*, or the challenge of providing a compelling rationale that explains why the distinction between intentional harm and incidental harm is relevant for the moral permissibility of conduct. I also survey six proposed rationales for the PDE and conclude that none of them is satisfactory. In Chapter 3, I present my own solution to the grounding challenge, the *solidarity rationale*, which develops and integrates ethical concepts from Foot and Anscombe. According to this rationale, the PDE flows from a moral standard of human solidarity. Intentional harm is morally objectionable because it successfully expresses malevolent desire, and in doing so, it deviates from the standard of solidarity that measures one's conduct in relation to others. Incidental harm does not share this wrong-making feature, though it can also deviate from the standard of solidarity if it is excessive or gratuitous. The standard of solidarity, in turn, is grounded in the inherent value or dignity of human beings.

The purpose of Chapter 4 is to give a more precise account of the intentional/incidental distinction. In order to do so, I expound an

[25] See note 23.

Anscombian account of intentional action. This chapter contributes to the overall scheme of the book in three ways. First, there are sometimes disagreements about how the PDE applies to particular (actual or hypothetical) situations, and these disagreements are often based on differing views about which effects or aspects of an agent's conduct are intentional and which are incidental. Therefore, it is important for practical purposes to have an account of intentional action, and I believe that Anscombe's is the best one we have. Second, the Anscombian account will prove helpful in framing a certain objection to the PDE, the closeness problem, in Chapter 5. Finally, I utilize the Anscombian account of intentional action in the course of replying to other objections to the PDE in Chapter 6.

In Chapter 5, I take up a long-standing objection to the PDE, the closeness problem. According to this objection, intentions are sufficiently fine-grained that an agent need not intend harm in almost any situation. The PDE therefore fails to rule out many instances of conduct that are intuitively morally objectionable unless it is supplemented by a criterion of excessive closeness, whose job is to identify things that are "too close" to harm to be considered incidental for purposes of applying the principle. The problem is that it is difficult to specify a criterion of closeness that is not arbitrary or subject to counterexamples. I argue in reply that proponents of double effect do not need a criterion of closeness; they have the resources to respond to the allegedly problematic cases without one. In Chapter 6, I then take up further objections to the PDE that have been put forward by philosophers who hold that an agent's intentions in acting are irrelevant to whether or not her conduct is morally permissible, including the objection that the PDE makes the morality of harmful conduct depend on what happens in the agent's mind rather than what happens in the world, the objection that it entails inconsistent judgments about cases, and the objection that it has absurd implications for moral deliberation.

The aim of this book is to provide a comprehensive defense of the PDE. My solution to the grounding challenge in Chapter 3 provides a reason to accept the principle, and my arguments in Chapters 5 and 6 demonstrate that the case against it has been overstated. Finally, in Chapter 7, I argue that my rationale for the PDE has an additional merit. It also helps nonconsequentialists respond to Joshua Greene's argument that recent findings from empirical psychology debunk deontological constraints on causing harm.

CHAPTER 2

The Grounding Challenge

2.1 Introduction

A common way of motivating the PDE is by appealing to intuitions about cases. It is widely accepted that it counts in favor of a moral principle if it coheres with our case-based intuitions, especially those that are strong and stable upon reflection. To be sure, in evaluating a moral principle or theory, coherence with our intuitions is not the only relevant consideration. Nonetheless, it is widely taken as a demerit of moral theories such as act-consequentialism that they have implications that clash badly with our intuitions about cases. It is therefore significant that the PDE accounts for common intuitions about a number of cases that might otherwise seem puzzling (Section 2.2).

We might also wonder, however, whether there is any deeper rationale for the principle. Warren Quinn asks, "What, apart from its agreeing with our particular intuitions, can be said in favor of [the PDE]? Indeed, why should we accept the intuitions that support it?" (1993a, 176). Quinn's questions are to the point. In Section 2.3, I give three reasons why the PDE cannot be sufficiently justified solely on the basis of intuitions about cases. Proponents of double effect face the *grounding challenge*, the challenge of providing a theoretical rationale that explains why the distinction between intentional harm and incidental harm is relevant for evaluating the moral permissibility of human conduct. In Sections 2.4–2.9, I examine six rationales and I argue that each of them is vulnerable to serious objections. The thrust of the discussion is therefore critical, but in Section 2.10, I draw some lessons from the failures of these proposals. This sets the stage for Chapter 3, where I turn to the constructive project of developing a novel rationale.

2.2 Intuitions

2.2.1 Precision Bombing/Terror Bombing

One of the canonical applications of the PDE contrasts two types of bombing:

> *Precision Bombing*: A bomber pilot's end is to help his country win a just war, and he pursues this end by targeting a munitions factory, though he foresees that a number of nearby noncombatants will be killed or injured from the explosions of his bombs.
>
> *Terror Bombing*: A bomber pilot's end is to help his country win a just war, and he pursues this end by dropping his bombs over the built-up area of a city in order to kill and injure noncombatants. He does this because he believes that the terror that results from the casualties will demoralize the enemy population and lead them to pressure their leaders to surrender.

These cases are modeled after the distinction between precision bombing and obliteration ("area") bombing during the Second World War (see Introduction). In the literature on double effect, the first case is often referred to as "strategic bombing" or "tactical bombing." Neither of these labels is felicitous, however. "Strategic bombing" is not because a country might adopt terror bombing as a strategy for aerial warfare, as the Royal Air Force did in 1942. "Tactical bombing" is no better because performing strikes on military targets can be part of strategy as well as tactics. As for the second case, Uwe Steinhoff claims that the label "terror bombing" is a subterfuge by proponents of double effect to bias people's intuitions (2018b, 238ff.). A more charitable explanation is that insofar as one of the defining aims of the sort of bombing in question is to produce fear and terror, it is accurately describable as a form of terrorism.[1]

That terrorism is a proper object of moral revulsion is uncontroversial. What is it that occasions such revulsion? Terrorism has an intentional structure that includes both a distal aim and a more proximate aim.[2] The

[1] That obliteration bombing constitutes a form of terrorism was recognized before and during the Second World War. Prior to the war's outbreak, Chamberlain denounced it with the words, "Whatever be the lengths to which others may go, his Majesty's government will never resort to the deliberate attack on women and children, and other civilians for purposes of mere terrorism" (qtd. in Garrett 2007, 168). And after the bombing of Dresden in 1945, Associated Press correspondent Howard Cowan wrote a newspaper article with the title "Terror Bombing Gets Allied Approval as Step to Speed Victory" (*Washington Star*, February 18, 1945).

[2] Cf. Coady (2008, ch. 8), Nathanson (2010, ch. 2), and Primoratz (2013, ch. 1). Primoratz speaks of terrorism as having a "direct" and "indirect" aim, but it is more accurate to describe its intentional structure in terms of its distal and proximate aims.

distal aim is the promotion of a social, political, or military agenda, which the agent of terror hopes to achieve by intimidating people to take actions that promote it. In the case of terror bombing, the distal aim is victory, and the bomber pursues this aim by pursuing the more proximate aim of killing and injuring noncombatants.[3] Part of the negative reaction to terror bombing is explained by the fact that it causes fear and terror both for its victims and for members of the wider population. But the moral horror that it induces is surely also explained in part by the fact that, like other forms of terrorism, it seeks to achieve its distal aim by deliberately killing and injuring innocent people (Nathanson 2010, 33). The terror bomber directs his attacks at noncombatants not because they have done something that would make them deserving of, or liable to, being attacked. Instead, he attacks them because they are vulnerable and because it is believed (by the bomber or his commanders) that harming them can advance his country's military agenda. By contrast, the precision bomber does not seek to harm noncombatants, and precision bombing therefore does not share an intuitively objectionable feature possessed by terror bombing.

Against this, Ezio Di Nucci contends that ordinary people do not in fact intuit a moral difference between precision bombing and terror bombing. Di Nucci's evidence for this claim comes from an online survey in which 299 participants were randomly assigned a version of either the terror bombing or precision bombing scenario. He found that the percentage of participants who judged that precision bombing is wrong (84 percent) was nearly the same as the percentage who judged that terror bombing is wrong (86 percent) (2014, 180). Di Nucci concludes that if there is a moral difference between the scenarios, it is not an intuitive one that can be used to motivate the PDE.

In response, we might note that Di Nucci's participants were all arts and humanities students at a single university. The inference that Di Nucci draws from his data is also problematic for two reasons. First, according to that data, a significant portion of participants did not correctly register the intentional structure of the precision bombing scenario: Nearly one-third (31 percent) judged that the precision bomber intends to kill noncombatants (2014). Therefore, a portion of the judgments that the precision bomber acts wrongly might be explained by the fact that some subjects incorrectly believed he intentionally kills noncombatants.

[3] In other cases, the terrorist's distal aim might be promoted by damaging people's property or by issuing credible threats to kill or injure people or damage their property (Coady 2008, 159).

Second, Di Nucci formulated the precision bombing scenario in such a way that it is not clear that a negative judgment about it conflicts with the PDE, even when its intentional structure is correctly discerned. Here is the description that was given to participants:

> A bomber pilot plans to bomb an enemy munitions factory because she thinks that the destruction of the munitions factory will force the enemy to a quick capitulation. The pilot knows it won't be possible to effectively bomb the munitions factory without also killing many children in a nearby school. As planned, the pilot destroys the munitions factory. As expected, many children in the nearby school also die. (2014)

The wording of this case creates difficulties for drawing any reliable conclusions about whether people's intuitions about it conflict with the PDE. For the PDE does not imply that precision bombing is *always* morally permissible; whether it is in any given situation will turn on factors such as whether the incidental harm to noncombatants is proportionate to the value of the objective being sought, whether the agent takes due care to avoid or minimize causalities, and whether there are any other wrong-making factors present. Several features of Di Nucci's description of the case are therefore significant. First, it does not specify whether the pilot is fighting for a just cause. This matters because many people believe that the value of the agent's more distal aims is relevant for assessments of proportionality (McMahan 2004; Hurka 2005). For instance, people might reasonably believe that *any* killing of schoolchildren by Nazi bombers is disproportionate and unjustified. Second, it is not specified whether there are other possible means to winning the war, and it is not specified how much longer the war is expected to last if other means of fighting are pursued. This is relevant because according to the Principle of Due Care (PDC), less costly means to victory should be taken if they are available, and this may be so even if taking them is expected to delay victory somewhat. Finally, Di Nucci's description *does* say that the bombing kills children in a nearby school, and this gives us some reason to presume that the bomber's conduct is not morally permissible. According to the PDC, for the bombing to be justified it must not be the case that the factory's destruction could be achieved in a way that would avoid or lessen harm to the schoolchildren. It is common knowledge, however, that children attend school only during certain hours of the week. Since no special circumstances are mentioned that would make bombing the factory impossible when there are no children present, it might be inferred that the bomber is being reckless in carrying out the bombing when she does.[4] Some of Di Nucci's participants could have judged that the precision bomber acts wrongly for one or all of the reasons I have described, and if they did so, their judgments would not conflict with the PDE.

2.2.2 *More Cases*

Foot also motivates the PDE by appealing to intuitions about cases. She raises the dilemma of a person who is considering whether to kill an innocent man in order to appease a mob and contrasts it with another dilemma involving the driver of an out-of-control trolley:

> *Scapegoat*: A person could kill an innocent man and pass him off as a criminal in order to prevent a mob of rioters from killing five hostages.
>
> *Trolley Driver:* The driver of an out-of-control trolley will run down and kill five workmen unless he steers the trolley onto a sidetrack. There is one workman on the sidetrack whom the driver will kill if he turns onto it (2002, 23).

Foot thinks we would say without hesitation that the trolley driver should steer to the less occupied track but that it is outrageous to think it is permissible for someone to kill an innocent person in order to appease the mob. The puzzle is that both dilemmas involve producing an outcome in which one person is killed and five others are saved. Why, then, can we not argue from the permissibility of *Trolley Driver* to the permissibility of *Scapegoat*? The PDE enables us to distinguish them insofar as the death of the man in *Scapegoat* would be brought about intentionally while the death of the workman in *Trolley Driver* would be incidental.

The PDE coheres with common intuitions about other cases as well:

> *Transplant*: A surgeon has five patients who are in need of organs – one needs a heart, two need lungs, and two need a kidney – and they will all die unless they are given transplants soon. Unfortunately, no organs are presently available. But then he learns that another person, Arnold, has just arrived for his yearly check-up and is a compatible donor for all five of the patients. The surgeon reasons that he could give Arnold a lethal injection

[4] Di Nucci's description states that the pilot knows it won't be possible to bomb the factory effectively without killing schoolchildren. This statement is ambiguous. It might mean that it is not possible to bomb the factory effectively without killing the children, supposing that they are present in the school. Alternatively, it might mean that it is absolutely impossible for the bomber to bomb the factory effectively without killing the children. I find the first reading more natural, since it would take a special explanation to make it intelligible why bombing the factory is absolutely impossible without killing children.

instead of the inoculation he is expecting, thereby making his organs available to save the five (Scanlon 2008, 15; cf. Foot 2002, 24; Thomson 1976, 206).

Tyrant: A tyrant credibly tells Philippa that he will kill five innocent people unless she kills one innocent person (Foot 2002, 25).

Hijacked Aircraft: Terrorists have hijacked an airplane with a dozen passengers on board and are headed toward the city. It is evident that they plan to crash the aircraft into a power plant, which will result in thousands of deaths. Attempts to communicate with the hijackers have proved futile, and several fighter jets have been scrambled. They can shoot down the airplane before it reaches the city but doing so will kill the passengers on board (Zamir and Medina 2010, 167).

Gate: The Huns have unexpectedly attacked the city and are galloping toward the open gate. Several children have been playing in the mechanism that closes the gate. If it is closed, they will be crushed, but if it is not closed, the Huns will enter through and sack the city, leading to scores of deaths. There is no time to get the children out before the Huns reach the gate (Sullivan and Atkinson 1985, 250).

It seems that it is wrong to kill the patient to make his organs available for transplant and to kill one person to prevent someone else from killing five, yet it also seems permissible to blow up the hijacked aircraft and close the gate to save a greater number. Standard forms of act-consequentialism conflict with the intuition that the conduct described in *Transplant* and *Tyrant* is wrong, and even sophisticated versions of consequentialism that give weight to the occurrence of *killings* (as opposed to deaths) in determining the value of outcomes conflict with the intuition about *Tyrant*. On the other hand, deontological constraints such as the constraint against doing harm or initiating lethal threats fail to explain the intuitive permissibility of the conduct in *Hijacked Aircraft* and *Gate*. The PDE offers an elegant explanation of our intuitions about all four cases.

2.3 Why Intuitions Are Insufficient

Intuitions about cases such as the ones described in the previous section provide initial motivation for the PDE. But friends of double effect are sometimes content to rest their case on intuitions, and in my view, this is a mistake. The intuitive case does not constitute a sufficient basis for holding the PDE.

One reason for this is that the PDE does not perfectly fit everyone's intuitions. Let us call a case that elicits intuitions that conflict with a principle a "counterexample" to that principle. Such cases are not counterexamples in the strict sense. No case or set of cases could demonstrate that a moral principle is false, only that it yields verdicts that are counterintuitive. Nonetheless, it is a cost of a moral principle that it has counterintuitive implications, and if a principle clashes with too many of our intuitions, the cost will be significant.

Some cases that have been raised as counterexamples to the PDE are not really counterexamples to the principle, at least as I defined it in Chapter 1 (Section 1.1). For instance, Frances Kamm believes that it would be wrong for a doctor to use a gas to run a machine for a surgical operation that will save five patients when some of the gas will seep next door and kill someone else (call this the *Gas* scenario) (1991, 573).[5] Kamm's intuition may depend on special obligations that arise in a hospital setting. If we change the case so that the five people in need are survivors of a plane crash on a deserted island with abandoned medical equipment, then it does not seem clear to me that it would be impermissible to use the gas. Even if we waive this point, the version of the PDE I endorse only implies that incidental harm is *sometimes* permissible in circumstances in which intentional harm is not. It is compatible with this that the doctor acts wrongly in using the gas even though the harm it causes is incidental. Anyone who thinks the doctor's conduct is wrongful should hold that the case involves some wrong-making feature not covered by the Principle of Proportionality or Principle of Due Care.

A better counterexample to the PDE would be a case in which the agent intuitively acts permissibly even though she intentionally brings about harm for an innocent person. The most notorious purported counterexample to the PDE has this structure:

> *Loop:* A runaway trolley is headed toward five people who will be killed if it continues on its present course. You can hit a switch that will turn the trolley onto a sidetrack that loops back and reconnects with the main track before reaching the five. There is one large person on the sidetrack and the trolley would be stopped if it hit him, preventing it from killing the five (Thomson 1985, 1402–3).[6]

Many philosophers think it is permissible to divert the trolley onto the sidetrack in order to save the five. But it appears that if you do so, you will

[5] This case is due to Foot (2002, 29).

[6] Thomson raises *Loop* as a counterexample to the Kantian principle that it is wrong to use one person to save others. But it is sometimes contended that it is a counterexample to the PDE as well (e.g., Scanlon 2008, 18).

intentionally cause the person on the sidetrack to be hit by the trolley as a means to saving the five.[7]

Despite its notoriety, there are reasons for doubting the strength of *Loop* as a counterexample to the PDE. It is not clear how widespread the intuition is that the agent in *Loop* acts permissibly. Empirical studies of trolley dilemmas have returned varying data about people's reactions to the case. While in one study 81 percent of subjects said that the action in *Loop* is permissible (Greene 2013, 221), in another study nearly half (44 percent) of respondents judged that the action is impermissible (Hauser et al., 2007). There is also evidence that people's intuitions about the case are sensitive to order effects (Liao et al., 2012). Since the order of presentation is not a morally relevant factor, the fact that intuitions about *Loop* are sensitive to it calls their reliability into question.

Moreover, it may be that not everyone conceptualizes *Loop* as a case of intentional harm. It is possible to see *Loop* as presenting a problem of protecting the five from the immediate threat of the trolley's traveling down the main track. That problem can be eliminated by diverting the trolley onto the sidetrack. However, because the sidetrack reconnects with the main track, this creates a secondary threat of the trolley's traveling down the sidetrack and rejoining the main track. At least, diverting the trolley *would* create this secondary threat if the sidetrack were unoccupied – as things stand, the presence of the person on the sidetrack prevents this threat from materializing. So, someone imagining themselves in the scenario might reason, "I'm diverting the trolley in order to eliminate the immediate threat of its going down the main track. A necessary condition for my doing this is that there is a person on the sidetrack who will stop it – otherwise the five would be killed by the secondary threat I create in eliminating the immediate threat. But I am not diverting the trolley *in order to* hit the person on the sidetrack" (Kamm 2000; Kaufman 2016).

I will not attempt to evaluate the cogency of this reasoning.[8] The point is not that it is a good way of reasoning about the case but that some people may in fact reason this way. This has implications for the value of *Loop* as a counterexample to the PDE. For if someone conceives the harm to the one as being incidental, her judgment that the agent acts permissibly does not conflict with the PDE.

One of the strongest counterexamples to the PDE involves cases with the following structure. The agent is pursuing a proportionately good end

[7] I argue in Chapter 5 (Section 5.3.2) that being hit by a trolley is a serious harm.

[8] See Otsuka (2008) for a critique.

and has a choice of two possible means. One option involves killing or harming one innocent person intentionally, while the other involves killing or harming several incidentally. In some of these cases, the PDE will condemn the first option but permit the second. One example is Gerhard Øverland's *Flamethrower and Rifle* case:

> *Flamethrower and Rifle*: Tom impermissibly attacks Mary and nineteen other people standing around her. Behind Tom is a house, and there are two bystanders on the roof. Mary could kill Tom with a nearby flamethrower, but using the flamethrower would also kill both bystanders. Mary also has a rifle, with which she can shoot one of the bystanders. That person would fall on Tom, rendering his attack ineffective. Since Tom is standing behind some trees, Mary cannot shoot him with the rifle (2016, 288).

Let us assume that if Mary uses the rifle, she will shoot the bystander in the head, this being the only clear shot. The PDE implies that Mary acts wrongfully if she shoots the bystander as a means to stopping Tom's attack.[9] Can she permissibly use the flamethrower? Assuming the PDC and any other relevant conditions are satisfied, the PDE says that she can.[10] So the PDE yields the verdict that Mary may not use the rifle to shoot one bystander, but she may use the flamethrower, which will kill both bystanders. I am sure this will strike many people as counterintuitive.[11] If Mary can save herself and the others from Tom's attack either in a way that results in the death of one innocent person or in a way that results in the death of two, why shouldn't she take the first option? To answer this question, proponents of the PDE need a convincing rationale that explains why the agent's mode of agency is so morally significant.

Beyond the fact that the PDE sometimes has counterintuitive consequences, there are three additional reasons why it is unwise for proponents of double effect to rest their case solely on intuitions.[12] First, while the

[9] A nonabsolutist who thinks the constraint against intentional harm has a relatively low threshold might claim that in this situation it may be permissibly infringed. As I stated in Chapter 1 (Section 1.3), I am interested in a version of the PDE on which the constraint against intentional harm is more robust.

[10] It might be that burning is such a terrible way to die that Mary may not use the flamethrower. I will bypass this concern; the details could easily be altered so that she has a less terrible weapon at her disposal.

[11] One way for proponents of double effect to avoid this verdict would be to invoke Kamm's Principle of Secondary Permissibility, which allows for an exception to the constraint against intentional harm in circumstances in which the people harmed intentionally could permissibly be harmed as a side effect (2004, 660). I find Øverland's criticism of this move compelling.

[12] In Chapter 7, I discuss another possible reason for not relying too much on case-based intuitions in supporting the PDE. Joshua Greene argues that understanding the origins of our deontological moral intuitions debunks their epistemic value.

PDE provides one way of making sense of some common nonconsequentialist intuitions, alternative explanations of these intuitions may be possible. It could be that some other principle, or set of principles, coheres with our case-based intuitions just as well or even better than the PDE. Some of these principles may even attribute moral significance to the agent's intentions in acting, without holding that the distinction between intentional and incidental *harm* is morally significant.[13]

Second, two recent empirical studies indicate that people's intuitions about moral dilemmas are not uniform across cultures or static across generations. In the largest survey of people's judgments about trolley dilemmas to date, Awad et al. (2020) collected responses of 70,000 participants from 42 countries to three cases: *Switch*, in which the agent can redirect a runaway trolley away from five people onto one; *Footbridge*, in which the agent can prevent a trolley from hitting five people by pushing a bystander off a footbridge into its path; and *Loop*. Awad et al. found that across cultures participants ranked sacrifice in *Switch* as most acceptable, *Footbridge* least acceptable, and *Loop* in between. However, they also found that there were significant variations across countries in people's willingness to endorse sacrificing one to save five in all three cases, with participants from Europe and the Americas being more willing to endorse utilitarian sacrifice than those from Japan, Taiwan, or China.[14] In another study, Hannikainen, Machery, and Cushman (2018) found that Millennials are more likely to make utilitarian judgments about hypothetical moral dilemmas than older cohorts. They note that this result is consistent with findings that younger people tend to be more secular and report lower empathy than middle-aged and older adults, as both of these factors have been linked to utilitarian judgments to moral dilemmas.[15] These studies suggest that philosophers who construct their moral principles on the foundation of case-based intuitions may be building on shifting sands.

[13] For instance, Quinn's (1993a) distinction between harmful direct agency and harmful indirect agency.

[14] Indeed, Awad et al. found that a majority of participants from many Western countries, as well as India, Singapore, Vietnam, Israel, and Turkey, endorsed sacrificing the bystander in *Footbridge*. This finding contradicts other empirical studies, in which only a minority of people judged that the conduct in *Footbridge* is morally acceptable (Hauser et al. 2007; Greene et al. 2009). It also conflicts with the intuition of most analytic moral philosophers. It is important to note, however, that the sample of participants in the study of Awad et al. was self-selected and unrepresentative (75 percent male, 75 percent younger than 32, and 75 percent college-educated).

[15] See, respectively, Gleichgerrcht and Young (2013) and Conway and Gawronski (2013).

The final reason to move beyond intuitions about cases is that, as Shelly Kagan (1991, 13–14) emphasizes, the goal of normative ethics is not merely to provide an axiomatization of our moral views. We also want an explanation *why* the various factors and distinctions we appeal to are morally significant. It may be that it is immediately obvious why a certain distinction is morally significant. But if it is not, then fulfilling the explanatory criterion will involve connecting the distinction with other moral concepts whose significance we can appreciate directly; that is, it will be a matter of providing the distinction with a compelling rationale.

While the distinction between intentional harm and incidental harm is not immediately implausible, its moral significance is not self-evident either. And upon reflection, many philosophers have found it difficult to understand why an agent's intentions in acting should be relevant in the way the PDE claims.[16] If you foresee that someone will suffer harm because of your conduct, it seems relevant to ask whether the good you are trying to achieve is sufficient to justify it. But why should it also matter whether the harm is intended? Wherein lies the "moral offensiveness of intending harm" (Kagan 1991, 131)? This is the grounding challenge. In the remainder of the chapter, I examine six proposed solutions to it.

2.4 The "Guided by Evil" Rationale

One of the most commonly cited rationales for the PDE is Thomas Nagel's. Nagel holds that intentional evil is especially morally offensive because it involves the agent's putting himself in a perverse or inappropriate relation to evil – the relation of "being guided by":

> [T]o aim at evil, even as a means, is to have one's action guided by evil . . .. But the essence of evil is that it should *repel* us. If something is evil, our actions should be guided, if they are guided by it at all, toward its elimination rather than toward its maintenance. That is what evil *means*. So when we aim at evil we are swimming head-on against the normative current. Our action is guided by the goal at every point in the direction diametrically opposite to that in which the value of the goal points. (1986, 181–2)

This passage is difficult to interpret, for the word "evil" has multiple senses and it is not clear which is at issue or whether Nagel is conflating several different senses. Nelkin and Rickless believe that Nagel faces a dilemma

[16] See, e.g., Bennett (1995), Kagan (1991, Ch. 4), McCarthy (2002), Hart (2008), Scanlon (2008), Greene (2013), Nelkin and Rickless (2015), and Steinhoff (2019).

depending on how we understand his talk of evil (2015, 403). They argue that "evil" may refer either to something morally wrong or to something very bad, such as a serious harm.[17] If we adopt the first alternative, the problem arises that it is circular to explain the wrongfulness of an agent's conduct by adverting to the fact that it aims at evil. The second alternative is also problematic, for it is not always wrong to aim at serious harm. In particular, it is not always wrong to aim at serious harm to people who are engaged in wrongful attacks on others. But if we amend the rationale to say that what is wrong is only aiming at serious harm for those who are not engaged in wrongful attacks, then our explanation once again becomes circular.

Nelkin and Rickless' first interpretation – that by "evil" Nagel means moral wrongdoing – is not very plausible. Moral wrongness is a property possessed by conduct, but an individual who intentionally kills another is not aiming at her own conduct; she is aiming at her victim's death. Their second alternative has more to be said for it. Nagel later asserts that the evil at which we are constrained not to aim is "*our victim's* evil" (1986, 182), and this lends support to the proposal that he intends "evil" to mean serious harm. The second horn of Nelkin and Rickless's dilemma does not seem fatal either. It would be only if it were impossible to spell out what it takes to be engaged in wrongful attacks on others in nonmoral terms.

A better objection to understanding "evil" in the quoted passage as meaning serious harm is that it does little to explain why it is wrong intentionally to bring about serious harm by adverting to the fact that in doing so one is being guided by serious harm. And despite Nagel's later reference to "our victim's evil," thinking of evil in terms of harm does not fit the passage very well. Nagel says there that the *meaning* of evil is that it should repel us. While it is true that we should be repelled by the thought of serious harm befalling people, it does not seem to be built into the very *meaning* of harm that it is repellent. The connection between harm and "repellentness" appears to be synthetic rather than analytic.

There is a third way that we can understand Nagel's talk of evil that Nelkin and Rickless overlook. According to what Scanlon calls the "teleological conception of value," value attaches to states of affairs (1998, 79ff.). For a state of affairs to be intrinsically valuable is for it to have the property of being "to be promoted" and for a state of affairs to be intrinsically disvaluable is for it so have the property of being "to be prevented." If Nagel is thinking of being evil as equivalent to being

[17] This corresponds to the two sense of evil I distinguished in Section 1.2.2.

disvaluable in this sense, then we can make sense of his claim that it is part of the very meaning or essence of evil that it should repel us. For it is indeed part of the very essence of "evil" on this conception that it is a proper object of repulsion, and if our action is directed at bringing about a state of affairs that is "to be prevented," then it seems that it is being directed in a way that is contrary to that in which the value of the state of affairs points.

The problem with this view is that from the fact that a state of affairs has intrinsic disvalue, it does not follow that it is always inappropriate to be guided by it all things considered. For, as Kagan points out, the fact that something possesses intrinsic disvalue does not rule out the possibility that it also possesses extrinsic value (1991, 168). In a case where a single state of affairs has both sorts of value we have, as it were, two competing normative forces, and it seems plausible that the appropriate thing to do is to side with whichever force is stronger. Consider a terror bomber who believes that considered in its own right the death of noncombatants ought to repel us. But he also thinks that in his circumstances the death of some noncombatants is an effective means to winning a just war, and he concludes that all things considered, it is therefore appropriate to bring them about. Of course, if the PDE is true, then the bomber acts wrongly if he intentionally kills noncombatants as a means to victory. But it is unclear how Nagel's rationale, on the present interpretation, can explain where his reasoning goes awry. If we point out to the bomber that his conduct is being guided by the goal of producing a state of affairs (noncombatant deaths) that has the property of being "to be prevented," he could reply that he is aware of this, but its instrumental to-be-promotedness outweighs its intrinsic to-be-preventedness.[18]

2.5 The "Treating as a Mere Means" Rationale

Kant's Formula of Humanity (FH) enjoins us to act in such a way that we treat humanity always as an end and never merely as a means (1996a, 80 [Ak 4: 429]). T. A. Cavanagh argues that FH can serve as a foundation

[18] Bennett considers yet another possible reading of the quoted passage, according to which being guided by evil is being guided in a way that essentially involves the *thought* of evil (1995, 224). The idea, I take it, is that a malicious agent begins with the end of doing evil (serious harm) to others, and then attempts to bring about certain effects, such as death and injury, precisely *because* they are evils. There is something undeniably vicious about such a character. However, as Bennett points out, a terror bomber need not be malicious in this way. He might bring about civilian casualties not because they are evils but because they contribute to victory.

for the strict constraint against intentional harm. Cavanaugh proposes to read FH disjunctively: It tells us that *either* (and ideally) we are to treat people as ends by benefiting them *or*, at a minimum, we are not to treat them as mere means to our ends (2006, 148–9). On his account, intentional harm is wrong because the agent thereby treats her victim as a mere means to her end, thereby violating the minimum prescribed by FH.

Cavanaugh's grounding works well for terror bombing. There is a straightforward sense in which, in harming and killing noncombatants, the terror bomber is using them as instruments for demoralizing the enemy population or their leaders. Unfortunately, it does not work as well at explaining the wrongfulness of other types of conduct condemned by the PDE. The problem is twofold. First, the constraint against intentional harm prohibits not only harming people as a means but also harming them as an end, and it is not clear how the prohibition on treating others as mere means could extend to the latter. Consider, for example, a scenario (*Crash Landing*) in which a pilot crashes his stricken airplane into a suburb in order to kill his wife's lover, who is a resident (Kenny 1995, 85). The pilot does not kill his wife's lover as a means to any further end – he kills her as an end in its own right. It might be objected that even in this case, the agent is using the man as a means to obtaining pleasure. This objection misrepresents the case, however. A sadistic agent might begin with the end of getting pleasure and then hit on killing someone as a means to obtaining it, but that is not how things are here. The vengeful pilot does not begin with the general end of obtaining pleasure and then calculate that he can achieve it by crashing his plane in the suburb and killing his wife's lover. Rather, upon noticing that he can crash his plane near the lover's residence, he forms the end of killing him and steers his aircraft toward the suburb as a means to achieving this aim. It is true that if the pilot were somehow to survive the crash, he would take pleasure in seeing the lover's lifeless body, but this pleasure would be the result of knowing that he accomplished his end.

The second problem with attempting to derive the constraint against intentional harm from the prohibition against treating people as a mere means is that there is a distinction between *harming someone as a means* and *treating someone as a mere means*: An agent harms others as a means when she causes them harm in order to further one of her goals, but she treats others as mere means when she employs them as tools or instruments without concern for their good. Cases in which someone harms others as a means without treating them as mere means will therefore not be covered by the rationale. Consider the type of bombing Cavanaugh calls "eliminative bombing":

> Eliminative bombing destroys non-combatants whose physical presence impedes the destruction of another legitimate military target. In such cases, persons obstruct the achievement of one's goal; one begins to pursue that goal by destroying them. (2006, 151)

The eliminative bomber kills noncombatants as a means to destroying a military target, but on any ordinary understanding of what it is to treat others as mere means, he does not treat the noncombatants as mere means: He treats them as obstacles to be removed rather than as tools to be employed. Cavanaugh might reply that he is stipulating a sense of "treating people as mere means" according to which intentionally harming someone constitutes treating her as a mere means. The trouble with this proposal, however, is that insofar as treating others as mere means is now being explained in terms of intentional harm, it can no longer serve as an independent ground for explaining the wrongfulness of intentional harm.[19]

2.6 The "Agential Involvement" Rationale

Ralph Wedgwood (2011a) defends a nonabsolutist version of the PDE, which states that it is harder to justify a course of action that has as a consequence a bad state of affairs if that state of affairs is intended than if it is not intended. On his account, what makes this true is that the normative reasons for and against a course of action are determined both by the value of its consequences and by what he calls the agent's "degree of agential involvement" in bringing them about. So, whenever the consequences of a course of action include a bad state of affairs, this generates a reason against it, but the strength of the reason depends not only on the badness of the state of affairs but also on the agent's degree of agential involvement in generating it (2011a, 392).

[19] FH may be a better fit with Quinn's (1993a) proposal that there is stricter constraint against harmful direct agency than harmful indirect agency. Quinn refers to his proposal as a version of double effect, but this is confusing because the constraint against intentional harm and Quinn's constraint on harmful direct agency involve different fundamental concepts (viz., intentional harm versus harm that comes from the agent's deliberately involving the victim in something in order to further his purpose by way of the victim's being so involved). As Quinn observes, it is possible to hold both that there is a moral objection to harmful direct agency and a further objection to intentional harm (1993b, 196).

Wedgwood distinguishes two dimensions along which a person can be agentially involved to a greater or lesser degree in bringing about a state of affairs. The first dimension is causal: One's agency is more involved with a consequence that one *actively causes* than with a consequence that one merely fails to prevent. The second dimension is intentional. One's degree of agential involvement in bringing about a consequence is greater if one *intends* it than if one does not intend it, even if one foresees that it will result from one's action. It follows that there is a stronger reason against a course of action that has a bad state of affairs as a consequence if that state of affairs is intended than if it is not intended. Wedgwood claims that the PDE is thus explained by a "pervasive and fundamental feature of the normative domain," namely, the significance for reasons for action of the agent's degree of agential involvement in an action's consequences (2011a, 393).

Even if Wedgwood's account can explain why there is a stronger reason against a course of action that has a bad state of affairs as a consequence if that consequence is intended than if it is not intended, it is not clear that it can explain why there should be a constraint against intentionally harming one person as a means to saving a greater number. Consider, for example, the *Transplant* scenario, where the surgeon's killing one patient and distributing his organs would save the lives of five others (Section 2.2.2). This course of action results in the bad consequences that one patient is dead and his organs have been removed, and it results in the good consequence that the lives of five patients are saved. The surgeon actively causes and intends the bad consequences, but she also actively causes and intends the good consequence of the five's being saved. Thus, while her high degree of agential involvement in the bad consequences of her action will strengthen the reason against it, her high degree of agential involvement in the good consequences should also strengthen the reason *for* it. It is therefore difficult to see why the weighted reason for killing the one and distributing his organs will not outweigh the weighted reason against it.[20]

A second difficulty for Wedgwood's rationale stems from the fact that it depends on the general principle that reasons against courses of action that have bad consequences are strengthened by the agent's degree of agential involvement. He highlights two dimensions of agential involvement, but it

[20] Kagan makes a similar objection to a Nagel-style rationale for the PDE (1991, 177).

seems there are others, and an examination of these casts doubt on the general principle. For example, it seems that your agency is more involved with a consequence of your action that you bring about *wholeheartedly* than with a consequence that you bring about reluctantly or halfheartedly. After all, the consequences that you are wholehearted about reflect "who you are" – your values and character – in a way that consequences you are ambivalent about do not. Yet intuitively, it is not the case that a course of action that has a bad state of affairs as a consequence is more difficult to justify if the agent brings it about wholeheartedly than if she brings it about halfheartedly. The fact that an agent is wholehearted in bringing about a bad state of affairs may make her more deserving of blame, but it does not seem relevant for evaluating whether the conduct was justified or unjustified. In another paper, Wedgwood also suggests that one's degree of agential involvement in generating a state of affairs may be determined in part by the amount of thought or effort that one had to put into bringing it about (2009, 335). It is surely not the case, however, that it is more difficult to justify turning a runaway trolley away from five people onto a sidetrack with one person on it if the switch is rusty and difficult to turn than if it is well-oiled.

Finally, even if these previous two difficulties can be overcome, it seems to me that Wedgwood's account would still not be a satisfactory solution to the grounding challenge. We saw in Section 2.3 that an adequate solution should connect the PDE with concepts whose moral significance we can directly appreciate. As applied to Wedgwood's rationale, the crucial question therefore is, *why* should degree of agential involvement be relevant to questions of permissibility and justification? To reply that this is a fundamental feature of the normative domain implies that no further answer can be given. But while I can see why it might be thought that there is a direct relation between an agent's degree of *responsibility* for a certain state of affairs and her degree of agential involvement in it – the more we are agentially involved in a state of affairs, the more it is "ours" – so long as the consequences of an agent's conduct are voluntary and within her control, it is opaque why her degree of agential involvement in them should be relevant for determining the permissibility of her conduct.[21]

[21] Chappell (2011) defends a version of the PDE that states that other things equal we are less responsible for actions under descriptions under which they are not intentional on the ground that actions under nonintentional descriptions have a lower degree of "action-hood." This is distinct from the version of the PDE that Wedgwood and I endorse, which concerns permissibility rather than responsibility.

2.7 The "New Natural Law" Rationale

The PDE plays an important role in the New Natural Law (NNL) moral theory, developed by John Finnis, Joseph Boyle, Germain Grisez, and collaborators.[22] The foundation of the NNL theory is a pluralistic account of human flourishing. Human flourishing has a number of constituents or "basic human goods." The basic human goods are distinct and irreducible, either to one another or to some other more fundamental value, and each is intrinsically desirable and capable of providing noninstrumental reasons for action. NNL theorists also make a distinctive epistemological claim, namely, that the basic human goods are known as principles of practical reason – that is, as goods that are to be rationally pursued in action – noninferentially by acts of direct insight upon reflection on the experience of participating in them. What are the basic human goods? Different authors answer this question in slightly different ways. Here is the list provided by Finnis in *Natural Law and Natural Rights*: life and health, knowledge, play, aesthetic experience, sociability or friendship, practical reasonableness, and religion.

NNL theorists hold that basic human goods, and their concrete instantiations, cannot be measured on a scale of objective goodness or desirability: "[B]asic values and their particular instantiations as they figure in options for choice cannot be weighed and measured in accordance with an objective standard of comparison" (George 1999, 93).[23] NNL theorists typically put this by saying that the basic goods are incommensurable; however, it would be more accurate to say that in their view the basic goods are objectively incomparable. Two items are incommensurable if and only if there is no cardinal unit of measure that can represent the value of both. On the other hand, two items are incomparable just in case they do not stand in any evaluative comparative relation (Chang 2015).[24] NNL theorists believe that incomparability holds at two different levels. First, basic human goods, considered as abstract categories of value, are incomparable in the sense that "No basic good considered precisely as such can

[22] Finnis (1980, 1983, 1991); Finnis, Boyle, and Grisez (1987a, 1987b). See also George (1999), Murphy (2001), Gómez-Lobo (2002), and Lee (2019).

[23] NNL theorists allow that basic human goods can be compared in certain ways. For instance, an agent may subjectively prefer one to another. But in their view, neither the basic goods themselves nor their instances are comparable with respect to what makes them objectively worth pursuing or choosing.

[24] Incomparability does not follow from incommensurability: It is possible for there to be an ordinal ranking of two items even if there is no cardinal ranking.

be meaningfully said to be better than another" (Finnis, Boyle, and Grisez 1987b, 110). Second, concrete *instantiations* or instances of basic goods that figure in options for morally significant choice are incomparable, and this holds even when the instances at issue are instances of the same category of basic good. Let us call the first sort of incomparability "abstract incomparability" and the second "concrete incomparability."

NNL theorists seek to justify ethical norms teleologically in considerations about the human good. However, unlike crude utilitarians who attempt to introduce metrics by which to measure value, NNL theorists do not believe that the basic goods and their instantiations can be measured on an objective scale of desirability or choice-worthiness. They hold that morality, which is identified with right practical reason, requires not that agents maximize the good but that they choose in line with respect for all the basic human goods (Finnis 1980, 118; 1983, 125; Finnis, Boyle, and Grisez 1987a, 283). It is this requirement that is supposed to ground the PDE. How so?

As a first pass, we might say that we fail to respect a basic good when we destroy, damage, or impede an instance of it, so that there is a prohibition against destroying, damaging, or impeding instances of basic goods. This cannot be quite right, however, for it is possible for there to be situations in which no matter what one does, some instance or instances of a basic good will be damaged, destroyed, or impeded. A rule that categorically prohibited any damage, destruction, or impediment of instances of basic goods would therefore be impossible for human beings to uphold. It is not impossible, however, for us to uphold a rule that prohibits *choosing* to destroy, damage, or impede any instance of the basic goods, either as an end or as a means to an end (Boyle 2004, 56–7; see also Finnis 1980, 120; 1991, 71; Finnis, Boyle, and Grisez 1987a, 292). NNL theorists thus maintain that the injunction to respect basic human goods grounds the following principle:

> (P): One should never intentionally destroy, damage, or impede any instance of a basic human good.

Since life and health are basic human goods, (P) entails an absolute prohibition on intentionally killing or seriously harming human beings. At the same time, (P) does not categorically exclude the incidental damage or destruction of instances of human life or health. The distinction between intentional harm and incidental harm is therefore morally significant.

Notice that (P) implies a stricter constraint on intentional harm than even the absolutist version of the PDE I discussed in Chapter 1

(Section 1.3). The scope of the PDE, as I defined it, is restricted to *innocent* people, whereas (P) makes no such restriction. According to NNL theorists, it is never permissible to bring about death or harm intentionally. Although they are not generally pacifists, they hold that all killing, even of enemy combatants in war, should be incidental (Finnis 1998, 286–7).[25] Soldiers should fight not with the intention of killing enemy combatants but only with the intention of stopping their attack. By contrast, though traditional just war theorists share the belief that the ultimate aim of just combatants should be to stop the adversary from perpetrating injustice, they hold that it is morally permissible for just combatants intentionally to inflict harm on enemy combatants, and even kill them, if doing so is a necessary and proportionate means to this aim.

One concern with the NNL theory is that it places such a severe restriction on what may be done permissibly in fighting a just war. We can press the point by way of one of Finnis's own examples. He claims that a person can spear an assailant in the heart in self-defense without intending to kill him (1998, 287). However, even if we grant this, as I believe we should, it is undoubtedly the case that if in order to incapacitate someone you spear him in the heart, you intentionally *spear him in the heart*. Being speared in the heart is a very serious harm in its own right. Therefore, if the scope of the PDE is not restricted to the innocent, it will prohibit intentionally spearing an unjust adversary in the heart. The concern then is that in order to incapacitate enemy combatants, just combatants often must inflict serious harms by shooting them, bombing them, and using other weapons that are designed to inflict harm. If just combatants are prohibited from doing these sorts of things, they will not be able to respond effectively to injustice.

A second worry about the NNL theory is that (P) has further implications that are very counterintuitive. For (P) says that there is an absolute prohibition against not only intentional harm to life and health but also against intentionally destroying, damaging, or even impeding *any* instance of a basic human good, including goods such as play, knowledge, and aesthetic experience. Consider then three versions of a scenario, which I will call *Parody*. In each version, Villain reliably informs you that he will kill a large number of innocent people unless you

[25] Finnis acknowledges that in this respect NNL theorists differ from Aquinas, who holds that it is permissible for public officials intentionally to kill unjust enemies of the political community so long as they are not motivated by hatred (*ST* II-II 64.7).

V1: Break up a children's football game that is occurring in the park across the street by shouting nonsense and flapping your arms like a bird until they disperse.

V2: Interrupt someone's contemplation of a replica of Michelangelo's *Pietà* at the local art gallery by uttering mildly rude statements under your breath until he leaves in annoyance.

V3: Give Joe a drug that will erase his knowledge of Newton's laws of motion (Joe remembers these from a high school physics class and never uses them, and he could easily re-learn them or look them up if for some reason he needs them).

It seems obvious that you would not act wrongly were you to break up the football match, disrupt the person's contemplation of the sculpture, or give Joe the drug in order to prevent Villain from committing mass murder. My intuitions here are maximally clear and stable, and if they are incorrect, then I do not see how any of my case-based intuitions can be relied on. But NNL theorists are committed to the claim that you would act wrongly if you were to act in any of these ways.

NNL theorists are committed to these counterintuitive verdicts because they hold that all instances of basic human goods are incomparable. Their argument is as follows.[26] The fact that a choice would involve intentionally destroying, damaging, or impeding an instance of a basic good provides a reason against it. The only way that reason could be overridden is if the destroying, damaging, or impeding of that instance were outweighed by the good or avoidance of evil that this choice produced compared with the alternatives. But since instances of basic goods are incomparable, such outweighing is not possible.

Making a complete evaluation of this argument would involve assessing the extent to which values are comparable. I will note only that one can resist the notion that all basic goods and their instances are comparable without subscribing to the NNL theory. There is room for a more modest position, which simply denies that *all* instances of value can be graded on a single objective scale of rational desirability or choice-worthiness. Robert Koons calls this view the "limited comparability" thesis.[27] The limited comparability thesis holds that some instances of basic goods are

[26] See Finnis (1980, 118–19; 1991, 54–5; 1995, 29). The clearest presentation of the argument I have encountered is Lee (2019, 86).

[27] Robert C. Koons, Unpublished manuscript, "Varieties of Value Incommensurability and Incomparability: In Defense of a Moderate Position." www.academia.edu/9523691/Varieties_of_Value_Incommensurability.

incomparable with respect to their overall desirability or choice-worthiness, while allowing that other instances are comparable. It seems right to say, for example, that a healthy and mutually respectful friendship that has lasted for many years is better, with respect to its overall choice-worthiness, than a trivial instance of aesthetic appreciation.[28] Or, returning to *Parody*, one need not be a consequentialist to judge that preventing the destruction of the lives of a large number of people is better, with respect to its overall choice-worthiness, than the goods that figure in *V1*, *V2*, and *V3*.

In conclusion, the NNL rationale for the PDE turns on accepting the proposition that one should never intentionally destroy, damage, or impede any instance of a basic human good. This proposition implies restrictions on fighting enemy combatants that would make it very difficult – if not practically impossible – to effectively fight a just war, and it has deeply counterintuitive consequences. Finally, it is based on the controversial claim that all instances of basic human goods are incomparable. These problems are sufficiently costly to motivate the search for a different rationale.

2.8 Character-Based Rationales I

Jonathan Bennett considers the view that the PDE can be grounded in considerations of character. Proponents of this view point to a range of attitudes that are characteristically possessed by agents who bring about harm intentionally and agents who bring about harm incidentally. Agents who intend harm characteristically *hope* to bring about the evils they cause, and they *welcome* them or *feel glad* when they are realized. By contrast, agents who simply foresee harm characteristically are *reluctant* to set in motion a chain of events that will culminate in harm and afterward experience *regret* for having caused it. These contrasts in attitude are supposed to support the claim that agents who cause harm intentionally manifest a worse character than agents who simply foresee harm. And this difference in character, in turn, is supposed to explain why intentional harm is more difficult to justify than incidental harm.

The problem with this proposal is that the differences in attitudes it picks out are not necessarily associated with the intentional/incidental distinction. Bennett observes that while a terror bomber will feel glad upon learning of the deaths of noncombatants, since their deaths are needed to achieve his end, a precision bomber "will also be glad when

[28] The example is Koons's.

he hears that civilians have died, because that is evidence that something has happened that he needs for his ultimate aim," namely, the destruction of a military facility (1995, 222). Likewise, both the terror bomber and the precision bomber hope for harm to noncombatants: the former because it is part of his plan, the latter because it is indicative of the facility's destruction. On the other hand, a terror bomber might also be reluctant to carry out his mission and feel regret afterward. For while reluctance and regret are incompatible with aiming at a goal for its own sake, they are not incompatible with aiming at a goal that one is pursuing only as a means to an end (Bennett 1995; McIntyre 2001, 227).

As for the claim that agents who cause harm intentionally manifest a worse character than those who cause harm incidentally, this is also not necessarily the case. We can see a dramatic illustration of this by considering two bombers: Sadistic Precision Bomber (SPB) and Reluctant Terror Bomber (RTB) (Delaney 2015). SPB drops his bombs intending only to destroy a munitions factory, but he does not care at all about the nearby noncombatants. He drops his bombs without hesitation, he positively revels in the fact that he causes noncombatant casualties as a side effect of destroying the factory, and he would be perfectly happy to target them on other occasions.[29] Meanwhile, RTB sincerely believes that the best means to winning the war is to induce terror in the enemy population, but he is horrified at the thought of killing noncombatants and he decides to target them only after a painful inner struggle. When they are compared in relation to their overall character, SPB seems worse than RTB. Yet, according to the PDE, RTB is guilty of wrongdoing, while SPB may act permissibly when he destroys the factory.

2.9 Character-Based Rationales II

The previous rationale attempted to ground the PDE in the claim that intentional harm reveals a worse character than incidental harm. Lawrence Masek (2018) proposes a different way of grounding the PDE in considerations of character. He argues that the intentional/incidental distinction is morally relevant because intentional harm *forms* the agent's character differently than incidental harm.[30]

[29] This description of SPB's psychology raises the question of why he does not also intend to kill the noncombatants in addition to intending to destroy the factory. Perhaps he knows he is being observed by high command and he is afraid that indulging his sadistic desires will lead him to make a technical error.

[30] A similar rationale is suggested by Boyle (1980, 536–7) and Finnis (2011b, 194).

Masek distinguishes two ways the wrongfulness of an agent's conduct can be related to the corruption of his character. Most familiarly, some types of conduct corrupt an agent's character because they are wrong, and they are wrong because they are ways of mistreating others. Masek claims that the direction of explanation can also go in the opposite direction. That is, it can also be the case that some types of conduct are wrong *because* they corrupt the agent's character, in the sense that they form his character in such a way that he is prevented from, or impeded in, participating in characteristically human goods. Thus, while some moral principles are based on the interests of others, other principles are based on what is in the agent's own interest. Principles of this latter sort direct agents against engaging in types of conduct that contribute to the formation or deepening of character traits that prevent or impede them from participating in characteristically human goods, thereby causing them to lead less fulfilling lives (2018, 14–15).

What does this have to do with the PDE? According to Masek, intentional harm contributes to the corruption of the agent's character (or corrupts it more deeply), though in similar circumstances causing harm incidentally may not corrupt the agent's character. This is so because people have a "closer" relation to intended effects than to incidental ones. An agent knowingly causes incidental effects, but she not only knowingly causes intended effects but also seeks them, aims at them, and is guided by them. The closer relation between the agent and the effects she intends means that intentional harm changes the agent's character more directly than incidental harm (Masek 2018, 19–20). For instance, a terror bomber seeks death, and this contributes to his becoming someone who is disposed to seek death or strengthens that disposition if it is already present, and such a disposition impedes him from participating in friendships and in peaceful relations with others. A precision bomber does not seek death, however. Depending on the circumstances, he might still act unjustly, and he might also develop character traits such as callousness that prevent him from participating in similar human goods, but since he does not intend to kill, his conduct does not contribute to developing a disposition to seek death.

Masek's claim that a person is more closely related to intended effects than to incidental ones is similar to Wedgwood's notion that a person is more agentially involved in intended consequences than in incidental ones. One might therefore see Masek's rationale as an attempt to explain why agential involvement is morally significant, something that Wedgwood's rationale left unexplained. Another noteworthy feature of Masek's rationale is the claim that the distinction between intentional harm and incidental harm is morally relevant because of the way in which intentional harm forms the agent's character rather than because of the way it mistreats others. In this respect, his account is reminiscent of Kant's view that we have a duty to treat nonhuman animals humanely not because of the way it treats them but because of the effects it has on our own character (1996b, 564 [Ak 6: 443]). But while for Kant treating animals inhumanely dulls emotions such as compassion and sensitivity that are "serviceable to morality" in our relations with other people, for Masek intentional evil contributes to a disposition that is detrimental to the agent's own happiness.

Masek's rationale is premised on a claim about the differential effects of intentional harm and incidental harm on the agent's character. Given the centrality of this claim, it is surprising how little he offers in support of it. Masek admits that engaging in conduct that involves bringing about harm incidentally can cause the agent to become callous to human life, and this sort of disposition prevents or impedes its subject from participating in goods like friendship and peaceful relations with others no less than a disposition to seek harm. When he considers an objection to this aspect of his theory, his reply is that "At some point, a justification of [the] PDE bumps up against the limits of rational analysis" (2018, 21). This overlooks the fact that the questions of whether and how intentional harm forms the agent's character differently from incidental harm are empirical ones, and Masek provides no serious empirical data to support his central claim.

Masek's rationale is also vulnerable to the charge that it is objectionably egocentric. It seems to confirm, rather than alleviate, the concern of some critics that there is something narcissistic about the PDE's focus on the agent's intentions in acting (Nye 2013). For example, imagine that Joe is a bomber pilot fighting in a just war against country Z. Z has won a number of decisive victories, and it now seems defeat is probable. Then it occurs to Joe that he could turn the tide by attacking a group of noncombatants who are especially vulnerable, and he asks himself whether it would be permissible for him to kill them. If Masek's rationale is correct, then if attacking the noncombatants is wrong, it is so because it would have certain downstream effects on Joe's character and his prospects for happiness. The effects of any course of action on a person's character likely vary, but it has been observed since Aristotle that character traits tend to be formed as the result of repeatedly engaging in similar types of conduct. Suppose then that Joe reasons that while a single terror bombing run will likely have some detrimental effect on his character, it will not corrupt it so much that he is significantly impeded in forming or maintaining friendships and peaceful relations with others. Since this is so, he concludes that it is morally permissible for him to kill the noncombatants. Even if Joe's beliefs about the effects of the attack on his character are true and justified, proponents of the PDE will not want to say that he acts rightly if he attacks the noncombatants.

Moreover, whether or not Joe's beliefs about the effects of the attack on his character are justified, his reasoning about whether it would be wrong to kill noncombatants seems to look to the wrong place. If it is our job to give ethical guidance to the military and a pilot, or one of his commanders, comes to us with a plan that involves making attacks on noncombatants in order to further larger military objectives, our explanation of why this is wrong will surely point to a consideration about the potential victims, namely that they are innocent and so should not be the target or object of attack. The key intuition here is that the wrongfulness of intentionally harming the innocent must be accounted for in terms of the fact that it treats *them* in an objectionable manner, even though they have done nothing that makes them deserving of, or liable to, such treatment.[31] In comparison with this sort of consideration, considerations about the downstream effects of intentional harm on the agent's own happiness are at best secondary.

2.10 Conclusion

In this chapter, I argued that it is incumbent on proponents of the PDE to provide a compelling rationale for the principle. I also argued that six rationales proposed in the philosophical literature are unsatisfactory. I would not be too disappointed if my criticism of one or more of these rationales misses the mark – far from it! From my perspective, the best state of affairs would be for several lines of argument to converge on the PDE. Assuming my objections are cogent, however, I think we can extract some lessons that will be helpful for constructing a better rationale.

In order to avoid the narcissism objection, a good solution to the grounding challenge should explain the wrongfulness of intentional harm primarily in terms of how the agent relates to the people he harms rather than its effects on the agent's own happiness (Section 2.9). If it is wrong to

[31] Primoratz invokes a similar intuition in his critique of consequentialist justifications for the Principle of Noncombatant Immunity (2007, 27).

be "guided by evil," then it is also not because doing so puts one in an inappropriate relation to the essence of evil (Section 2.4) but because it puts one in an inappropriate relation to *the persons* whose evil one is guided by. Cavanaugh's rationale attempted to cash out the nature of the inappropriate relation at issue as being one of treating others as mere means, but it foundered on the observations that an agent can harm others intentionally as an end and intentionally harming others does not always involve treating them as mere means (Section 2.5). More promising, I think, is the idea that conduct that involves bringing about harm intentionally essentially involves the manifestation of a certain attitude. We have seen, however, that the attitude in question cannot be that of welcoming evil or feeling glad about it, as these attitudes are not necessarily connected with intending evil as opposed to simply foreseeing it (Section 2.8). In the following chapter, I will argue that the morally objectionable attitude that is expressed or manifested in intentional harm is a certain sort of *desire*, namely a desire to bring about harm or evil to an innocent person. This idea is at the heart of my proposed rationale for double effect, the solidarity rationale.

CHAPTER 3

Double Effect and the Morality of Solidarity

Wise men, Callicles, say that the heavens and the earth, gods and men, are bound together by fellowship and friendship, and order and temperance and justice, and for this reason they call the sum of things the 'ordered' universe, my friend, not the world of disorder or riot.

—Plato, *Gorgias* (507e–508a)

3.1 Introduction

According to the PDE, the moral constraint against bringing about evil as a foreseen side effect is less stringent than the constraint against bringing about evil intentionally:

> *PDE*: There is a strict moral constraint against bringing about serious evil (harm) to an innocent person intentionally, but it is permissible in a wider range of circumstances to act in a way that brings about serious evil incidentally, as a foreseen but nonintended side effect.

The grounding challenge is the task of providing a compelling rationale for the PDE. In this chapter, I present my own solution to the challenge.

As a starting point, I recall the just war theory argument for the Principle of Noncombatant Immunity (PNCI) (Section 1.5.1). The argument is that war is justified only as a response to a precedent injustice – in the paradigm case, as a defense of ourselves or others from unjustified aggression by the adversary. Since noncombatants are not engaged in perpetuating injustice, the justification for waging war against the agents of injustice does not extend to them. Therefore, noncombatants may not be the objects or targets of military operations. The presupposition of this argument is that the default norms that govern human interpersonal relations exclude intentional harm.[1] Noncombatants have done nothing

[1] This presupposition is made explicit by Walzer: "We are all immune to start with; our right not to be attacked is a feature of normal human relationships" (2015, 145n).

to justify a departure from the default, so it is wrong to harm them intentionally. At the same time, just war theory also presupposes that the default norms do not always preclude incidental harm to noncombatants in the course of carrying out attacks on military targets.

One way to approach a rationale for the PDE is therefore via the question, why should the default norms that govern human relationships include a more stringent constraint against intentional harm than incidental harm? My goal in this chapter is to ground these norms in a standard of human solidarity. In doing so, I am developing a rationale that was once gestured at by Philippa Foot. At the end of an essay that is devoted to defending double effect and the principle of doing and allowing, Foot makes the following, rather cryptic, remark:[2]

> Nor is it impossible to see the rationale of the principle that one man should not want evil, serious evil, to come to another even to spare more people the same loss; it seems to define a kind of solidarity between human beings, as if there is some sense in which no one is totally to *come out against* one of his fellow men. (2008a, 103–4)

Foot speaks of not *wanting* serious evil to come to others rather than not intending it, but given the context, I think it does no violence to her thought to take it to include the idea that the wrongfulness of bringing about evil to others intentionally consists in the fact that doing so is contrary to solidarity with them.

Foot's remark poses several questions. What sort of solidarity might undergird the PDE? What is the basis of this solidarity? And in what sense does someone who harms another intentionally totally "come out against" her? My way of proceeding will be to articulate a conception of a region of morality that provides a framework within which to answer these questions. This region encompasses what Ross (1930) calls the duty of beneficence and the duty of nonmaleficence. My conception of the content of these duties owes more to Strawson than Ross, however. In his essay "Freedom and Resentment," Strawson claims that reactive attitudes such as gratitude, resentment, and indignation are reactions to the manifestations, or lack thereof, of other attitudes on the part of others in our interpersonal dealings. In particular, the reactive attitudes "rest on, and reflect, an expectation of, and demand for, the manifestation of a certain

[2] Foot changed her mind about double effect. She does not endorse it in her early essay "The Problem of Abortion and the Doctrine of Double Effect," but she came to accept it in her paper "Morality, Action, and Outcome," in which the quoted passage appears. The only other discussion of Foot's remark in the context of double effect I am aware of is Wiggins (2009, ch. 9).

degree of goodwill or regard on the part of other human beings ... or at least the expectation of, and demand for, an absence of the manifestation of active ill will or indifferent disregard" (1974, 14). In this chapter, I argue that these demands can be unified around a standard of solidarity.

In Section 3.2, I describe a notion of solidarity that is relevant to our topic. As I define it, one person is in solidarity with another when the first has concern for the second that is founded on something shared in common between them. In Section 3.3, I propose that our conduct is measured by a standard of solidarity in relation to others insofar as they are fellow human beings. The topic of Section 3.4 is the precept of beneficence. Beneficence occupies a central place within the morality of solidarity because beneficent actions express benevolent desire, and a paradigmatic way in which we manifest concern for others is by acting in ways that express benevolence. These sections provide a view of the wider moral landscape within which, in my view, the PDE is properly situated. It is only after this landscape has been surveyed that I turn to the constraint against intentional harm. In Section 3.5, I argue that intentional harm is morally objectionable because it expresses a desire to bring about an evil for another rather than a good, and in doing so deviates from the solidarity standard. I also describe the relation between intentional harm and the concept of an attack, and I illustrate how the constraint against intentional harm circumscribes the duty of beneficence. Next, in Section 3.6, I turn to the two principles governing incidental harm I identified in Chapter 1 (Section 1.4): the Principle of Proportionality and the Principle of Due Care. I argue that these principles can also be grounded in the solidarity standard. Finally, in Section 3.7, I argue that the normative foundation of the solidarity standard is the principle that Anscombe identifies as the basis for the prohibition on murder, namely, the dignity of human beings.

3.2 Solidarity

Recent theorists have called solidarity a "multiply ambiguous notion" (Mason 2000, 27), a term with "unsettled meaning" (Schwarzenbach 2015, 4), and a "nebulous concept" (Stjernø 2004, 2). The notion of solidarity is employed in a variety of ways in contemporary social and political discourse, and I will not attempt to delineate them all or map their relations. Rather, my aim is to describe one concept of solidarity – or perhaps one aspect of a multidimensional phenomenon – that will be fruitful for developing the remark from Foot quoted above.

As I will understand it, to be in solidarity with someone is to possess concern for him or her, where one's concern is grounded on something that is shared in common between oneself and the other, something that enables one to think of oneself and the other as constituting a "we."[3] The examples of solidarity that most readily come to mind involve people coming together in order to fight injustice, such as *Solidarność* in Poland and the Civil Rights Movement in the United States. But the things that are shared in common between people are highly diverse and include shared interests and values, shared family or ethnic ties, shared history, shared religion, shared citizenship, and other sorts of community membership. An individual might thus be in solidarity with one person as a co-religionist, a second as a fellow citizen, and a third as a fellow member of the working class. Sharing something in common is the foundation for being in solidarity with others, but when one individual is in solidarity with another, the first has concern for the second person *himself* or *herself* and not just for the thing they share.

Concern for a person is an integrated bundle of cognitive, affective, and motivational states and dispositions. One of the most salient aspects of the phenomenology of concern is that it involves appearances of value. When we have concern for someone, we see her good – her welfare or flourishing – as being good, and we see the prospect of harm befalling her as bad. We would not hesitate, for instance, to say that it is a "bad thing" or a "bad state of affairs" when someone we care about is killed or injured, either at the hand of another human being or as the result of a natural disaster. But when we care about someone, we also see the person herself as having value, as being someone who *matters* and so is worthy of concern. Indeed, the value of the person is more fundamental than the value of her good, for when we have concern for someone, her good seems to us to matter precisely because *she* seems to matter (Darwall 2002, 70).

These appearances of value ground the further elements of concern. Because the object of concern and her good seem to matter, how she is faring will be perceptually salient, we will be attentive to her needs, and we

[3] In order to think of oneself and another as a "we," one must recognize that oneself and the other share something in common. But the ultimate ground of solidarity is the thing shared – the thing the agent recognizes – and not the agent's act of recognizing it.

My account of solidarity dovetails with that of Mason (2000), Cureton (2012), and Bommarito (2016). It is also not far removed from Rorty's (1989) description of solidarity as a sympathetic desire to alleviate another's suffering upon recognition of her as being "one of us" in some respect. Although concern for an individual is broader than a desire to alleviate suffering, concern includes a desire to sympathetically tend to its object's needs.

will notice possible ways in which our own conduct might improve her lot or detract from it. We will feel joy when things are going well for her, distress at her misfortunes, and compassion when she is suffering. And we will be motivated to contribute to her good to the extent that we are able.

I will call this final, motivational element of concern "goodwill." I believe that Aristotle's analysis of this attitude is still the most insightful.[4] According to him, goodwill is the wish for the good of an individual. This description is so far incomplete, however, for there are two further features that are essential to it. First, goodwill is oriented toward action. It is not an idle wish but a desire or inclination to benefit its object, at least "so far as you can."[5] Second, goodwill is a desire for the good of an individual *for his or her sake*.[6] One of Aristotle's examples helps clarify this feature.[7] It would ordinarily be absurd to think of a man who "loves his wine" that he bears goodwill for it. The man might want his wine to remain unspoiled, but even if we allow ourselves to suppose that it makes sense to think that the wine has a good and that being unspoiled is a constituent of it, it would still take a special explanation to make it intelligible how the man could want his wine to remain unspoiled *for the sake of the wine*. In ordinary circumstances, when a person wants his wine to remain unspoiled, he wants it not for the wine's sake but for the sake of some person or persons – say, himself or his dinner guests.

When one person possesses goodwill for another, he has an action-oriented desire for the other's good. But this desire is not like the wine-lover's desire. In bearing goodwill for another, one does not want the other's good merely for the sake of oneself or a third party; one wants the other's good for the sake of the person herself. As Darwall puts it, a desire for someone's good that springs from concern for her has both a "direct" and "indirect" object: Its direct object is the person's good, and its indirect object is the person herself (2002, 1). Since an end is *that for the sake of which* something is done, when one performs a beneficial action for a person that is motivated by goodwill, that person is an end of one's action. She is not an end to-be-produced, however, for in most circumstances she will already exist prior to one's action. She is rather what Kant calls a self-standing end (*selbstständiger Zweck*), that is, an entity for the sake of which some producible end is brought about (1996a, 86 [Ak 4:437]).

[4] Aristotle refers to the attitude as "love" or "liking" (*to philein*) (*Rhetoric* [*Rh.*] 1380b36–1381a1) and "goodwill" or "being well-disposed" (*eunoia*) (*Nicomachean Ethics* [*NE*] 1156a3–5).

[5] *Rh.* 1381a1.

[6] *NE* 1155b32, *Eudemian Ethics (EE)* 1240a23–5, *Rh.* 1381a1.

[7] *NE* 1155b29–31.

As I have defined it, *being in solidarity* is a relation that one individual can stand in to another, and there is no implication that the relation is reciprocated. When two or more persons are in solidarity with one another, I will say that a *relation of solidarity* obtains between them. Likewise, a group can be said to be in solidarity to the extent that its members stand in relations of solidarity with one another. Affective bonds between kin, comradeship among members of a sports team or military unit, and concern for others as fellow citizens are different determinations of the generic notion of relations of solidarity.[8]

Although I have not attempted to analyze everything that might intelligibly be meant in speaking of solidarity, the above account illuminates some of the core cases of it. Consider three examples of paradigmatic acts of solidarity:

(1) Farmworkers in our community have gone on strike against local fruit growers, who are paying them an unjust wage. In solidarity with the workers, we support their strike through collecting donations, participating in boycotts, and picketing (Blum 1980, 144).
(2) In solidarity with their black neighbors, the white residents of a city join in peaceful protests advocating for reform of the police and criminal justice system, which have unjustly and disproportionately harmed black residents.
(3) A young girl is undergoing chemotherapy for leukemia, and the treatment causes her hair to fall out. Her parents and older siblings shave their own heads in solidarity with her (Zhao 2019, 1).

In (1), our aim is to support the farmworkers, and we do so by undertaking public acts such as picketing and boycotting. These actions are intended to raise awareness of their plight, putting economic pressure on the growers, and influencing the political climate in ways that favor the farmworkers' interests. Our actions *manifest* or *express* our concern for the good of the farmworkers, and we take them because they are our fellow citizens and fellow human beings.[9] Similarly, in (2), by joining in the

[8] Aristotle refers to relations of reciprocal goodwill with the abstract noun *philia*, a term that is commonly translated as "friendship." However, Aristotelian *philia* can obtain between soldiers and sailors, members of religious guilds, and citizens of a political community. Konstan argues that for Aristotle friendship is a particular *kind* of *philia*, namely the kind that obtains between *philoi* (friends) (1997, 68). Whether or not this is correct, if *we* want to reserve "friendship" for affective bonds that are intimate and voluntary, we need a term that covers the mutual exchange of a more generic form of concern, and my term "relations of solidarity" fills this need.

[9] I further discuss the concept of manifesting or expressing a desire in Section 3.4.1.

protests, the white residents aim to affect change in institutions that discriminate against the black residents, and they do so out of recognition that the black residents are neighbors who are worthy of concern.

Case (3) may seem puzzling for my view, for it might appear that the actions of the other family members do not make the cancer-stricken girl better off. However, the contention that the other family members' actions do not make the girl better off overlooks the fact that not all benefits are material benefits. Shaving their heads is meant to be a sign on the part of the parents and siblings of their loving support for the girl as a member of the family, communicating to her that she does not have to undergo her ordeal alone. The knowledge that she does not have to bear the burden of the cancer treatment on her own but that it will be shared by those who care about her is itself a great good, one that it is likely to be psychologically uplifting for the girl as she battles the illness.

Besides explaining these paradigmatic cases, my account also explains three further features of solidarity. The first is that being in solidarity with others is a matter of being somehow *united* with them. One of the salient features of solidarity is the feeling of unity with others, the sense that one is "in it together" with those who are in solidarity with oneself. What accounts for this is the fact that goodwill is a kind of psychological bond or nexus between persons. As Aquinas explains, goodwill – in his terminology, love (*amor*) – is a form of interpersonal union, one which he calls the "bond of affection":

> There is also a union which is essentially love itself. This union is according to a bond of affection, and is likened to substantial union, inasmuch as the lover stands to the object of his love, as to himself .... (*ST* I-II 28.1 ad 2)

By "substantial union," Aquinas means the unity that a substance has with itself. It is impossible for one human being to be substantially united with another, for that would destroy the distinction between them. But when one person has goodwill for another, the first relates to the second in a way that is *similar* to the way he relates to himself. Aquinas is here recalling the Aristotelian doctrine that a friend is "another self."[10] We do not ordinarily seek to promote our good only because we believe that doing so is in the interest of others. Rather, when we act to further our good, we do so at least in part for our own sake. But if you have goodwill for another person, you desire her good for her sake and so you affectively relate to her in the

[10] *NE* 1166a1–4, *EE* 1240a23–5.

same way that you affectively relate to yourself.[11] Therefore, we can say that when relations of solidarity obtain between persons, none of the parties are "in it alone," for each cares about the good of the others in the same way he cares about his own good.

Second, the account explains the historical relation of solidarity to *fraternity*, the concept of which was the immediate ancestor of solidarity. Fraternity also includes the idea of mutual support and cooperation: In the focal case, siblings are supposed to act together in ways that are conducive to the flourishing of the family, and to the extent that they do not, their relationship is defective. However, fraternity cannot be analyzed in exclusively behavioral terms, for that would leave out the essential notion that the cooperative behavior of siblings is supposed to be a manifestation of their *love* or *concern* for one another, a concern that is based on their kinship.

Finally, my account explains how solidarity serves to realize its characteristic function, which is to produce social harmony or social cohesion.[12] It does so in at least two ways. First, relations of reciprocal concern and goodwill among members of a group foster social trust and willingness to cooperate. Second, relations of solidarity also serve as a counterweight to forces that threaten to break the group into hostile factions, such as competing interests, differences in evaluative outlook, and the sort of petty tribal attitudes that Freud called the "narcissism of minor differences" (1961a, 72). Social harmony, in turn, facilitates cooperative activities that are conducive to achieving a wide variety of shared ends that benefit the members of the group.

The aim of this section was to outline a conception of solidarity, one that is relevant to developing a solution to the grounding challenge. Having accomplished this task, in the following section I discuss the role of solidarity in the moral domain.

3.3 The Morality of Solidarity

The guiding idea of this chapter is that a central region of morality is structured by a standard of human solidarity. The proposal is that we

[11] Relatedly, Kant observes that everyone treats himself as an end in the sense I identified above (1996a, 86 [Ak 4:437]). It follows that in treating others as ends one is treating them as one treats oneself.

[12] In summarizing the contributions of French sociologists from Fourier to Durkheim, Stjernø writes they all "underscore the need to have a broadly inclusive understanding of solidarity, to include and encompass all essential parts of society in the great social task that is embodied in their common goal, the promotion of a harmonious society" (2004, 39).

ought to be in solidarity with others and that our conduct is measured by a standard of concern and goodwill in relation to them. The basis for this solidarity is simply our shared humanity – that is, our rational nature.[13]

The proposal is not that we should be in solidarity with collective entities such as aggregate welfare or with humanity considered as an abstract whole. The idea is rather that we should be in solidarity with each of our fellow human beings *as individuals* because they are our fellow human beings.[14] It is not possible for us to have the same sort of personal knowledge of, and intimate affection for, every human being that we have for our friends and family members, and this probably would not be desirable even if it were possible. But we can have the basic elements of concern even for strangers, such as recognition of their value and a desire for their good for their sake.[15] This sort of basic solidarity is not always reciprocated, but there is a normative expectation that it will be, and when it is, we stand in relations of human solidarity with others.[16]

An agent's conduct is morally defective, and thus morally wrong, when it deviates from the standard of solidarity that measures her conduct in relation to some other person or persons.[17] In the remainder of the chapter, I will describe three ways in which an agent can act in a way that deviates from the solidarity standard. These three ways of acting wrongly correspond to the precept of beneficence, the strict constraint against intentional harm, and the Principles of Proportionality and Due Care.

[13] Bayertz (1999) refers to this form of solidarity as universal solidarity. Rorty (1989) denies that there is a human essence that could ground a notion of human solidarity. I think his skepticism about essences is unwarranted, but it would take me too far afield to argue for this claim here.

[14] One problem with Ivan Karamazov in *The Brothers Karamazov* is that while he claims to love humanity he detests individual human beings.

[15] Tania Singer and Olga Klimecki describe a technique, loving kindness training, which is designed to cultivate concern for other people in general. Someone practicing this technique begins by visualizing a person he or she feels close to and then gradually extends the feeling of kindness toward others, including strangers and even personal enemies. Singer and Klimecki's research found that people who practiced loving kindness training increased their helping rates toward strangers in a computer game when compared with a control group (2014, R876).

[16] My proposal in this section is similar in some respects to Scanlon's conception of morality in Scanlon (2008, ch. 3). Scanlon conceives of morality as specified by a normative ideal for a relationship, and like me he sees the relevant relationship as one that holds between human beings generally. He also believes that the moral relationship is defined by a kind of mutual concern. However, Scanlon slides from speaking about concern for others to speaking about concern for the justifiability of our actions, thereby linking his account to his contractualist ethical theory. By contrast, in the view I am proposing, norms of solidarity are specified directly in terms of concern for others and the goodwill that is a constituent of it. This is not a minor difference: It leads to opposing views about the truth of the PDE and the correct way to understand the duty of beneficence.

[17] Or when it deviates voluntarily from it (see Section 5.6).

Before discussing these norms, I want to emphasize that human solidarity governs only one region of morality. Most evidently, this region is anthropocentric, but nothing I say here excludes the idea that there are other regions that are nonanthropocentric.[18] Second, norms of solidarity are, in the first instance, interpersonal,[19] but they do not constitute the whole of interpersonal morality. This is because they deal only with duties that we have to others insofar as they are fellow human beings – what have sometimes been called the "offices of humanity." I assume though that we also have special duties to certain other people that are grounded in more particular relationships, e.g., as parents, children, friends, or fellow citizens of a political community. These relationships define more local forms of community and solidarity. Third, norms of solidarity do not exhaust what we owe to others; for example, they do not determine in any direct way norms of promise-keeping or distributive justice.

Finally, the norms of solidarity I discuss are *default* norms for human interpersonal dealings (Section 3.1). To say they are default norms is to say there are circumstances under which departure from them is justified. In relation to the constraint against intentional harm in particular, commonsense morality recognizes two such circumstances. First, a person who voluntarily transgresses moral norms, and so is subjectively culpable for his transgression, deserves censure for engaging in wrongdoing and sometimes also sanction. But sanctioning wrongdoers involves intentionally imposing harms or burdens on them that it would not otherwise be permissible to impose. Second, commonsense morality also recognizes that persons and communities are entitled to defend themselves and others from harmful conduct that is undertaken without a just cause even if the perpetrators are not subjectively culpable for it (e.g., as a result of extensive propaganda). Agents of harmful and objectively unjust actions therefore make themselves liable to proportionate harm inflicted in the course of defensive action. What these two sorts of cases have in common is that for departure from the default to be justified, there must be some answer to the question, "What *offense* has this person committed that makes treating him or her in this way appropriate?" The concept of "innocence" serves to mark out those persons who have committed no offense and who are thus not suitable objects of intentional harm.[20]

[18] In particular, it does not preclude the existence of moral norms pertaining to the treatment of nonhuman animals or care for the environment.

[19] But see note 48 on self-directed duties.

[20] In addition, nonabsolutists about the constraint against intentional harm also hold that it may be permissibly infringed when a great enough good is at stake (Section 1.3).

It must also be emphasized that while punishment and self- and other-defense involve some departure from the norms of solidarity, those norms are never completely suspended. Even wrongdoers retain their human dignity (Section 3.7), and this is reflected in the morality of warfare and punishment. For instance, punishments must not be excessive or degrading, combatants fighting a just war may only employ the degree of violence that is necessary to stop injustice, and war must be fought with the aim of restoring peaceful relations with the adversary.

3.4 The Precept of Beneficence

3.4.1 Beneficent Conduct

In our ordinary interactions with others, we expect that they will manifest some degree of concern for us, and the paradigmatic way this concern is manifested is in conduct that promotes our good. It is not the case that every action that benefits someone is an expression of concern for the beneficiary, however. One person, A, might realize that some good will accrue to another person, B, as a side effect of a course of action he has undertaken even if he does not care at all about B. A may be pursuing the course of action simply because it is the easiest or cheapest way of obtaining some object he wants for himself. In the central case, beneficial conduct is an expression *of concern* for the beneficiary when it expresses goodwill for the beneficiary, a desire for the beneficiary's good for his or her sake (Section 3.2).

When you are in solidarity with someone, you desire her good for her sake. If this desire is not an idle wish, you will also be disposed to bring about more determinate states of affairs you take to further her good. Let us call a desire to bring about or secure a good (including the prevention of an evil) for a person for that person's sake a *benevolent* desire.[21] Desires – at least, the sort of desires that interest us here – are dispositions, and dispositions are manifested or expressed in characteristic sorts of action. The main difference between desires and simple physical dispositions, such as fragility and solubility, is that desires are expressed teleologically in action that is aimed at their satisfaction (Hyman 2015, 107).[22]

[21] What about cases where the agent mistakenly believes that something is a good when it is not? "Benevolence" suggests an act of will that has a good for its (direct) object. But when someone makes an erroneous judgment, the object of her desire is not a good but a merely apparent good. Therefore, the desire is not a benevolent one, even if the agent believes it is and it is motivated by a more general desire for the good of the other.

[22] As Anscombe puts the point, "The primitive sign of wanting is *trying to get*" (1963, §36).

I will call the sort of conduct that successfully expresses benevolent desire "beneficent conduct." Since desires are expressed in action that is aimed at their satisfaction, beneficent conduct may be defined as follows:

> *Beneficent Conduct*: Conduct – broadly construed to include omissions – that is aimed at bringing about or securing a good for S for S's sake, and that succeeds in bringing about or securing that good for S.

Beneficent conduct is the sort of conduct that paradigmatically expresses goodwill for others.[23] But there are two ways that someone's conduct can fall short of the paradigm. First, A might act with the aim of bringing about G for B for B's sake but fail to secure G. In that case, A tries to act beneficently but is unsuccessful (with respect to G). Second, someone's conduct might fall short of the paradigm due to a mistaken belief about the good. Suppose that N is not a good (that is, N is an evil or neither a good nor an evil) and that A aims at and succeeds in bringing about N for B in the mistaken belief that N is a good. Perhaps it's not as clear what to say about this sort of case, but it seems to me that A is not acting beneficently toward B (with respect to N). Rather, A is trying to act beneficently, but she fails to do so because of her mistaken belief.

Notice also that whenever an agent acts beneficently, she expresses a benevolent desire. The reason is that an agent's aims in acting are the contents of the desires that are expressed in her action (Hyman 2015, 128). Therefore, when an agent acts beneficently, her conduct can be explained by reference to the benevolent desire it expresses. For example, suppose that John helps Sally with her homework with the aim of helping her learn the material, for Sally's sake. It will then be true that John helps Sally with her homework *because* he wants her to learn the material for her sake.

3.4.2 *Privations of Beneficence*

Beneficent conduct successfully expresses the concern for others that is constitutive of solidarity. Conversely, failure to aid others (or at least attempt to aid them) sometimes betrays a lack of concern, or sufficient concern, for them. These failures to aid deviate from the standard of solidarity that measures our conduct in relation to others and are therefore wrongful.[24]

[23] My definition of beneficent conduct corresponds to what Audi calls "altruistic conduct" (2016, 85).

[24] Germany is one of a number of jurisdictions with a Good Samaritan law criminalizing failures to provide reasonable assistance to others in emergency situations. The commenters on the German Penal Code justify this legal obligation as arising from a "minimum humanitarian solidarity"

Utilitarianism has been recommended on the ground that it reflects the duty of beneficence recognized by virtuous agents (Smart 1973, 31). But utilitarians misconstrue the duty of beneficence in two ways. First, beneficent actions aim at promoting or securing a good for some particular person or persons for their sake, not at maximizing the net balance of aggregate welfare of all humankind or all sentient beings.[25] Second, as Foot observes (2008a, 2008b), from the fact that a virtuous agent cares about the good of others and consequently has among his general ends the aim of benefiting them, it does not follow that anything one does with the aim of improving the lot of others will be morally required or even morally permissible. For as it appears in commonsense moral thought, the *content* of the duty of beneficence is circumscribed by other kinds of considerations.

Another way of putting Foot's point is that the precept of beneficence is one that holds *semper sed non ad semper*. This means that the fact that we could benefit someone by ϕ-ing is always a relevant consideration, but it does not always impose a moral requirement to act beneficently by ϕ-ing because it is possible for there to be other considerations that countervail sufficiently against doing so.[26] Let us call a *privation of beneficence* a failure to act (or attempt to act) beneficently when one can and ought to do so. Privations of beneficence are wrong, but not every omission of beneficent conduct is a privation of beneficence.

Here are four sorts of considerations that countervail decisively against beneficent action (the list is intended to be illustrative, not exhaustive). First, the potential beneficiary would use the good in question to harm others who are not liable to, or deserving of, harm. Second, there is some more important matter that the agent should be attending to instead. For instance, a person ought not to spend the evening working at the local food pantry when doing so would mean leaving her young children at home unattended. Third, engaging in beneficent conduct would require the agent to make an unreasonable sacrifice to her own good, e.g., one is not required to give her own life, or even run a substantial risk of doing so,

(*humanitären Mindestsolidarität*) (Kindhäuser, Neumann, and Paeffgen 2010, 2749, Commentary on §323c).

[25] A fortiori beneficent actions do not aim at increasing the total net quantity of intrinsic good in the universe. I concur with Wiggins (1998) that Ross, under the influence of Moore, went astray in his conception of beneficence on this point.

[26] Cf. Cullity 2004, 18–19. The source of the Latin phrase is Aquinas, who states that sins of omission are contrary to affirmative precepts, which always impose an obligation but not "for all times" (*contrariatur praecepto affirmativo quod obligat semper sed non ad semper*) (*ST* I-II 71.5 ad 3).

in order to prevent others from suffering harm. Fourth, if the only physically available means of effecting a good are themselves wrongful, then there is no privation of beneficence if one forgoes taking them. If acting in a certain way is morally impermissible, then the agent ought not and ethically *cannot* act in that way even if doing so would have good results.

It follows that it takes a degree of practical wisdom to discern when a situation imposes a duty to act beneficently. Nevertheless, it is not difficult to stipulate conditions in which a failure to act beneficently would constitute a privation of beneficence. The shopworn example is that of the drowning child whose life you could save at trivial cost to yourself in circumstances in which there are no other countervailing factors (Singer 1972). In that case, it would obviously be wrong for you to stand by and allow the child to drown. But it is worth calling attention to an implication of my view that is more controversial. Consider a variation on the rescue case by Ramon Das:[27]

> *Swimming Pool*: Aaron dives into a swimming pool and saves a woman's child from drowning. He does not save the child for the child's sake, however. Instead, he saves the child in order to impress its mother as a means to sleeping with her (2003, 326).

Suppose that Aaron is able to save the child for the child's sake and that there are no considerations that sufficiently countervail against doing so. Then on my account, there is a privation of beneficence on Aaron's part and he acts wrongly. There is a privation of beneficence because although he saves the child, he does not do so even in part for the child's sake but only with a view to satisfying his lustful desire.

Das thinks we should reject the notion that Aaron acts wrongly for two reasons. First, he claims that the idea that Aaron acts wrongly conflicts with the intuition that Aaron does the right thing for the wrong reason. Second, he claims there are no grounds for doubting that Aaron does in fact act rightly.

I agree that saving the child is the right thing for Aaron to do. The value of the child's life means that it is a bad thing if the child drowns. This generates a reason for Aaron to save him, and I have stipulated that no considerations countervail sufficiently against doing so. The crucial point for responding to Das's first objection, however, is that there is in fact no

[27] Das raises this case as objection to Michael Slote's (2001) agent-based virtue theory.

conflict between judging that Aaron does the right thing for the wrong reason and the claim that Aaron acts wrongly.

Compare the idea of doing the right thing in the wrong manner. Suppose that Charles disciplines his misbehaving child in a way that is excessively harsh. If discipline is merited by the child's behavior, then disciplining her is the right thing for Charles to do. Still, the fact that Charles disciplines the child in such a harsh *manner* surely means that his conduct is morally defective. In light of this, I think we would be right to judge that he acts wrongly.

We can consistently judge both that Charles does the right thing and that he acts wrongly because the judgment that he does the right thing is a judgment of what he does – what act-type his conduct instantiates – while the judgment that he acts wrongly is a judgment that assesses his overall concrete action or conduct.[28] Charles's conduct includes what he does as one of its dimensions, but it has other dimensions as well, namely, its manner and motivation (Audi 2016). So even if *what* he does is right or appropriate, his conduct may nonetheless still be wrong in virtue of a defect in one of these other dimensions. And this possibility is realized in the case at issue: Charles's conduct is wrong even though it instantiates the right act-type (*discipline the child*) because its excessively harsh manner is a wrong-making feature of it.

It is possible to say something similar about Aaron's conduct in *Swimming Pool.* His conduct instantiates the act-type *save the child* and saving the child is the right thing for him to do. It is compatible with this, however, to say that Aaron's lack of the right motivation is a wrong-making feature of his conduct. Just as we can consistently judge that Charles both does the right thing and that he acts wrongly in virtue of doing the right thing in the wrong manner, so too we can consistently judge both that Aaron does the right thing and that he acts wrongly in virtue of doing the right thing for the wrong reason.

There is thus no conflict between the intuition that Aaron does the right thing for the wrong reason and the claim that he acts wrongly. But does Aaron really act wrongly? Das thinks it is clear he does not, but I do not find this at all obvious. We might say that what the situation *calls for* or *demands* is a response of basic solidarity on Aaron's part to the child's plight. Aaron fails to make the called-for response, though, because he saves the child only for a self-regarding reason. In the terms I developed in

[28] For more on the distinction between judgments of act-types and judgments of concrete actions, see Section 6.3.1.

this section, Aaron's conduct deviates from the standard of solidarity that measures it in relation to the child, and for this reason, he is guilty of a privation of beneficence.[29]

3.5 The Constraint against Intentional Harm

3.5.1 Maleficent Conduct

According to the proposal in Section 3.3, our conduct is measured by a standard of solidarity toward our fellow human beings and we act wrongly when our conduct deviates from this standard. Privations of beneficence are "sins of omission," insofar as they consist in the agent's failure to manifest benevolent desire in circumstances in which she can and ought to do so. In this section, I show how the strict constraint against intentional harm can also be derived from the standard of solidarity.

Why should intentional harm be morally objectionable on the morality of solidarity? We can answer this question by comparing intentional harm to privations of beneficence. Many privations of beneficence involve a failure to engage in conduct that aims at the good of others. However, in *Swimming Pool* (Section 3.4.2), Aaron acts wrongly even though he does aim at saving the child and indeed succeeds in achieving this aim. Aaron aims at a good for the child, and his conduct thus expresses a desire with the same *valence* as a benevolent desire. It deviates from the standard of solidarity, however, because it does not express a desire for the good of the child *for the child's sake*. An agent who brings about harm intentionally engages in conduct that involves an even greater deviation from the solidarity standard. Instead of aiming at promoting or securing a good for his victim, the agent of intentional harm aims at bringing about an evil for her. In doing so, the agent's conduct expresses a desire whose valence is *contrary* to benevolence: the desire for an evil for a person, or *malevolent* desire.[30]

[29] This is compatible with the true proposition that Aaron's omitting to save the child altogether would be *morally worse* – even *much* morally worse – than his saving him but failing to do so for the right reason. It is also compatible with the proposition that in jurisdictions with Good Samaritan laws there are good pragmatic reasons not to hold people criminally liable for failing to provide assistance to others with the right sort of motivation (Tadros 2011, 164–6).

[30] Jorge Garcia makes a similar point by saying that when an agent fails to act for the sake of securing a good for someone she acts inofficiously, but when an agent acts for the sake of preventing or eliminating someone's having a good, she acts *counter*-officiously (1993, 8).

Consider the concept of maleficent conduct, which I define as follows:

> *Maleficent Conduct*: Conduct – including omissions – that is aimed at bringing about or securing an evil (harm) for S and that succeeds in bringing about or securing that evil for S.

Since a person who intentionally harms someone successfully aims at bringing about an evil for the victim, an agent of intentional harm acts maleficently. Conversely, if a person acts maleficently, her conduct expresses a malevolent desire: Because an agent's aims in acting are the contents of the desires expressed by her action, when A ϕ-s with the aim of bringing about E for B, A's ϕ-ing expresses the desire to bring about E for B.[31] Therefore, when one person harms another intentionally, not only is the victim harmed, but the harm is the result of conduct that manifests malevolent desire. But malevolent desire constitutes an *inversion* of the correct orectic orientation toward the victim. For this reason, conduct that brings about serious harm intentionally grossly deviates from the standard of human solidarity.[32]

It may be objected that an agent of intentional harm does not necessarily desire for her victim to suffer harm. In Chapter 2 (Section 2.8), we met Reluctant Terror Bomber (RTB). This figure sincerely believes that the best means of winning a just war is to induce fear into the adversary's population, which he can do by killing and injuring noncombatants. But he is also horrified at the thought of intentionally harming innocent people. He decides to target them only after a long inner struggle and afterward feels regret for doing so. RTB intentionally harms noncombatants, yet it would be intelligible if later he were to say, "I hurt them because I thought it was the surest path to victory, but no way did I *want* to harm them!"

My response begins with the observation that the terms "desire" and "wanting" have both a narrow and a broad sense.[33] The narrow sense corresponds roughly to what the Greeks called *epithumia* and which we might call "appetite." In this sense, we desire something only when we

31 If E is an evil but A mistakenly thinks E is a good, A qualifies as acting maleficently. However, if A's mistake is a reasonable one, then there will be grounds for excusing or exonerating her for the deviation in her conduct (see Section 5.6).

32 It may appear that there should be an exception for cases of life-saving medical amputations. I do not believe that these are genuine cases of intentionally inflicting evils on others in order to benefit them, however. A human being's body parts are good to the extent that they contribute to the good of the whole person. If the condition of a body part is in some way threatening a person's survival, then the part is not a good and its removal is not an evil.

33 Cf. Anscombe (1963, §34); Thompson (2008, 103–4); Finnis (2011b, 175).

believe it will give us pleasure or be conducive to pleasure. It is in the narrow sense that RTB can truly say that he did not want to harm noncombatants: He had no appetite for it and took no pleasure in doing so. However, there is also a broader sense of "desire" according to which a desire is a state of being motivated by a goal (Alvarez 2010, 93). Even if RTB took no pleasure in harming noncombatants, harming them was a goal that motivated his action. It was not his ultimate goal, which was victory, but it was a more proximate goal and his motivation to pursue this goal helps explain why he dropped his bombs on them. Thus, RTB's desire enters into a true explanation of his conduct: He dropped his bombs *because* he wanted to harm the noncombatants and believed that dropping bombs on them would harm them, and he wanted to harm the noncombatants because he wanted to help procure victory.[34]

In this respect, even a reluctant terror bomber compares unfavorably with a precision bomber (Section 2.2.1). A terror bomber's ultimate goal is victory, but one of his more proximate goals is to kill and injure noncombatants. His conduct therefore expresses the desire to bring about harm for his victims, and I think this is the sense in which we can say – in Foot's language – that he *comes out against them* in it. By contrast, a precision bomber drops his bombs in order to destroy a military target and not in order to kill or injure noncombatants. While a precision bomber may or may not have a desire to harm nearby noncombatants, his conduct is not motivated and explained by this desire and thus is not an expression of it. Of course, this does not mean that precision bombing is always morally justified. It simply means that whatever else is true of the precision bomber's conduct, he does not "come out against" noncombatants in the way the terror bomber does, for his conduct does not express malevolent desire for them.

3.5.2 Attacks

There is something more we can say about the difference between the precision bomber and the terror bomber: The former attacks a military target while the latter attacks noncombatants. There is a close connection between the concept of intentional harm and the concept of an attack. This is because, as R. A. Duff notes, *attack* is an intentional concept: Attacks have objects, at which they aim and direct some harm (2007, 149).

[34] See Davidson (1963) and Section 4.3.1.

These objects may be identified in highly specific terms (e.g., The Prime Minister of Nation Z) or in more generic ones (e.g., the next passer-by). But insofar as attacks involve bringing about harm intentionally, they necessarily express malevolent desire.

Nonetheless, the extension of the concept of intentional harm is broader than that of an attack. Consider the case of a woman who, in order to escape the burdens of motherhood, kills her children by omitting to feed them. The woman intentionally brings about the deaths of her children: Since they depend on her for nourishment, in withholding it she is responsible for their deaths (Section 1.2.1). However, it seems wrong to say that the woman attacks her children. She would attack them if she decided to carry out her murderous intention by, say, stabbing them or shooting them. But starving someone to death is not attacking him. Attacks are essentially "active" in the sense that A attacks B only if A actively intervenes in the world in order to cause B harm. Since it is sometimes possible to cause death intentionally without actively intervening in the world, not all cases of intentional harm are attacks.[35]

Paradigmatic attacks also have two further properties: (1) they involve the use of force or violence, and (2) they are perpetuated against the will of their victims. Neither of these two properties is essential to attacks, however. The queen who intentionally kills the sleeping king by pouring a vial of poison in his ear does not kill him by using force or violence, but she still attacks him, albeit in a stealthy manner. And while it is unusual, people do sometimes freely consent to being seriously harmed or killed, even in circumstances in which death is uncontroversially an evil. In 2001, Bernd Brandes voluntarily answered an advertisement to be killed and eaten by Armin Meiwes; Meiwes killed Brandes by stabbing him in the throat and was eventually found guilty of murder. It seems right to say that Brandes consented to being attacked by Meiwes, though this is a marginal case of an attack.

While not all cases of intentional harm are attacks, attacks are surely the most common form that intentional harm takes. This is worth flagging because intuitively attacks on others are *the* paradigm of unsolidarity with them. The account I have offered in this section explains why this is so: Insofar as they are intentional, attacks manifest malevolent desire and, in doing so, grossly deviate from the standard of solidarity. In addition, my

[35] Here I depart from Duff, who classifies omissions intended to cause harm as attacks (Duff 2007, 149).

account also explains why cases of intentional harm that are not attacks, such as that of the parent who kills her children by starving them, are morally on a par with attacks.

3.5.3 *Acting Maleficently vs. Acting out of Malice*

The claim that agents who intentionally bring about harm for others act maleficently toward them should be distinguished from the claim that agents who intentionally bring about harm for others act *out of malice* for them. When we say that someone acted out of a certain motive, we are identifying the most final desire that explained his conduct (Sverdlik 2011, ch. 2). In particular, if A acts out of malice for B, then the desire that ultimately explains why A acts as he does is the desire *to do harm to* B, under just that description. So, if you were to kill one person only in order to save five others from being killed, you would not be acting out of malice for the person you kill but rather out of a desire to save the five. However, you would be acting maleficently toward the one.

In fact, even an agent who kills another person as an end does not necessarily act of out malice for him, as the following example illustrates:

> *Lost File*: Alice is a physician and has a patient, Bert, who has been in a coma for many years. One day while searching the hospital records, Alice discovers a lost file, which is a request by Bert to be disconnected in the event he falls into a coma. Alice gets permission from the hospital and disconnects Bert. She disconnects him in order to kill him because she thinks his continuing to live is a senseless indignity and that death would be good for him (Thomson 1999, 514).

It is controversial whether death is an evil for Bert in these circumstances. We can simply note that Alice's belief that death is a good for Bert is either true or false. If it is true, then she does not act out of malice for him. On the other hand, if Alice's belief is false, then she intentionally brings about an evil for Bert in the mistaken belief that it is a good. In that case, Alice acts maleficently, but she does not act out of malice, for the most final desire that explains her conduct is not a desire to do harm to Bert but a desire to do good for him.

It is not just agents who bring about harm out of malice who act in a way that deviates from the standard of solidarity. *Whenever* a person intentionally causes harm, he successfully expresses a desire to bring about an evil for his victim – that is, a malevolent desire. And any conduct that successfully expresses malevolent desire toward an innocent person constitutes a gross deviation from the standard of solidarity in relation to the victim because of the objectionable valence of this desire.[36] It may be that agents who intentionally harm others in order to see them suffer harm deviate even further from the solidarity standard than do agents who bring about intentional harm out of better motives, but both sorts of agents engage in conduct that is morally defective.

This final point sheds some light on the concept of murder. The common law *mens rea* for murder is "malice aforethought," and in the case of intentional killing, this malice is said to be express rather than implied.[37] This has given rise to puzzlement, for intentional killing need not involve any malice in the sense of spite or hatred (Perkins 1934, 537–8). A contract killer may bear no personal hatred for his victims – it is, as they say, "just business." Yet, while the contract killer does not kill his victims out of malice but out of a desire for money, his conduct does express malevolent desire toward those he kills, and this is what constitutes the "malice" of which the law speaks in the case of intentional killing.[38]

3.5.4 Intentional Harm and the Precept of Beneficence

I have argued that both the precept of beneficence and the constraint against intentional harm can be grounded in a standard of human solidarity. Here it is worth reiterating that the duty of beneficence is circumscribed by other sorts of considerations, including moral constraints (Section 3.4.2). For an illustration of how the constraint against intentional harm interacts with the duty of beneficence, consider the *Transplant* dilemma:

> *Transplant*: A surgeon has five patients who are in need of organs – one needs a heart, two need lungs, and two need a kidney – and they will all die unless they are given transplants soon. Unfortunately, no organs are presently available. But then he learns that another person, Arnold, has just

[36] For the same reason, deviating from the standard of solidarity in one's conduct does not require expressing a desire to bring about harm for a person "for her sake." It is not even immediately clear what it is to desire a harm for someone for that person's sake. To me it suggests wanting to harm someone because one thinks it will have some downstream beneficial effect for him. Think, for example, of an abusive father who claims that the beating he is inflicting on his son is not for his (the father's) sake but for the son's, because it will "teach him a lesson." This sort of case is a deviation from the standard of solidarity, but so too are cases where the agent brings about harm intentionally though not "for the victim's sake."

[37] I am here prescinding from the distinction between murder and voluntary manslaughter, which arose as a device for mitigating the severity of punishment for intentional killings that resulted from sufficient provocation.

[38] In the case of intentional killing because there are other cases of murder that do not involve the intention to kill (or even harm) the victim (Section 3.6).

> arrived for his yearly check-up and is a compatible donor for all five of the patients. The surgeon reasons that he could give Arnold a lethal injection instead of the inoculation he is expecting, thereby making his organs available to save the five.

Let us suppose that you are the surgeon and that your options are O_1: give Arnold the lethal injection, remove his organs, and give them to the five patients in need of transplants, or O_2: forgo giving Arnold the lethal injection. The outcome of O_1 will be that Arnold dies and the five live, while the outcome of O_2 will be that Arnold lives and the five die. Let us also stipulate that if you kill Arnold and remove his organs, no one will ever find out the real cause of death.

Assuming that the utilities are not affected by such things as undermining confidence in the medical community, act-utilitarianism approves of taking O_1 – indeed, it requires killing Arnold and giving his organs to the five. The morality of solidarity assesses the case differently. If you were to take O_1, your conduct would express benevolence for the five patients in need of transplants, for your actions would be aimed at saving their lives for their sake. However, taking this option would also involve killing Arnold and procuring his organs as a means to saving the five. Since death is an evil for Arnold, your killing him would constitute a gross deviation from the solidarity standard *in relation to him*, and this would make your conduct wrong.

We might imagine someone retorting to this analysis, "Yes, but since death is an evil for the five, your *not* killing Arnold to procure his organs for them (option O_2) would constitute a gross deviation from the solidarity standard *in relation to them*." The theory I have presented in this chapter provides the materials to answer this objection. It is correct that if you take O_2, you would not be acting beneficently toward the five. Crucially, however, not all failures to act beneficently are deviations from the solidarity standard. What are deviations are *privations* of beneficence, which are failures to act beneficently when the agent can and ought to do so. But if the only available means of effecting a good for someone are themselves wrongful, then there is no privation of beneficence if the agent forgoes taking them (Section 3.4.2). From this and the fact that intentionally killing Arnold to procure his organs is wrong, it follows that you are not deviating from the solidarity standard if you forgo killing him in order to save the five.

3.6 Incidental Harm: The Principles of Proportionality and Due Care

According to the PDE, it is sometimes permissible to act in a way that brings about harm incidentally in circumstances in which it would not be permissible to bring about that harm intentionally. I stated in Chapter 1 (Section 1.4) that I doubt it is possible to provide a set of sufficient conditions for the permissibility of incidental harm. But while I disavowed an algorithm, I described two principles that provide partial guidance for the production of incidental harm:

> *Principle of Proportionality (PP)*: It is permissible to pursue a course of action that brings about incidental harm only if the harm is not disproportionate to the value of the end being pursued.
>
> *Principle of Due Care (PDC)*: It is permissible to pursue a course of action that brings about incidental harm only if all reasonable steps are taken to avoid or minimize that harm.

The motivation behind these principles is that incidental harm should be neither excessive nor gratuitous. They are necessary conditions for the permissibility of incidental harm, but they are not sufficient: To be permissible conduct that causes harm incidentally must also not have any other wrong-making features.

The PP and PDC are often associated with double effect. This has led to the criticism that the PDE attempts to combine norms that rest on incompatible foundations in an ad hoc manner (Riisfeldt 2019). The constraint against intentional harm makes the PDE a deontological principle, but when judging the permissibility of incidental harm, the PP and PDC appear to be consequentialist in character, inasmuch as they focus on considerations about the harmful effects of the agent's conduct. In this section, I argue that the PP and PDC can also be grounded in the standard of human solidarity. Far from being an ad hoc combination, the constraint against intentional harm, the PP, and the PDC spring from a common moral source.

In seeking justification for the PP and PDC, the place to begin is the point of view of an agent who has concern for others as fellow human beings. We noticed earlier that the phenomenology of concern involves appearances of value (Section 3.2). If you care about someone, the good of that person seems to be something good, and this is because the person herself seems to be valuable. Conversely, her suffering harm seems to be not just something that is bad for her but something that is simply bad – a bad thing or a bad state of affairs – because it negatively impacts someone who is valuable. Let us suppose that these perceptions of value are veridical (as I believe they are – see Section 3.7). Then it really is a bad thing when a fellow human being suffers harm. The badness of this state of affairs, in turn, generates a strong reason against pursuing any course of action that will cause serious incidental harm. In most circumstances, this reason will be decisive. One should either pursue one's ends in some other way or forgo them if they cannot be pursued without causing harm.

There can also arise extraordinary circumstances, however, in which certain objectives are especially urgent and important. In such circumstances, the agent will still have a strong reason against pursuing means to them that she expects will produce incidental harm, but she will also have a strong countervailing reason in favor of pursuing those means, a reason that is generated by the fact that they are conducive to attaining her end (provided that no less costly means are available). Hence, the reason against acting in a way that one foresees will produce incidental harm is not always conclusive: While there is a presumption that any conduct that causes incidental harm is wrong, that presumption is defeasible.[39]

Compare on this point the concept of recklessness in criminal law. In modern penal codes, the *mens rea* of recklessness is often defined as the conscious disregard of a substantial and unjustified risk that the material element of an offense exists or will result from one's conduct (e.g., Model Penal Code §2.02(2)(c),). Applied to the case of harming others, an agent is reckless if he consciously disregards a substantial and unjustified risk that harm to others will result from his conduct. There are two points to notice about this definition. First, in order to be reckless in causing harm, the agent must be aware that his conduct threatens it. This element of awareness or foresight is what distinguishes a reckless agent from one who is merely negligent. A negligent agent fails to realize that his conduct poses a substantial and unjustified risk to others though he should be aware that it does (Model Penal Code §2.02(2)(d)). Second, not all conscious risk-taking constitutes recklessness. It has often been observed that many everyday activities, such as driving motor vehicles and operating heavy machinery, impose some degree of risk on others, but drivers and machine operators do not necessarily engage in reckless conduct. Risk-taking is reckless only when it is *unjustified* or *unreasonable* in the circumstances, that is when "its disregard involves a gross deviation from the standard of conduct that a law-abiding person would observe in the actor's situation" (Model Penal Code §2.02(2)(c)). An agent who acts in a way that imposes even a great risk of causing harm thus does not necessarily act recklessly.

[39] One is of course also not acting beneficently toward the people who are harmed, but given the importance of the end one is aiming to achieve, it is very likely that one's not acting beneficently toward them does not constitute a privation of beneficence in the circumstances.

For, all things considered, he may be justified in engaging in the risky conduct.

Modern penal codes also typically distinguish between cases in which the agent believes it is *possible* or *probable* that his conduct will result in a certain outcome and cases in which the agent is *certain*, or *nearly certain*, that his conduct will have that outcome. Thus, the Model Penal Code lists "knowledge" as a form of *mens rea* distinct from recklessness: An agent "knows" his conduct will bring about a certain result when he is "practically certain" it will have that result (§2.02(2)(b)). Unlike the case of recklessness, there is no reference here to reasonability: An agent "knows" his conduct will produce a result if he is practically certain it will bring that result about, regardless of whether it is reasonable to engage in that conduct.

I suggest that for purposes of ethical evaluation, "knowledge" should be treated as the limiting case of recklessness when it comes to causing harm. Recklessness is about running unreasonable risks, and when an agent is practically certain that his conduct will cause some harm, he foresees that the risk he is running of causing it is close to 1. Therefore, agents who are sure that their conduct will cause harm to others also act recklessly, but only on the condition that engaging in that conduct is unreasonable in the circumstances.[40] Of course, in order for her conduct to be reasonable, an agent who is practically certain that a contemplated course of action will cause harm to others requires stronger justification for embarking on it than does an agent who foresees that embarking on a course of action carries with it only a moderate risk of causing harm.

An incident from the film *Master and Commander: The Far Side of the World*, based on a novel by Patrick O'Brien, illustrates the point.[41] During the Napoleonic Wars, Captain Jack Aubrey of the British frigate *HMS Surprise* is charged with hunting down the French privateer *Acheron*. During a terrible storm, one of the ship's masts is broken and crashes into the sea, taking with it the sails and rigging – and a sailor named Will Warley. The wrecked mast is still attached to the ship by its rigging and Warley is furiously struggling to swim toward it, knowing it is his only hope for making it back aboard the ship. Unfortunately, the mast is also pulling the ship over, and the midshipman warns Aubrey that the *Surprise* will sink unless it is immediately cut away from the wreckage. The captain

40 L. Alexander argues that this is how criminal law ought to handle cases of "knowledge" of harm (2000, 940).

41 This incident is also discussed by Biggar (2013, 94–5).

does what is necessary to save the ship, and with the help of another sailor, he cuts the ropes that are connecting it to the mast, knowing that in doing so, he is also condemning Warley to certain death. The scene is presented as exemplifying one of the perils that attend life at sea and is infused with a sense of tragedy and loss. But though we, the audience, are meant to experience Warely's death as tragic, we are not supposed to see Aubrey's conduct as being reckless.

Aubrey faces a practical problem set by his role as captain of the *Surprise*, which is to save the ship from the imminent threat of sinking. One way that morality constrains the way he may pursue this end is by prohibiting him from killing, or otherwise seriously harming, innocent people as a means to it (Section 3.5.1). But intentional harm is not at issue here: Aubrey is not contemplating killing Warley *in order to* prevent the *Surprise* from sinking. The possible means that present themselves are rather to cut the ropes that are linking the wrecked mast to the rest of the ship. Aubrey realizes that a side effect of cutting the rope will be that Warley will surely drown, and he recognizes that this generates a reason against cutting away the mast, but he concludes that avoiding the loss of the ship and its crew outweighs this reason. We recognize these facts about Aubrey's reasons too, and it is this recognition that underwrites the judgment that his conduct is not reckless or morally wrong, even though it has a consequence that is tragic.

In evaluating Aubrey's conduct, it also matters that the threat of the ship's sinking is imminent. Even when the PP is satisfied, the value of human life generates a reason to pursue the available option that minimizes incidental harm, in accordance with the PDC. Suppose, for instance, that the wrecked mast was only slowly pulling the ship over and that the available evidence indicated that Aubrey could afford to wait several minutes before cutting away the mast – crucial minutes during which the sailor might be able to make it back on board. In that case, there would be a strong reason in favor of waiting to cut the rope and little to be said in favor of cutting it immediately, and it would therefore be reckless for the captain to do the latter.

Part of what it is to have concern for others is to recognize that their well-being matters and therefore to recognize that the consideration that a course of action would cause excessive or gratuitous harm counts decisively against it. We respond correctly to this reason by refraining from performing such actions, pursuing our goals by other means, or forgoing them altogether. Hume said that no man would tread as willingly on another's gouty toes, whom he has no quarrel with, as he does on the pavement

(2006, 227). He seems to have overestimated the moral goodness of human beings. Nonetheless, it is true that if you are walking down a sidewalk and notice that if you continue on your present course, you will step on someone's gouty toes, and *if* you care about his good, you will alter your path and walk around him. In this case, your act of stepping aside is a manifestation of your concern for him. There is thus another way that concern for others can be expressed or manifested, besides performing actions that aim at their good (Section 3.4.1). Concern for others can also be expressed by constraining one's pursuits of one's ends when they will cause or threaten to cause them harm.

An agent who knowingly causes incidental harm that is excessive or gratuitous manifests – in the sense of *making manifest* or making apparent – a lack of sufficient concern for the human beings his conduct harms.[42] This in turn constitutes a deviation from the solidarity standard, which is a standard of concern and goodwill. It may be that the agent is totally indifferent to the good of the people his conduct affects and so fails to recognize any reason against acting in a way that threatens to harm them. Apart from cases of psychosis, it is rare to find anyone who is totally indifferent to the good of others. But it is not rare to find agents who care nothing about certain groups or classes of people because they regard those groups as being somehow subhuman or *Lebensunwertes Leben.* Here the tactic of dehumanization tacitly acknowledges the standard of human solidarity even while attempting to undermine its application to the disfavored group. Agents who rationalize away the humanity of certain individuals will also be prone to harming them intentionally when it suits their purposes. More commonly, the problem is not that an individual fails to care at all about his fellow human beings but that he does not care *enough.* He discounts the value of their good and holds their lives cheap in comparison with the value of his own objectives. Agents with this mindset may adhere to the constraint against intentional harm but violate the PP or the PDC because they discount the reasons that stem from the incidental harm their actions bring about.

Coady suggests that the term "collateral damage" is a euphemism that disguises the human costs of incidental harm. In the context of warfare, it frequently serves both to belittle the death and destruction that are the

[42] Sadistic Precision Bomber (SPB) (Section 2.8) does not intentionally kill noncombatants, but he also does not have any concern for the noncombatants he harms incidentally. But if he refrains from causing incidental harm that is unnecessary or disproportionate (say, because he scrupulously obeys his commander's orders), then his lack of concern is not manifested in his conduct, for he acts in just the way that someone with a proper concern for the noncombatants would act.

predictable results of military operations and to insinuate that the agents of it should be excused since it was not what they were aiming at (2008, 133). However, it is no part of double effect to give *carte blanche* for incidental harm. Incidental harm is sometimes just as morally objectionable as intentional harm, and when it is, it merits the same degree of censure. This point is recognized in the common law concept of murder. In a case of depraved indifference murder, the defendant did not intend to kill the victim, but her conduct was "so wanton, so deficient in a moral sense of concern, so devoid of regard of the life or lives of others, and so blameworthy as to warrant the same criminal liability as that which the law imposes upon a person who intentionally causes the death of another" (*People* v. *Suarez* 844 N.E.2d 721 [2005]; qtd. in Dressler 2018, 486–7).

3.7 The Normative Foundation of the Morality of Solidarity

I have argued that the precept of beneficence, the constraint against intentional harm, and the PP and PDC can be derived from the proposal that our conduct is measured by a standard of solidarity in relation to others. I believe this proposal has a good deal of intuitive appeal. We might ask, however, whether the solidarity standard itself admits of any further grounding. Can the truth of our proposal be explained by any more fundamental considerations?

One possibility is broadly utilitarian. According to this view, the solidarity standard measures our conduct because general conformity to it is socially beneficial. For the sake of comparison, consider a possible rationale for the rules that govern respect for private property. If I take something that belongs to you without your consent, then I wrong you, but what makes my conduct wrong is the fact that it violates a system of conventions that has assigned the item to you rather than me. This system of conventions stands in need of justification, and in the view under consideration, what justifies it is the benefits it has for the people living under it. For, the argument goes, human flourishing is better served in a social and political context in which some property is owned by private individuals than in one in which all property is owned collectively.[43] In a similar way, it might be contended that what grounds the standard of solidarity is the good that people stand to gain from conforming to it. Our flourishing also depends on living a shared life with others, and not just any sort of shared life, but one that is peaceful and cooperative. To the extent that people within a

[43] This is how Aristotle justifies private ownership of property (*Politics* 1263a8–b30).

community conform their conduct to the solidarity standard, relations of solidarity obtain among them. These relations facilitate cooperation, foster trust, and mitigate conflict, and this in turn is conducive to a whole host of benefits that are instrumental for human flourishing (Section 3.2). On the other hand, deviations from the standard of solidarity, such as attacks on others and reckless disregard for their good, impede the good functioning of the group.[44]

I do not doubt that this line of argument is basically correct. But I do not believe that it is the whole story. Consider Anscombe's incisive critique of the utilitarian rationale for the prohibition on murder:

> You can argue truly enough . . . that general respect for the prohibitions [*sic*] on murder makes life more commodious. If people really respect the prohibition against murder life is pleasanter for all of us – but this argument is exceedingly comic. Because utility presupposes the *life* of those who are to be convenienced, and everybody perceives quite clearly that the wrong done in murder is done first and foremost to the victim, whose life is not inconvenienced, it just isn't there anymore. He isn't there to complain: so the utilitarian argument has to be on behalf of the rest of us. Therefore, though true, it is highly comic and is not the foundation: the objection to murder is supra-utilitarian. (2008, 187)

Anscombe does not deny that the prohibition on murder contributes to the well-ordering of society, and so to the material advantages that a well-ordered social life brings. Her point is that when it comes to explaining what makes murder wrong, the primary focus should be on the victim and how it treats *him*. The principal explanation of the wrongfulness of murder is not that it violates a rule whose general observance is socially beneficial, but that it treats the victim in a way that is intrinsically inappropriate. This is what it means to say that the objection to murder is "supra-utilitarian."

Elsewhere Anscombe locates the objection to murder in the way it treats human beings as creatures with dignity. There is, she says, "a special worth and dignity in being a human" (2005f, 68), and there are certain virtues, such as the virtue of justice, which have as an integral component a knowledge of the dignity of human nature (2005b, 63). The wrongfulness of murder consists primarily in the fact that it is a violation of this dignity.

What is meant in speaking of the value and worth of being a human? In elucidating this notion, I will return to something I noted earlier about the

44 Foot appears to envisage something like this rationale for the constraint against intentional harm. The good of the rule, she says, lies in the benefits that people stand to gain from a system that includes it (2008a, 103–4).

phenomenology of concern, namely that it involves appearances of value (Section 3.2). When you care about someone, she appears as someone who *matters*, as someone who is *worthy* of concern. We might think, for example, of parents' love for their children. It is common for a parent to experience her child as being valuable. But this value is of a higher and different kind than the value of material goods. A parent might indicate the value of her child by saying that he or she is precious or cherishable, a treasure that is incomparably greater than the sort of treasure that might be put in a bank vault or safety deposit box. And it is common for parents to experience their love for their children as being a response not simply to the fact that the children are *theirs*, but as being a response to a value that the children have in themselves, one that the parents' intimate relation puts them in an especially good position to appreciate. We might also return to one of our paradigmatic examples of solidarity from Section 3.2. When the white residents of a city join their black neighbors in protests aimed at instigating change in institutions that have treated the black residents unjustly in solidarity with them, it is because the white residents recognize that the black residents are people who matter. Finally, we can observe that as human beings we characteristically possess some degree of self-concern – self-love – and insofar as we do we experience ourselves as being valuable. This experience is most clear when we think about how we want others to treat us. We want and expect that others will not be indifferent to our good, and we are apt to complain that we are being treated "like dirt" if we believe that someone is treating us in a way that denigrates our worth.

To say that human beings have "a special worth and dignity" is to say that these appearances should be taken at face value. When you experience someone you care about as being valuable, your experience is not illusory because he or she really is valuable. Moreover, every human being is valuable in just the same way. The sort of value in question is picked out by terms such as *preciousness*, *irreplaceability*, and *inviolability*, and it is a sort of value that makes appropriate attitudes such as concern, respect, and even reverence.

In virtue of what do human beings possess their dignity? The traditional view, to which I subscribe and which is shared by Anscombe and Kant, is that human beings have dignity in virtue of their rational nature.[45] Because

[45] Although Kant is the philosopher who is today most closely associated with the concept of dignity, the idea goes back to ancient Stoicism. The term *dignitas* was originally used by the Romans to denote the honor or worth of the social and political elite, but it was repurposed by the Stoics to

of our rational nature, human life involves, as Anscombe puts it, "a leap to another kind of existence from the life of other animals" (2005c, 267). In virtue of our rational nature, we are oriented toward the transcendent values of truth and goodness. This orientation is manifested in our ability to reflectively step back from our beliefs and pursuits and ask whether we have good reason for believing or going on as we presently do. Our rational nature is also the basis of our freedom. Our conduct is not determined by our pre-rational instincts; rather, we shape our lives in view of a more or less determinate conception of how it is good for us to live.

Kant held that rational beings are the only beings with intrinsic value or "inner worth." The value of everything else depends on its relation to human desire. However, it does not follow from the notion that rational beings possess a special dignity that nothing else has intrinsic value. For my own part, I find more plausible a pluralistic view according to which there are a variety of forms of intrinsic value (Anderson 1993, ch. 1). These forms of value differ in degree, and they also differ in kind, in the sense that their bearers are properly valued in different ways on account of them. For instance, we properly value the natural world by responding to it with awe, appreciation, and wonder, and we properly value sentient creatures by treating them humanely. We do not need to be nihilists about the intrinsic value of the nonhuman world to hold that beings with a rational nature have a distinctive and higher sort of value.

Our rational nature is the basis of our exalted status in comparison with other creatures. But it is also the basis of the fundamental equality between human beings. To say that human beings have a rational nature is to say that they are members of a kind whose nature is characterized by certain tendencies or potentialities, such as the potentiality to understand the world conceptually and the potentiality to engage in deliberation about how to shape their life in light of that understanding. These natural potentialities for thought and action must be distinguished from capacities that the subject is in a position to exercise immediately (Lee and George 2008). An infant lacks immediately exercisable capacities for rational thought and action, but he or she still has a natural tendency to develop these capacities given a suitable environment. Mental and biological defects can also prevent or impede the development of a human being's natural potentialities for rational thought and action or impede the subject from exercising them once they have developed. But these are *defects* and

refer to the high worth possessed by human beings in comparison with other things, especially nonhuman animals. On the history of the concept of dignity, see Rosen (2012).

impediments precisely because they prevent the development or actualization of the subject's rational nature.[46] Infants and human beings with severe cognitive defects have a rational nature and so possess full human dignity. Since human dignity belongs to us in virtue of our natural kind, every human being possesses the same basic worth, and they possess it for as long as they exist.

An ordinary virtuous person's knowledge of human dignity need not be philosophically articulate. She need not grasp, or fully grasp, the concept of rational nature or have any distinct notion of what it is about human beings in virtue of which they matter as they do. Her knowledge might rather consist simply in the conviction that human life is precious, and so worthy of regard and concern, and even reverence. Anscombe calls this a "religious attitude" toward human life, but she emphasizes that it is not necessarily connected to any particular religious creed (2005c, 269–70).

The ultimate ground for the standard of solidarity, then, is the dignity of human nature. The reason that our conduct is measured by a standard of concern and goodwill toward others is that as rational beings they are, by their very nature, worthy of our concern and goodwill. Conduct that accords with this standard is a fitting or appropriate response to human beings in virtue of their dignity.[47] On the other hand, conduct that deviates from the solidarity standard mistreats people because it is an unfitting or incorrect response to them on account of their dignity (assuming they have committed no offense that would make them deserving of, or liable to, some departure from the standard).[48] One way to mistreat people is to act in a way that shows a lack of sufficient concern for them, but we also mistreat others when we "come out against them" by seeking evil for them rather than good.

Although this grounding for the solidarity standard is nonutilitarian, we ought to recognize that general conformity to it makes an immense contribution to human flourishing. I have already remarked that relations

[46] It is not a defect or lack of development in, say, a cat or an olive tree that they cannot engage in rational thought or action, and the reason is that unlike human beings cats and olive trees do not possess a rational nature.

[47] It is often said that in virtue of their dignity human beings should be treated with *respect*. But to respect an object is, roughly, to respond appropriately to it on account of its having a feature that warrants the response. Since conduct that accords with the solidarity standard is an appropriate response to human beings on account of their dignity, treating them in ways that accord with that standard is also treating them with respect.

[48] Since one is oneself a human being, the standard of solidarity also gives rise to corresponding self-directed duties. These duties are not *de se* duties, however; that is, they are not duties to oneself considered precisely *as oneself* (Darwall 2002, 49). They are rather duties one has to oneself insofar as one is a human being.

of solidarity are beneficial insofar as they facilitate cooperative activities. The instrumental value of these relations is not the only sort of value they possess, however. When relations of solidarity that are based on human dignity prevail within a community, its members are partners in pursuing one another's good, and they are partners in this endeavor because they recognize that each of them is someone who matters. This sort of partnership is valuable in its own right. As Talbot Brewer writes, "It is a different activity, and a far more valuable one, to live and work side-by-side over a lifetime with people who affirm one's basic worth as a human being than with people who merely find it beneficial to appear as if they do" (2011, 169). When Brewer says that it is highly valuable for a person to work alongside others who affirm his basic worth, I take it that the claim is that it is good *for* the person himself, that it contributes to his flourishing. Let us call this good the *good of solidarity*. The good of solidarity is a very great good, but it is not a good that a person is capable of achieving on her own. Like the good of friendship, the good of solidarity is a component of our flourishing that can only be obtained in concert with others and in the right sort of social context. And this sort of social context exists only to the extent that people conform their conduct to the solidarity standard.

3.8 Conclusion

The purpose of this chapter was to articulate a rationale for the PDE. The argument was complex, so I will summarize its main components here. I began by outlining a conception of what it is to be in solidarity with others (Section 3.2). To be in solidarity with another is to have concern for him or her based on something that is shared in common between oneself and the other. An essential element of concern is the attitude of goodwill, an action-oriented desire for the good of the other for his or her sake. According to the morality of solidarity, human conduct is measured by a default standard of solidarity in relation to others, which is a standard of concern and goodwill (Section 3.3). The normative foundation for this standard is the dignity of the human person. In virtue of their rational nature, human beings have a distinctive value or worth, a value that may be described as being precious or inviolable (Section 3.7).

Conduct that deviates from the solidarity standard is typically morally defective, and hence morally wrong. I described three ways in which an agent's conduct can deviate from the standard. First, privations of beneficence occur when an agent fails to act in a way that manifests or expresses benevolent desire in circumstances in which he can and ought to do so

(Section 3.4). Second, an agent deviates from the solidarity standard by causing incidental harm that is either excessive or gratuitous (Section 3.6). This sort of conduct is reckless, and in engaging in it the agent manifests a lack of sufficient concern for the good of others. Finally, an agent's conduct deviates from the standard of solidarity when it intentionally brings about harm (Section 3.5). Conduct that involves harming others intentionally successfully expresses malevolent desire, which deviates from the standard of solidarity in virtue of being a desire for an evil rather than a good.

While the standard of solidarity rules out some incidental harm, it does not rule out conduct that brings about incidental harm that is neither excessive nor gratuitous, so long as it does not possess any other wrong-making features. On the other hand, intentional harm is, just as such, a deviation from the standard of solidarity, and there is therefore a strict constraint against it. Taken together, these two propositions are tantamount to the PDE.

CHAPTER 4

An Anscombian Account of Intentional Action

4.1 Introduction

The PDE accords moral significance to the distinction between what an agent does or brings about intentionally and what she foresees or expects but does not intend. The task of the previous chapter was to provide a rationale for the PDE. The topic of this chapter is the distinction between intention and foresight. An agent who acts intentionally typically foresees that she will bring about a number of effects and that her conduct will fall under a variety of different descriptions. Which of these effects and descriptions are intentional and which are incidental?

The intentional/incidental distinction is standardly illustrated by cases in which it is clear where the line between them falls:

> A cancer-stricken patient undertakes a round of chemotherapy, but she does not do so with the intention of losing her hair, though she knows hair loss is an inevitable effect of the treatment.
>
> A marathon runner does not intentionally cause wear on his shoes though he is certain that running a long distance will have that effect.

There are many scenarios, however, where it is not obvious where to draw the line between intention and simple foresight. Here are three:

> *Fly and Hammer*: Austin, who has a great hatred of flies, finds a fly in his apartment, and the only swatting implement to hand is a hammer. The fly eventually settles on the bald head of his friend. Austin smashes the hammer down on the fly, which also severely injures and kills his friend. Does Austin injure or kill his friend intentionally (i.e., are the head injury or death intended)?[1] (Coady 2008, 139)

[1] It bears repeating that I use "intentionally" as a cognate of "intention" (Section 1.2.1). In a broad sense, an agent does or brings about intentionally whatever she is aware of doing or bringing about. It is not controversial that Austin injures and kills his friend intentionally *in the broad sense*. The question is whether the injury and death were intended by Austin – and thus intentional in the narrower sense.

> *Burning Building:* Beth jumps out the window of the 100th floor of a skyscraper to avoid a fire that is consuming the building in the belief that being slowly burned to death would be far worse than a quick end from hitting the pavement. Does Beth kill herself intentionally? (Tollefsen 2006, 443)

> *Fleeing London Airport*: In order to escape some pursuers, Charles boards a plane at London airport that he knows to be bound for Manchester. Although Manchester is the last place he would like to be, Charles boards the plane because he wants to escape his pursuers and it is the first one he sees. Does Charles board the plane with the intention of traveling to Manchester? (Lord Bridge, *R* v. *Moloney* [1985] AC 905 at 926)

Cases like these show the need for a theoretical account of intentional action, which will help us to determine the contents of an agent's intentions in acting.

In Chapter 1 (Section 1.2.1), I distinguished the intentional from the incidental as follows:

> An agent intends to ϕ when it is her aim, goal, or purpose to ϕ, she ϕ-s intentionally when ϕ-ing is among her aims, goals, or purposes in acting, and she brings about an effect intentionally when it is her aim, goal, or purpose to bring it about.

> An agent ϕ-s incidentally when ϕ-ing is not among her aims, goals, or purposes in acting, but she knows or is aware that she is ϕ-ing; she brings about an effect incidentally when it is not among her purposes, but she is aware (knows, foresees, expects) that it will result, or likely result, from her conduct.

This way of distinguishing the intentional and the incidental is due to Anscombe. In *Intention*, Anscombe argues that intentional action characteristically has a teleological order and this order is self-consciously known by its agent because it is determined by her own calculation of means to an end. The purpose of this chapter is to elucidate Anscombe's account of intentional action.[2] This contributes to the overall aim of the book in three ways. First, applying the PDE to particular (actual or hypothetical) cases requires us to make judgments about what the agent does or brings about intentionally, and I believe that Anscombe's account is the best on offer. Second, in Chapter 5, I will discuss the closeness problem for the PDE, and this problem is usually thought to be particularly acute for fine-grained

[2] I will not attempt to provide a defense of Anscombe's account against its competitors, which would be a major undertaking. My discussion will also be limited to elements of Anscombe's theory of intentional action that are relevant to the aims of this book. For comprehensive overviews of *Intention*, see Wiseman (2016) and Schwenkler (2019).

accounts of intention such as Anscombe's. It will therefore be useful to have that account on the table before proceeding to Chapter 5. Finally, in Chapter 6, I will critically examine further objections to double effect, and I will draw on the material I develop in this chapter in responding to these objections.

In Section 4.2, I show how Anscombe uses a special sense of the question "Why?" to elucidate the teleological order internal to intentional action. In Section 4.3, I explain how the teleological order of an agent's intentional action is determined by the calculation on the basis of which she acts, where the concept of calculation is illuminated by the notion of practical reasoning. Getting clear about the concept of calculation is therefore essential for correctly drawing the intentional/incidental distinction, which is the topic of Section 4.4. Finally, in Section 4.5, I apply the Anscombian account of intentional action to the three controversial cases described above.

4.2 The Teleological Order of Intentional Action

According to Anscombe, an action is intentional under a certain description just in case a certain sense of the question "Why?" is applicable to it under that description. The relevant sense of the question is "that in which the answer, if positive, gives a reason for acting." (1963, §5). Positive answers to the question "Why?" are diverse; they may look to the past ("He killed my brother") or to the future ("For profit"), or they may place the action in a certain interpretive light ("Because I admire her"). Moreover, the question is not refused application by answers such as "No particular reason" or "I just thought I would." Just as the question "How much money do you have in your pocket?" is not refused application by the answer "None," so too the question "Why are you ϕ-ing?" is not shown to be inapplicable by the answer "No reason" (Anscombe 1963, §17).

Although the question "Why?" admits of diverse answers, one sort of answer is central to Anscombe's theory of intentional action, namely, the sort in which the agent explains what she is doing by mentioning another action. For instance:

(a) Why are you walking upstairs?
– I'm going to get my camera.

(b) Why are you lying on the bed?
– I'm doing Yoga.

In (a), the response to the "Why?" question mentions something future, something that the agent is *going* to do (get her camera), while in (b), the response mentions a wider description of something else the agent is currently *doing* (Yoga).[3] In both sorts of case, the agent explains something she is doing by citing another thing she is doing or going to do. And in both sorts of case, the question "Why?" could also be answered by employing the locution "in order to" (or simply "to") along with a description of an action. Thus, the respondent in (a) could say that she is walking upstairs "(in order) to get my camera," and the respondent in (b) could say that she is lying on the bed "(in order) to do Yoga." These answers give a teleological explanation of what the agent is doing in terms of another action that it subserves.

Anscombe makes two further observations about this mode of action explanation. First, if a person answers the question "Why are you ϕ-ing?" by saying "In order to χ," then it must be the case that she sees an intelligible connection between ϕ-ing and χ-ing (1963, §22). There are various forms this connection might take. It may be that doing the first will lead to doing the second (as going upstairs will lead to getting my camera), that the first is constitutive of the second (as lying on the bed is constitutive of doing Yoga), or that the first is a stage or phase of a larger action (as cracking an egg is a stage of making an omelet). But if the agent is ϕ-ing in order to χ, then she must know or believe that ϕ-ing is somehow conducive to χ-ing.

Second, in many cases, the question "Why?" can be reiterated, and when this is so, the answers to the reiterated question provide further explanations of the agent's conduct by revealing the further aims or goals that she is pursuing in it. This is illustrated by Anscombe's example of the gardener at the pump (1963, §23). Someone has found a way of contaminating the water supply of a house with a deadly poison. The house is inhabited by a small group of party chiefs – it is suggested that they are Nazis who have gotten control of the state and are planning a world war. The person who contaminated the water source believes that if these men are killed, then some others will get into power, and these good men will govern well and perhaps even institute the Kingdom of Heaven on earth. He has revealed his calculation to the house's gardener, who is now pumping water into the cistern that supplies the house's drinking water. Suppose we come upon the scene hoping to understand the gardener's conduct and he answers our questions honestly, perhaps because we are his trusted confidants. The following conversation ensues:

[3] Schwenkler calls the form of explanation exhibited by (a) "forward-looking explanation" and the sort exhibited by (b) "outward-looking explanation" (2019, 64).

(c) Why are you moving your arm up and down on the pump handle?
– I'm operating the pump.

Why are you operating the pump?
– I'm replenishing the house's water supply.

Why are you replenishing the house's water supply?
– I'm poisoning the inhabitants.

The man's answers to the successive applications of the question "Why?" reveal "a special sort of developing series" (2005e, 150) or an "order that is there whenever actions are done with intentions" (1963, §42). This order, which can be represented by a series of letters, is an explanatory order: The man is doing A (moving his arm up and down on the pump handle) *because* he is doing B (operating the pump), he is doing B *because* he is doing C (replenishing the house's water supply), and he is doing C *because* he is doing D (poisoning the inhabitants). It is also a teleological order, for the man is doing A *in order to* do B, which he is doing in *order to* do C, which he is doing in turn *in order to* do D. And the teleological-explanatory order uncovered by the question "Why?" is one that is present *in* the man's conduct as he pumps water.[4]

There are many reasons why the gardener might be poisoning the inhabitants of the house, and the question "Why?" can be asked again in relation to poisoning them. Suppose his answer is "To inaugurate the Kingdom of Heaven on earth." This is a further element in the series of answers, which we can label E. This element is also different from the previous ones, however, for instituting the Kingdom of Heaven on earth is sufficiently remote from poisoning the Nazis that it cannot be said to be something the gardener *is doing*; rather, it is a goal that is at a distance from his present conduct that he is aiming to accomplish by means of poisoning the Nazis.[5] Yet even in this case, it is still a fact about the gardener's conduct here and now that it is *ordered to* and *directed at* this goal.

In revealing the nested order of aims, goals, or purposes for the sake of which the agent is acting, the question "Why?" reveals her intentions in acting. The fact that the gardener answers the question "Why are you moving your arm up and down on the pump handle?" by saying "I'm

[4] Cf. Lavin (2016); Schwenkler (2019, ch. 3).

[5] Anscombe makes the point by saying that there is a "break" between cases where we can say of someone that he *is doing* B in doing A and cases where we can say only that he is *going* to do B or that he is acting *in order to* do B. She emphasizes that this break is not a sharp one: Its location depends on how normal it would be to take B-ing to result from A-ing as a matter of course, and this is a highly contextual matter (1963, §23).

operating the pump" shows that his conduct is intentional under the description "moving my arm up and down on the pump handle." Each element in the series that follows (B–E) corresponds to a *further intention with which* he is moving his arm up and down on the handle: He is moving it with the intention of (i) operating the pump, (ii) replenishing the house's water supply, (iii) poisoning the Nazis, and (iv) inaugurating the Kingdom of Heaven on earth.

Of course, there are also countless other things that the gardener is doing as he pumps water. He is making disturbances in the surrounding air molecules, sweating, generating certain substances in his nerve fibers, making a peculiar clicking rhythm, generating a pattern of shadows on the nearby rockery that looks somewhat like a face, and so on. None of these things fall within the teleological order identified above. It is possible, however, that some of them fall within a different teleological order that could be identified by the question "Why?", for example,

(d) Why are you making that clicking rhythm?
– To entertain myself.

This shows that beating out the clicking rhythm is also intentional and done with the further intention of getting some entertainment. But many of the things that the gardener is doing or bringing about will not fall under any teleological order that can be identified by the question "Why?" These are *byproducts* or *side effects* of the gardener's conduct. If he is aware of them, he is doing or bringing them about incidentally rather than intentionally. As such, he would reject the application of the question "Why?" in relation to them. If we were to ask, for example, "Why are you making a shadow shaped like a face on the rockery?" his answer might be not "Because I'm ϕ-ing" or "To χ" but "I don't care about that" or "It's just an interesting effect of the light." This means that making the shadow on the rockery is a foreseen but nonintended side effect of the man's pumping activity.

4.3 The Calculative Order of Practical Reasoning

In the previous section, we saw that on Anscombe's account an action is intentional when a special sense of the question "Why?" applies to it, and we saw that repeated applications of the question "Why?" help reveal a teleological order that characteristically belongs to intentional action. Our analysis of intentional action would be incomplete, however, without a discussion of practical reasoning. Anscombe claims that the teleological order elicited by the question "Why?" is in fact the same as the order of practical reasoning (1963, §42), and this order is a *calculative* one. In this section, I will argue that practical reasoning is significant for understanding intentional action because the teleological order of an agent's action is determined by the calculation on which she acts, and the notion of calculation may be fruitfully approached by way of practical reasoning.

4.3.1 Practical Reasoning

In Anscombe's view, practical reasoning is not "ordinary" theoretical reasoning with a special subject matter, such as what one ought to do or what it would be best to do. The difference between theoretical reasoning and practical reasoning is a difference in *form* rather than matter. Theoretical reasoning is reasoning about what is true. In the paradigmatic case, the reasoner believes a certain set of propositions (the premises) and reasons from those propositions to another proposition (the conclusion) that they prove (or at least make probable), and she thereby comes to believe that the conclusion is true (or likely true). On the other hand, practical reasoning is "another type of reasoning than reasoning from premises to a conclusion they prove" (1963, §33). It is not reasoning about what is true but reasoning about *what to do*.

Anscombe states that practical reasoning has the form of a calculation about what to do (1963, §33). She is here following Aristotle, who says that practical reasoning ("deliberation": *bouleusis*) is a search (*zetēsis*) (*NE* 1112b20–5). It is a calculation or search for effective and acceptable means to an end that the deliberating agent wants to achieve, and it is undertaken with a view toward achieving the end through action. The problem that practical reasoning seeks to solve is the problem of how to get or do or bring about one's end. Its characteristic question is therefore not "Why?" but "How?" where the "How?" question is not a question about the manner of the agent's conduct, but one that asks about possible *means* to the agent's end.

For example, suppose my end is to avoid trouble with my co-conspirators.[6] I ask myself how I can do so and hit upon a possible means: I could take part in a campaign to get some men tortured under interrogation. I reason further that I can take part in the torture campaign by joining a petition to the governor and that I can join the petition by signing my name on a piece of paper. I then proceed to sign my name.

[6] This example is based on Anscombe (2005e, 149).

This example helps illustrate several features that are characteristic of practical reasoning. First, the *starting point* of practical reasoning is the *thing wanted*, that is, the end or goal that the agent desires (1963, §34). Practical reasoning does not proceed from the fact *that* one wants something; rather, it begins with *what* one wants – in this case, to avoid trouble with my co-conspirators.[7] Practical reasoning is undertaken for the sake of achieving this end, and the wanting of the end, which is not a mere wish but a desire to achieve it *through* some means, is what provides the "motor force" for the reasoning, making it genuinely *practical* reasoning and not just idle speculation about how the end could be achieved *if* one wanted to do so.

Second, what makes the agent's desire for the end intelligible is the fact that it appears to her to be desirable in some respect. The agent need not judge that her end is *morally* good or that it is the *best* thing for her to pursue in the circumstances (as in cases of weakness of will), but we will find the agent's desire for the end unintelligible if we cannot see how anything about its object could seem to her to be desirable.[8] In the example above, my desire to avoid trouble with my co-conspirators is intelligible because I care about my own safety and well-being, and I know that these will be in jeopardy if I do not please them. More generally, the agent desires her end because it appears good in its own right and she desires whatever means she settles on because of their instrumental value – their usefulness – for achieving or realizing her end.[9]

Third, in order for practical reasoning to reach a successful conclusion, any possible means the agent hits on must be ones she finds acceptable, compatibly with her other aims and values. If I am the sort of person who finds torture morally intolerable, then the possibility of participating in a torture campaign probably will not even occur to me, and if I do consider it, I will immediately dismiss it. Possible means might also be rejected because their foreseen effects are too costly or otherwise unsatisfactory. For instance, even if I have no qualms about participating in a torture

[7] It is possible, though, that in an unusual sort of case *what* the agent wants has to do with one of his desires. For example, I notice that I have a desire to kill my parents and so I make it my end to get rid of this awful desire. In this case, my end is to rid myself of the desire to kill my parents, but the desire that motivates my practical reasoning is not the desire to kill my parents but the desire to rid myself of the homicidal desire (Anscombe 2005d, 115).

[8] Anscombe illustrates this point with an example of a person who says he wants a saucer of mud. His saying this would immediately raise the question "What for?" (1963, §37). Does he believe the mud has some nutritional value? Is he using it to make something, such as a mud hut? Does he just want something to call his own? If we can find no answer to the "What for?" question, we will not be able to make sense of the desire.

[9] Anscombe adopts Aristotle's threefold categorization of the good as the useful, the fitting, and the pleasurable (1963, §37). For an extended discussion of this categorization, see Vogler (2002).

campaign, if I am running for political office and I foresee that word of my involvement will get out and harm my chances of winning the election, then I might also reject participating in the campaign. If the agent is unable to find any effective and acceptable means for achieving her end, then her practical reason will terminate unsuccessfully.

Finally, an agent's practical reasoning will not reach a successful conclusion unless she can connect the chain of means she is constructing with something that she immediately knows how to do. In the example above, my practical problem is to avoid trouble with my co-conspirators, and I reason that I can do so by taking part in the torture campaign. But my practical problem is not yet solved, for I still face the question of *how* to take part in that dark enterprise, and if I cannot find an answer to *that* question, I will not be out of my predicament. My problem will not be solved unless I can bring my reasoning to bear on the particulars of my situation. I do this by reasoning that I can take part in the torture campaign by joining a petition to the governor, which I can do by signing my name on *this* piece of paper with *this* pen.[10]

4.3.2 *The Practical Syllogism*

Practical reasoning is a conscious activity engaged in by a deliberating agent. But it is an activity that operates over conceptual contents, and we can represent these contents in the form of a *practical syllogism*. In this respect, practical reasoning is similar to theoretical reasoning. Theoretical reasoning is an activity that involves forming a belief that the conclusion of an argument is (probably) true. The argument whose conclusion one comes to believe is not itself an activity, though, but an abstract conceptual structure that can be given linguistic expression and evaluated for its reasonableness.

In her essay "Practical Inference," Anscombe proposes that the premises of a practical syllogism can be construed as a set of hypothetical statements linking the agent's end with an ordered series of means.[11] The hypotheticals represent the agent's knowledge (or belief or opinion) about how a series of actions will be efficacious toward achieving her end. In a case where the agent is calculating what to do here and now, the conclusion of a practical syllogism is a specification of something the agent immediately knows how to do in her present circumstances. A practical syllogism will

[10] Anscombe (1963, §41). See also A. Ford (2016).

[11] Although the agent's end is not itself a premise of the practical syllogism, it is still useful to specify it at the outset (Anscombe 2005d, 116).

therefore take the following form (for reasons that will become apparent shortly, I'll call this the Pattern 1 form):

(e) End: E
If D, then E
If C, then D
If B, then C
If A, then B
So: A[12]

For instance,

(f) End: Avoid trouble with my co-conspirators.
If I take part in the torture campaign, I will avoid trouble with my co-conspirators.
If I join the petition to the governor, I'll be taking part in the torture campaign.
If I sign my name on this piece of paper with this pen, I'll join the petition to the governor.
Conclusion: Sign my name on this piece of paper with this pen.

One might wonder why reasoning in accordance with a practical syllogism such as (f) should count as *reasoning*. After all, the hypothetical statements do not show that what I have labeled the "conclusion" is true or likely to be true – indeed, the conclusion is not the sort of thing that has a truth value. But, to repeat a point made above, practical reasoning is not reasoning about what is true but about *what to do*; in particular, what to do to achieve a desired end. Although the premises of a practical syllogism do not prove its conclusion, the syllogism shows that the action that is specified in the conclusion has a sort of *reasonableness*, given the assumption that the premises are true. It shows that it *makes sense* for an agent with the specified end to perform the relevant action by displaying the action as an effective way of pursuing it.[13]

In her discussion of practical reasoning in *Intention*, Anscombe's example of a practical syllogism follows a different pattern. She envisions a man

[12] In rare cases, there will be only one way of achieving a goal, so that doing A is necessary in order to get/do/bring about B. Anscombe mentions Aristotle's example of a doctor who has the goal of restoring his patient to health, where the only way to restore the patient's health is to make him "homogenous." In this case, the corresponding premise of the practical syllogism will take an "only if" rather than "if, then" form: "Only if this patient is homogenous will he be healthy" (Anscombe 2005d, 118).

[13] To say that the action specified in the conclusion of a practical syllogism such as (f) has a sort of reasonableness, assuming the truth of the premises, is not to say that it is *fully* reasonable. The action in question could still be criticized as being rationally unacceptable in other ways, for example, as thwarting other ends that the agent has or ought to have. And if to act in a way that is morally wrong is to act in a way that is unreasonable, then moral criticism of the action is also a form of rational criticism.

who eats some pigs' tripes on the basis of a practical syllogism whose premises are as follows (§33):

(g) Vitamin X is good for all men over 60.
I'm a man over 60.
Pigs' tripes are full of vitamin X.
Here's some pigs' tripes.

Anscombe endorses Aristotle's doctrine that the conclusion of practical reasoning is an action, and she says that the conclusion of the syllogism is the action of taking some pigs' tripes and eating them. I have drawn a distinction between practical reasoning and the practical syllogism that represents the content of a piece of practical reasoning, and I think it would therefore be better to say that the conclusion of the syllogism is the specification of an action, namely, eat some of *these*. We can still accommodate the Aristotelian doctrine, however, if we say that when the man reasons in accordance with this syllogism, his *drawing* the conclusion is his embarking on eating some of the pigs' tripes (McDowell 2010, 422).[14]

In a practical syllogism of the pattern we find in *Intention* (call it "Pattern 2"), the premises are categorical statements rather than hypothetical ones. It is not difficult to transform a Pattern 2 syllogism into a Pattern 1 syllogism. Following Anscombe's suggestion in "Practical Inference," we can put the two forms side by side (Anscombe 2005d, 118):

(h)

Pattern 2 Syllogism:	*Pattern 1 Syllogism:*
Vitamin X is good for all men over 60.	End: Get something good for me.
I'm a man over 60.	If I get some vitamin X, I'll be getting something good for me.
Pigs' tripes are full of vitamin X.	If I eat some pigs' tripes, I'll get some vitamin X.
Here's some pigs' tripes.	If I eat some of these, I'll eat some pigs' tripes.
Conclusion: Eat some of these.	Conclusion: Eat some of these.

[14] The Aristotelian doctrine can be understood through a parallel with theoretical reasoning. Suppose that a person forms the belief that q because he believes that p and that <if p, then q> and he recognizes that these jointly imply q. This person has reasoned through a modus ponens argument, and the conclusion of this argument is the proposition that q. But in drawing that conclusion, he thereby comes to believe that q. So we can also say that his drawing the conclusion that q is the *conclusion* of his reasoning activity. Similarly, one way to interpret the Aristotelian doctrine is that, in paradigmatic cases, when the time for acting is now, the conclusion of one's practical reasoning is embarking on the action specified in the conclusion of a practical syllogism.

The Aristotelian doctrine is controversial. For a defense, see Fernandez (2016) and Dancy (2018). People who deny it might instead say that drawing the conclusion of a practical syllogism is the formation of an intention (Broome 2013, ch. 14).

What is the relation between the two patterns? The premises of the Pattern 2 (left-hand) syllogism show the *rationality* of the agent's belief in the corresponding premises of the Pattern 1 (right-hand) syllogism. For instance, if the man eating the pigs' tripes is asked, "What makes you think that if you get some vitamin X you'll be getting something good for you?" he could reply, "Because vitamin X is good for all men over 60, and I am a man over 60." In addition, the premises of the Pattern 2 syllogism are among the man's motivating reasons for acting. They are considerations *in light of which* he eats the pigs' tripes and which together show the favorable light in which he sees eating them: Eating the pigs' tripes is instrumentally desirable because they are full of vitamin X, which helps him stay healthy, and he sees health as being desirable for its own sake.

When human beings act intentionally, they characteristically act on the basis of a means-end calculation, and the content of this calculation can be set out in the form of a practical syllogism.[15] Practical reasoning is significant for understanding intentional action because it is a familiar and salient example of calculation. Nonetheless, the scope of calculation is wider than that of practical reasoning if the latter is understood as a conscious activity that occurs prior to action. A person can act on a certain calculation spontaneously or out of habit. For instance, a man might see some pigs' tripes lying out on the table and immediately eat some in order to get some vitamin X without engaging in any reasoning. The reason for speaking of calculation even in such cases is that when a person acts intentionally and for the sake of an end, she will have some grasp or understanding of how what she is doing subserves her end.[16]

4.3.3 *Bringing the Two Orders Together*

We are now in a position to return to Anscombe's contention that the teleological order of intentional action revealed through successive applications of the question "Why?" is the same as the order of practical reasoning. Here the Pattern 1 form of the practical syllogism is significant. We can arrange the actions that appear in the antecedents and consequents

[15] We can accommodate cases where the agent is ϕ-ing for no reason by representing ϕ-ing as a conclusion of a practical syllogism that has no premises (Hanser 2005, 448).

[16] For this reason, it is misleading to say that agents who act intentionally act on the basis of a "plan of action." The term "plan" suggests the result of planning activity, and planning involves deliberately considering various options prior to action. Finnis (2011a) uses the term "proposal" instead of "plan," but this is also potentially misleading, for an agent need not consciously propose anything to himself before acting, as the example of spontaneously eating some pigs' tripes also demonstrates.

of the hypothetical statements of a Pattern 1 syllogism in a certain order, beginning with the consequent of the first premise and ending with the antecedent of the final premise. In the case of the man who is eating some pigs' tripes, the relevant order is as follows:

(i) Get something good for me [D]
Get some vitamin X [C]
Eat some pigs' tripes [B]
Eat some of these [A]

There are two ways that one can read the order set out in (i). On the one hand, it can be read from top to bottom, as the order D–A. In that case, it is a *calculative order* of means to an end: D (get something good for me) is the man's end, and C–A are the series of means that he has settled on as answers to the question "How?" On the other hand, the order can also be read from bottom to top, as the order A–D. In that case, it describes the *teleological order* of further aims or goals B–D for the sake of which the man is doing A (eating some of these), and which can be elicited through the question "Why?" The calculative order of practical reasoning and the teleological order of intentional action are one and the same order considered from two different points of view.[17]

Of these two orders, the calculative and the teleological, the calculative order has explanatory priority.[18] When a human being is doing A *in order to* do B, and doing B *in order to* do C, this will be the case *because* she has calculated that she can do C *by* doing B, and she can do B *by* doing A. Put another way, an agent's intentions in acting are determined by the calculation on which she acts. Furthermore, since the teleological order of intentional action depends on the agent's own means-end calculation, when such an order is present in the agent's conduct, the agent herself will know what she is doing intentionally, which is manifested by her ability to *give* the explanation of what she is doing in terms of her further aims or goals in response to the question "Why?"[19]

17 Aquinas makes the same point when he writes, "Although the end be last in the order of execution, yet it is first in the order of the agent's intention" (*ST* I-II 1.1 ad 1). What Aquinas calls the "order of intention" corresponds to the calculative order of practical reasoning, while the "order of execution" corresponds to the teleological order of intentional action.

18 This point is emphasized by A. Ford (2017).

19 Cases where the agent is deceiving herself about what ends she is pursuing may seem to be exceptions. Eric Marcus (2019) argues, however, that in cases of self-deception the agent's knowledge of what she is doing intentionally is not negated but *masked*.

4.4 The Intentional/Incidental Distinction

The finding of the previous section is that an agent's intentions in acting are determined by the calculation on which she acts (or *calculations* in a case where the agent is pursuing two or more independent ends simultaneously through a single course of action). The calculation includes the agent's end and the means she has settled on for achieving it, and it can be represented by a practical syllogism. On the other hand, effects or aspects of the agent's conduct that fall outside her means-end calculation are not intentional. If she is aware of these effects or aspects, they are incidental.

We can illustrate this way of drawing the intentional/incidental distinction by returning to the man from *Intention* who is eating some pigs' tripes. There are a whole host of true descriptions of what he is doing: He is eating the pigs' tripes, of course, which consists in his taking them off the plate, moving them to his mouth, chewing them, and swallowing them. He is getting some vitamin X and raising his cholesterol level. He is also, we might suppose, eating some of last night's leftovers and some of his deceased grandmother's favorite dish. But what he is doing and bringing about intentionally is determined by the calculation on the basis of which he is acting, which we represented earlier by the following (Pattern 1) practical syllogism:

(h) End: Get something good for me.
If I get some vitamin X, I'll be getting something good for me.
If I eat some pigs' tripes, I'll get some vitamin X.
If I eat some of these, I'll eat some pigs' tripes.
Conclusion: Eat some of these.

The man is therefore intentionally (i) eating some of *these*, (ii) eating some pigs' tripes, (iii) getting some vitamin X, and (iv) getting something good for him. He may also be aware that by eating the pigs' tripes, he is raising his cholesterol level. He is not raising his cholesterol level intentionally, though, for raising it is not part of his means-end calculation. Moreover, as he ingests the pig's tripes, he might warmly remember that they were his late grandmother's favorite food. But while his action can truly be described as "eating my grandmother's favorite food," this description is not relevant to his calculation of what to do to eat something good for him. Therefore, his action is not intentional under the description "eating my grandmother's favorite food," though he knows that in eating pigs' tripes he is, in fact, eating his grandmother's favorite food.

4.4.1 *Rejecting "Cartesian Psychology"*

Anscombe's account should be distinguished from an error about intention and intentional action she labels "Cartesian psychology" (1981e, 58–9). The Cartesian psychologist makes two claims. First, an intention is an "interior act of the mind" that a rational agent can produce at will and direct at any aspect or effect of his action that he wishes. Second, this direction of intention is accomplished by the agent's making a little speech to himself of the form "What I *mean* to be doing is such-and-such" (cf. 1963, §27).

Anscombe calls this conception of intention a "perverse doctrine" and condemns it on the ground that it leads to the abuse of double effect. Here's how the abuse works. A person is doing (or about to do) something that he realizes is morally dubious by the lights of the PDE. He then tries to justify his conduct by telling himself that he is "directing his intention" away from the evil effects that would bring it under the prohibition on intentional harm. For example, a Royal Air Force commander in World War II might try to justify authorizing the obliteration bombing of German cities by telling himself that all he really means to be authorizing is destroying the houses of the industrial workers, with a view to lowering their morale.[20] He knows that a large number of the workers, their families, and other civilians will undoubtedly be killed and injured when the residential districts of the cities are destroyed, but he eases his conscience by telling himself that these causalities are "merely" incidental.

This commander is deceiving himself, however, if he thinks the policy can be justified in this manner. He deceives himself in thinking that if civilian casualties are incidental, then they are thereby justified – as if "I didn't mean to do it!" automatically absolves one from guilt. Even if the harm to civilians were incidental, that does not negate the fact that the bombing kills and injures massive numbers of them in an attack that is aimed at the destruction of their property and without good evidence that an attack of this sort will reduce morale rather than stiffen it (as was in fact the case). But even more important is that there is no doubt that the *actual calculation* behind the policy of obliteration bombing was to try and affect

[20] In March 1942, Lord Cherwell wrote a minute to the Prime Minister arguing that "having one's house demolished is most damaging to morale. People seem to mind it more than having their friends or even relatives killed." (qtd. in Garrett 2007, 173). Garrett notes that the official history of Bomber Command states that Cherwell's intervention "did much to ensure the concept of strategic bombing in its hour of crisis" (qtd. in 2007, 173).

enemy morale by way of producing multiple effects, including not only damage to civilian property but also death and injury to civilians themselves. And it is the actual calculation on the basis of which the agent acts that determines which effects of his conduct are intentional. Therefore, if he were being truthful with himself, the commander would have to acknowledge that he cannot reject the question "Why?" asked in relation to bringing about civilian casualties.

4.5 Application to the Controversial Cases

With our account of the intentional/incidental distinction in hand, let us revisit the three controversial cases from Section 4.1.

> *Fly and Hammer:* Austin, who has a great hatred of flies, finds a fly in his apartment, and the only swatting implement to hand is a hammer. The fly eventually settles on the bald head of his friend. Austin smashes the hammer down on the fly, which also severely injures and kills his friend. Does Austin injure or kill his friend intentionally?

Coady thinks it would be absurd for Austin to plead that he did not intend his friend's injury or death (2008, 139). If we accept the Anscombian account, we will disagree. Austin's end is to kill the fly, and his means to this end is to crush it with the hammer. The friend's injury and death are outside the means-end calculation on which Austin acts, and both are therefore incidental. It might be suggested that Austin's means to killing the fly is to smash his friend's head, but I think this suggestion is incorrect. He brings down the hammer not *in order to* smash his friend's head but in order to smash the fly, though he of course foresees that the hammer will do great damage to his friend's head. This judgment about Austin's intentions in no way implies that he is not guilty of serious wrongdoing. As Coady recognizes, Austin's conduct egregiously violates the proportionality requirement for incidental harm.

Resistance to the claim that Austin does not intentionally kill or injure may also be due to the belief that Austin is surely guilty of committing murder, together with the belief that murder requires an intention to kill or cause grievous bodily harm (as it does in current English law). But instead of abandoning the Anscombian account, I think we should instead reject the notion that an intention to kill or cause grievous bodily harm is necessary for murder. As Anscombe puts it, while the intentional killing of the innocent constitutes the "hard core" of murder, this hard core is surrounded by a fuzzy penumbra, in which fall some killings that are not intentional (2005c, 262).[21] Given that Austin's conduct manifests extreme indifference to the well-being of his so-called "friend," it is not difficult to believe it falls squarely within the penumbra.

> *Burning Building:* Beth jumps out the window of the 100th floor of a skyscraper to avoid a fire that is consuming the building in the belief that being slowly burned to death would be far worse than a quick end from hitting the pavement. Does Beth kill herself intentionally?

Beth does not kill herself intentionally. Her end is to avoid an agonizing death in the fire, and her means to doing so is to remove herself from the building, which she does by jumping out the window. Thus, if we could somehow ask Beth why she is jumping out the window, she would answer, "To escape the flames." But if we asked her, "Why are you killing yourself?" she would refuse the question application, responding with an answer such as "If only I could avoid it! But it can't be helped that death will be the result of jumping out the window." In this respect, Beth's case can be distinguished from one in which the agent – call her Brenda – has been contemplating committing suicide for some time and jumps out the window of a burning building both in order to avoid the flames and in order to end her life (Tollefsen 2006, 449). Beth's conduct is behaviorally similar to Brenda's, and the actions of the two women might even be indistinguishable to an observer on the street who sees them both jump. But Beth's and Brenda's actions embody different calculations, and hence, different intentions.

> *Fleeing London Airport:* In order to escape some pursuers, Charles boards a plane at London airport that he knows to be bound for Manchester. Although Manchester is the last place he would like to be, Charles boards the plane because he wants to escape his pursuers and it is the first one he sees. Does Charles board the plane with the intention of traveling to Manchester?

Lord Bridge claims that Charles certainly intends to go to Manchester. A careful analysis with the Anscombian account, however, returns the verdict that Charles does not board the plane with the intention of traveling to Manchester. Charles calculates that in order to escape his pursuers, he must get away from the airport; any plane will be sufficient

[21] Similarly, Finnis proposes to define the mental element in murder disjunctively, as either an intention to kill or certainty that death will be brought about by something one does without lawful justification or excuse (2011b, 186). See also the discussion of depraved indifference murder in Section 3.6.

for doing this, so he boards the first one he sees. The calculation on which he acts can thus be represented by the following practical syllogism:[22]

(j) *Charles's Calculation*
If I get away from the airport, that will help me escape my pursuers.
If I board the first plane I see, it will take me away from the airport.
If I board this plane, I'll board the first plane I see.
So, I'll board this plane.

The fact that the plane happens to be bound for Manchester is irrelevant to Charles's calculation. In this respect, we can compare it to the calculation of another agent, Cody, who finds himself in similar circumstances. Cody arrives at the terminal and calculates:

(k) *Cody's Calculation*
If I get away from the airport, that will help me escape my pursuers.
If I go to Manchester, that will take me away from the airport.
If I board this plane, I'll go to Manchester.
So, I'll board this plane.

Here part of the means that Cody settles on for escaping his pursuers is to travel to Manchester. Thus, if a fellow passenger were to ask him as he boards the plane "Why are you traveling *to Manchester*?" he would answer (if he was being honest) "To escape my pursuers." By contrast, if Charles were asked the same question, he would refuse it application, saying something along the lines of "That's the last place I want to be, but it's where this plane is headed." This means that Cody boards intending to travel to Manchester while Charles does not.

4.5.1 Intention and Success

Further support for this analysis of Charles's intentions comes from the fact that a person's intentions in acting define the success conditions for her conduct. This is illustrated by a memorable story in *Intention*.[23] A man is going to the supermarket with a shopping list and, unbeknownst to him, he is being followed by a detective who is making a record of everything he purchases. Anscombe observes that what happens in the world has a different relation to the shopper's list than it does to the detective's record:

> [I]f the list and the things that the man actually buys do not agree, and if this and this alone constitutes a *mistake*, then the mistake is not in the list but in the man's performance (if his wife were to say: "Look, it says butter

[22] Cf. Finnis (2011c, 274n10). [23] See also Murphy (2004).

> and you have bought margarine," he would hardly reply: "What a mistake! we must put that right" and alter the word on the list to "margarine"); whereas if the detective's record and what the man actually buys do not agree, then the mistake is in the record. (1963, §32)

The detective's record aims to reflect what goes on in the world independently of it. As such, what happens is a standard or measure for the record in the following sense: If there is any discrepancy between what the shopper buys and what appears on the record, that shows the record is defective. It has failed at being what it is supposed to be, namely, a recording of what the man bought. On the other hand, the shopper's list is an expression of what he intends to purchase, and in that capacity, it is a standard for what he does. It is not a moral standard, but rather a standard that measures whether and to what extent his shopping activity is a *success*. That is, supposing that the man did not change his mind about what to buy, if there is a discrepancy between what he buys and what appears on the list, that shows he has *failed* to do what he intended.

The tale of the shopper and the detective illustrates how an agent's intentions in acting define the things she does as being successful or unsuccessful. This point requires some care, however, because a person's actions can be *partially* successful and partially unsuccessful. Suppose, for instance, that I put poison in my uncle's tea with the intention of killing him and coming into my inheritance. My uncle recovers from the poisoning, but in an unusual act of generosity, he immediately bequeaths me his entire fortune. In this case, I succeeded in getting my uncle's money. My actions were not *fully* successful, however. For I did not just intend the end of getting his money, I also intended a certain means for achieving that end, namely killing him. I did not succeed in killing him, though, and in that respect, my action was a failure. I may be pleased to have received my uncle's money without his death, but that does not mean that my actions were fully successful. It just means that I do not mind that I partially failed to do what I set out to do since I still achieved what I ultimately cared about through a stroke of good luck.

Let us return now to the escape from London airport. Imagine that both Charles, the star of the case, and Cody have boarded the plane that is headed for Manchester. Halfway through the flight, there is an emergency and it is re-routed to Liverpool, where both men escape and go into hiding. In this version of the scenario, Cody's actions will be partially successful since he will have lost his pursuers. But he will count them as being at least in part a failure, for his intention was to escape his pursuers *by* traveling to Manchester and the plane never arrived there. On the other hand, Charles will not count his actions as even partially a failure. He boarded the first plane he saw, got away from London airport, and escaped his pursuers, and he therefore accomplished every element of his calculation. The point that the agent's intentions in acting determine the success conditions for his actions thus supports the conclusion that Charles did not have an intention to travel specifically *to Manchester*.

4.6 Conclusion

According to the Anscombian account, an action is intentional under a certain description when the question "Why?" has application to it under that description, where the question asks for a reason for acting. The question "Why?" can often be reiterated, and answers to successive applications of it identify a teleological order in the agent's conduct, that is, a nested sequence of aims, goals, or purposes for the sake of which she is acting. This order of aims/goals/purposes in turn corresponds to the agent's intentions in acting. The answers to the "Why?" question that can truthfully be given are determined, in turn, by the agent's own means-end calculation. Since this is so, "It is nonsense to pretend that you do not intend to do what is the means you take to your chosen end" (Anscombe 1981e, 59). If doing X figures in the means-end calculation on the basis of which one acts, then doing X is intentional and one cannot change this fact by concentrating on some other aspect of one's conduct, Y, and saying to oneself, "What I really mean to be doing is Y." On the other hand, whenever an agent acts intentionally, there will be many effects and aspects of her conduct that do not fall within her means-end calculation, and these are not intentional. If the agent is aware that she is bringing them about or doing them, they are incidental.

CHAPTER 5

The Closeness Problem

5.1 Introduction

The aim of this chapter is to respond to an objection to the PDE known as the closeness problem. According to philosophers who advance this objection, the problem arises because intentions are sufficiently fine-grained that an agent need not intend harm in nearly any situation. The PDE therefore fails to rule out conduct that is intuitively objectionable in a whole host of cases unless it is supplemented with a criterion of excessive closeness, whose role is to identify things that are "too close" to harm to be considered incidental for purposes of double effect. However, it also proves extremely difficult to specify a criterion of closeness that is not arbitrary or subject to counterexamples.[1] The closeness problem is often thought to be particularly acute for accounts like Anscombe's, according to which an agent's intentions in acting are determined by the means-end calculation on the basis of which she acts.

The central claim of this chapter is that the magnitude of the closeness problem has been exaggerated. Friends of the PDE have a variety of resources for defusing cases that allegedly demonstrate the need for a criterion of closeness. In Section 5.2, I discuss the origins of the problem in classic essays by Philippa Foot and Jonathan Bennett. In the remainder of the chapter, I then argue that the PDE does not need to be supplemented by a criterion of closeness. In Section 5.3, I show how many of the cases that populate the literature on the closeness problem can be dealt with in other ways, namely, by correcting mistaken analyses of the agent's intentions, by reminders that the PDE covers intentional harms short of death, and by invoking moral principles other than the constraint against intentional harm. There are, however, a remaining class of cases that still appear to be problematic, which I describe in Section 5.4. In Section 5.5,

[1] This formulation of the closeness problem draws on Nelkin and Rickless (2015).

I introduce a candidate criterion of closeness that seems promising for handling the problem cases, but I ultimately argue that it should be rejected. Finally, in Section 5.6, I argue that the problem cases should be resolved instead by a more precise articulation of the *content* of the constraint against intentional harm.

5.2 Origins of the Problem

The closeness problem originated in a pair of essays by H. L. A. Hart and Philippa Foot published in *Oxford Review* in 1967 (Foot 2002; Hart 2008). Hart noted that some early twentieth-century Catholic moralists attempted to use the PDE to distinguish two cases in biomedical ethics:

> *Hysterectomy*: A pregnant woman has cancer of the uterus. Her physician removes the gravid uterus in order to save her life, foreseeing that the nonviable child will die as a result.
>
> *Craniotomy*: A woman's labor is obstructed due to the fact that the head of her unborn child is too large to pass through her birth canal (cephalopelvic disproportion). This condition threatens the life of both mother and child, so her physician performs an obstetric craniotomy, a procedure in which he crushes the child's skull (typically after making an incision in its head and evacuating its contents) and then removes its corpse from the birth canal.[2]

The moralists argued that in *Hysterectomy* the death of the child is a foreseen side effect of removing the woman's uterus while in *Craniotomy* the death of the child is intended as a means to ending the obstructed labor. The first procedure is therefore morally permissible while the second is not. Hart doubted, however, that a physician who performs a craniotomy intends to kill the child.

Given that craniotomy reliably leads to death, a physician certainly *could* perform one with the intention of killing, and I do not think that Hart would disagree. The issue is better framed as whether, given the nature of the procedure, the physician *need* intend the child's death. I will give my own analysis of the case below (Section 5.3.2). For now, I simply comment that, on the Anscombian account, Hart is correct that it is possible to perform the procedure without intentionally killing the child. The physician's practical problem is to end the obstructed labor threatening the woman's life. In order to do so, he must remove the child from her body,

[2] The invention of cesarean section has made obstetric craniotomy obsolete in the developed world, though apparently it is still occasionally performed in areas where health services are under-resourced. See Duffy 2007 (cited in Gormally 2016, 153n55).

and he does this by crushing its skull. Crushing the child's skull inevitably causes its death, but it is not the child's *death* that enables its body to be removed from the woman's body. Indeed, the physician would face the same practical problem even if the child had died prior to his performing the craniotomy, and he would proceed in the same way. The means-end calculation that defines what the physician does intentionally thus need not include bringing about the child's death.

In discussing the *Hysterectomy/Craniotomy* pair, Hart did not mean to be raising a general objection to the PDE: He simply doubted one application of it. His main complaint about double effect was that he could not see why the intentional/incidental distinction should be morally significant (2008, 124). However, Foot saw Hart's discussion as raising a fundamental *problem* for the PDE. She thought the contention that the physician could perform a craniotomy without intending the child's death makes "nonsense of [the PDE] from the beginning" (2002, 21). To strengthen this claim she introduced another case as an analog to *Craniotomy*:

> *Potholer*: A party of potholers (cave explorers) have allowed a large man to lead them out of a cave and he has gotten stuck in the cave's entrance, leaving the others trapped behind him. One of the explorers has a stick of dynamite that they can use to blow up the stuck man. This would clear the entrance and enable their escape.

Foot imagines the trapped explorers decide to use the dynamite. They admit they intentionally blow up the stuck man in order to clear the cave entrance, but they also claim that they do not intend *to kill* him – they merely foresee his death as a side effect of blowing him up. Foot finds it absurd that the PDE would not forbid blowing up the stuck man. Furthermore, she assumes that the ground of this condemnation could only be that his death is so "close" to his being blown up that it counts as intentional for purposes of applying double effect. The problem for proponents of the PDE lies in specifying what counts as excessive closeness: "What is to be the criterion of 'closeness' if we say that anything very close to what we are literally aiming at counts as if part of our aim?" (Foot 2002, 22).

The other source of the closeness problem is Bennett. Bennett noticed that some proponents of double effect agree with Hart that a physician who performs a craniotomy need not kill the unborn child intentionally. But Bennett believed that other absurd results follow if the constraint against intentional harm is not supplemented with a criterion of closeness. He notoriously claims that on an Anscombian-style account of intention even a terror bomber does not intend to kill noncombatants but only to bring it about that their "bodies should be in a state that would cause a general belief that they were dead" (1995, 210). The intentional structure of terror bombing is therefore similar to the intentional structure of precision bombing, insofar as neither involves intentional killing. This is a major problem, for while proponents of double effect disagree about the permissibility of craniotomy they are united in wanting to distinguish terror bombing from precision bombing.[3] Bennett thought that in order to avoid the result that terror bombers do not kill intentionally we require a "tight-binding principle," which specifies when two items are too close for an agent to intend one and not the other if he foresees both.

We can formulate the closeness problem as a dilemma. Proponents of the PDE must either (1) provide a criterion of excessive closeness or (2) be stuck with consequences that are absurd and that render the principle unable to do the work they want it to do.[4] There are also two distinct ways one might understand the notion of excessive closeness:

(1) If E is too close to M and the agent intends M, then E counts *as if* it is intended for purposes of applying the PDE.
(2) If E is too close to M, then an agent who intends M and foresees E also intends E.

Foot thinks of the notion of excessive closeness along the lines of (1) while Bennett conceives of it along the lines of (2). Whether we think of excessive closeness as (1) or (2), however, we run into problems.

The problem for (1) is that, however, we fill out the notion of excessive closeness, it is bound to seem arbitrary. A rationale for the PDE explains why intentional harm is morally objectionable, but a person who intends something *close* to harm on this account does not intend harm. It is therefore difficult to see how the rationale for the PDE will apply to something close to harm (Tadros 2015, 58–9).

The problem for (2) lies in specifying a criterion of closeness that is not subject to counterexamples. Consider, for example, the proposal that M and E are too close to separate in intention when M causally necessitates

[3] For the distinction between terror bombing and precision bombing, see Section 2.2.1.

[4] Another way out of the dilemma is to attempt to replace the PDE with a different moral principle that distinguishes many of the cases the PDE is supposed to distinguish. The principle in question might even be sensitive to the agent's intentions, even if it does not accord moral significance to the distinction between intentional and incidental *harm*. This is the strategy employed by Quinn (1993a). Quinn muddies the waters, however, by calling his distinction between harmful direct agency and harmful indirect agency a "version" of double effect.

E (so long as the agent is aware that M causally necessitates E). Since in *Potholer* the death of the stuck man is causally necessitated by his being blown up, and since the explorers intend to blow him up, it follows by this criterion that they also intend his death. However, if a military facility is located next to a hospital, then it might be that the facility's being destroyed causally necessitates the deaths of the noncombatants in the hospital. Yet, it seems clear that a bomber pilot could intend to destroy the facility without intending to kill the noncombatants, even though he foresees their deaths.

Or consider another criterion that combines causal necessity and causal immediacy (roughly, M immediately produces E when M produces E without any intermediate causal links). In "Action, Intention and 'Double Effect'," Anscombe considers a variation of *Potholer*, in which the trapped explorers have no dynamite but instead can move a rock that will both open an escape route and crush the stuck man's head. Anscombe claims that if the rock must roll along a path before it crushes the man's head then there is room to say that the resulting head-crushing is not intentional. But if the rock is instead positioned *next to* the man's head, so that his head's being crushed will be an immediate effect of moving it, then if one intends to move the rock, one intends to crush his head (2005a, 224).

Finnis observes that this proposal seems to conflict with Anscombe's own account of intentional action in *Intention*, where it is posited that what an agent does intentionally is determined by the means-end calculation on the basis of which she acts (2011b, 192). In both the case where the rock must roll along a path and the case where it is positioned next to the man's head, the explorers' calculation is the same: Their end is to exit the cave, and their means to doing so is to open an escape route by moving the rock. In neither case do the explorers move the rock *in order to* crush the man's head, and this implies that in neither case is the head-crushing intentional by the lights of *Intention*.

It might be retorted that this only shows that Anscombe changed her mind. But there are other scenarios where it seems intuitively clear that a certain effect is not intentional though it is a causally necessary and immediate effect of the agent's intended means. Consider, for example, a case by Patrick Lee:

> *Lee's Knee*: Lee has severe osteoarthritis in his left knee. The cartilage in the knee has worn down to such an extent that any walking at all further damages it and even the bone. One evening Lee decides to take a walk for the purpose of getting some exercise, which he knows will immediately and inevitably damage his knee (2017, 235).

Lee's walking inevitably damages his knee, and it does so without any causal intermediaries. Yet, it seems plain that he is walking with the intention of getting some exercise and not with the intention of causing damage to his knee, just as a marathon runner runs with the intention of exercising and not with the intention of wearing out his shoes. This supports the account from *Intention*.

Other criteria of closeness have been proposed and I will not attempt to review them all here. The preceding discussion is intended to illustrate the nature of the challenge involved in grasping the first horn of the closeness dilemma. Since I am pessimistic about the prospects of finding a satisfactory criterion of closeness, my strategy will be to argue that the second horn is not nearly as bad as those who push the closeness problem contend.

5.3 Doing without Closeness

5.3.1 A Mistaken Analysis of Intention: Bennett on Terror Bombing

I begin with Bennett's analysis of terror bombing since his claims about it are everywhere repeated. Bennett considers an account of intention very similar to Anscombe's in *Intention*, according to which an agent's intentions in acting encompass her end and the means to her end but not any further effects, even ones that are causally necessary and immediate. His case that we need to supplement this account with a criterion of closeness rests on the contention that unsupplemented it has implications that are "outright crazy." As proof, he submits the following:

> I said [earlier] that the [terror bomber] intended to kill the civilians so as to lower morale, but the truth is finer-grained than that. Really, he intended only that the people's bodies should be in a state that would cause a general belief that they were dead, this lasting long enough to shorten the war: nothing in that scheme requires that the dismaying condition of the bodies be permanent; so nothing in it requires that the people become downright dead rather than seemingly dead for a year or two. It would not enter the bomber's head that he could achieve the lesser thing without achieving the greater; but the greater thing is complex, and only one constituent is intended as a means. (1995, 210–11)

Bennett's argument consists in three claims. (1) The Anscombian account implies that a terror bomber does not intend that the noncombatants he kills should be dead but only that they should *appear* to be dead for a period of time. (2) There must be some sense in which a terror bomber does intend noncombatant deaths. This shows (3) that the Anscombian account needs to be supplemented with a criterion of closeness. I agree with (2): Terror bombers intend to kill noncombatants.[5] But I disagree with (1): The Anscombian account does in fact have that result. The problem lies not with it but with Bennett's faulty application of it.

The key point is that the terror bomber intends to make the noncombatants appear to be dead *by* killing them (Cavanaugh 2006, 115). We can concede that the bomber intends to make the noncombatants appear to be dead since it is their appearing dead to others that will, he believes, cause them to become demoralized. But that still leaves unresolved the practical problem of *how* to make the noncombatants appear to be dead. It seems the answer to this question must be: by killing them, which he does by dropping his bombs on them. It has been claimed that things would be different if the bomber had at his disposal special "knock-out" bombs (FitzPatrick 2006, 590). Yet, even if he had knock-out bombs, in ordinary circumstances using them would not be sufficient to cause the appearance of death: The fact that the unconscious victims do not appear to be otherwise injured would surely make the others wonder what sort of weapon they had been hit with, and whether it had killed them, and a quick check of their vital signs would reveal they were still alive. Clever philosophers can of course construct cases in which there is no possibility of examining the bodies, but this is emphatically not the sort of case Bennett has in mind. He is explicit that he is talking about terror bombing in ordinary conditions. And, looking ahead to the next section, we should also not forget that being knocked unconscious for a significant period of time is itself a serious harm (Shaw 2006a, 219).

Some defenders of Bennett counter that this reply is inadequate. FitzPatrick (2006, 591) and Nelkin and Rickless (2015, 406n13) claim that, actually, the terror bomber's intended means of making noncombatants appear to be dead is not killing them but only *impacting them sufficiently with his bombs to put them in a condition of appearing to be dead.* According to these authors, proponents of PDE need a criterion of closeness to connect being impacted with ordinary lethal bombs and death.

Against this, however, I think we need only point out that calculations typically have multiple elements and that there must be some intelligible

[5] At least the sort of terror bombers Bennett has in mind. It is possible that seeing a number of their comrades seriously injured would be sufficient to demoralize a certain population, even if none of the wounded were dead. But intentionally causing serious injury is also prohibited by the strict constraint against intentional harm.

connection, in the mind of the agent, between her end and the means she adopts for realizing it. Recall, for instance, the gardener who is poisoning a house's water supply in order to kill its inhabitants (Section 4.2). If he is going to poison the water supply by operating the pump, he must have some idea of how operating the pump is supposed to cause the water supply to become poisoned (Anscombe 1963, §26). The connection is obviously that operating the pump causes the poisoned water to flow through some pipes into the house's cistern. Thus, if we were to ask the gardener "Why are you causing the water to flow through the pipes?" he would not refuse the question but answer "In order to get it into the cistern." This means that he is also intentionally making the water flow through the pipes, even if we did not make this element of his calculation explicit in our initial presentation of the case. Similarly, if a terror bomber intends to make some noncombatants appear to be dead *by* impacting them with his bombs, he must have some idea of how their being impacted with the bombs is supposed to lead to their appearing to be dead. But the only connection between these that makes sense is that the noncombatants' being impacted by the bombs causes them to die, by doing such things as burning them, rupturing their vital organs, and blowing them to pieces. Therefore, provided the terror bomber is not seriously deluded about how his bombs work, he must intend to cause the deaths of the noncombatants.

There is another confusion about the terror bombing case that we should also clear up. In his sympathetic presentation of Bennett's argument, Quinn observes that the terror bomber would not complain if "by some miracle" his victims came back to life unharmed after the war's conclusion (1993a, 178). Quinn infers from this that the terror bomber does not intend the deaths of the noncombatants. However, Quinn's observation does not show this at all. What it shows, rather, is that in order to achieve his end the terror bomber does not need the noncombatants to *remain* dead permanently.

Bennett is partially responsible for this confusion. In his discussion of terror bombing, he equates being dead with the state of being permanently inoperative or dismantled (1995, 212). This is a strange understanding of death. As Steinhoff notes, it makes resurrection from the dead conceptually impossible (2018a, 77). What Bennett calls "death" might more aptly be called (to coin a neologism) "perma-death." Our ordinary concept of death is not that of perma-death, which is why the idea of resurrection from the dead is not incoherent. The ordinary concept of death is rather the cessation of vital activity, and in biological organisms, this amounts to the cessation of integrated organic functioning. We can concede that the terror bomber does not (or at least need not) intend to bring it about that noncombatants are dead permanently (perma-death). But this in no way impugns the analysis above, which shows that he does intend to bring about their deaths.[6]

Bennett has not shown that the terror bomber does not intend the death of his victims. It might be objected, however, that his argument nonetheless shows that the bomber does not violate the constraint against intentional harm, on the ground that what is really a harm is not death but perma-death, or at least death for a significant period of time. Imagine you are a doctor who works at a hospital that has a resurrection machine, a device that can bring a corpse back to life if it is not too decayed. In that event, it might be argued, a person would not be seriously aggrieved if you painlessly killed him and then immediately resurrected him. This in turn supports the claim that it is not *death* that is a serious harm but rather death for a significant period of time. But if death is not a serious harm, then intentionally bringing it about is not prohibited by the constraint against intentional harm.

Even if this objection is successful, it would not acquit Bennett's terror bomber, since Bennett specifies that the noncombatants need to be dead for a significant period of time ("a year or two") in order for the war to be successfully concluded. But we can imagine variations of the case in which the noncombatants would only need to be dead for a few hours or even minutes to secure victory, and in these variations, it seems that terror bombing would be equally difficult to justify. The objection is therefore not frivolous.

My response is twofold. First, the argument's premise is dubious. I *would* feel seriously aggrieved if my doctor painlessly killed me and then brought me back to life if he did it without my permission. More importantly, the thought experiment does not show that death is not a serious harm. I think it shows rather that facts about the circumstances can sometimes reduce the *magnitude* of certain evils. In particular, if someone suffers E in circumstances in which it is or will be immediately reversed,

[6] Steinhoff argues that Bennett confuses death with perma-death because he is misled by an analogy he tries to make between terror bombing and the case of a political leader who intends to bring about a month-long state of disintegration in a trade union to avoid a strike at Christmas. In the case of the trade union, we might say that the politician does not intend the "death" of the union, meaning by this its permanent dissolution. But it is an error to infer from this metaphorical use of "death" that when it comes to biological organisms, death is permanent dissolution. Death is the cessation of integrated biological functioning, not the permanent cessation of it.

then the magnitude of E is less than it would be otherwise. As support for this, consider another case. Suppose I have in my home a machine that can instantly re-grow a lost limb and I lose my arm while working on some equipment outside. If I know that I am going to immediately go inside and re-grow the arm, I might regard its loss as a relatively minor harm, comparable to a nasty scratch (though more painful).[7] Nonetheless, it would be ludicrous to think that it follows that a person who loses a limb in the actual world does not suffer a serious harm. Similarly, in the actual world where death is permanent,[8] to inflict death on a person is to inflict on him a very serious evil.[9]

I conclude that Bennett's argument is unsuccessful. On the Anscombian account of intentional action, ordinary terror bombers do indeed kill their victims intentionally, and in doing so, they cause them serious harm.

5.3.2 *Intentional Harms Other Than Death*

Many discussions of the PDE focus on intentional killing. According to the version of the principle that I endorse, however, there is a strict constraint against intentionally bringing about serious harm more generally. This enables the PDE to handle the other cases that were supposed to give rise to the closeness problem, *Craniotomy* and *Potholer*.

Foot thought that it would be absurd if the PDE failed to condemn blowing up the man stuck in the cave entrance. The PDE does condemn this, but not because being blown up is somehow "too close" to death. Rather, the PDE condemns the trapped explorers' conduct because they intentionally blow up the man as a means to clearing the entrance and being blown up is itself a serious injury for the man. A similar analysis

[7] We must also assume that I am somehow able to prevent my body from going into shock and bleeding out before I can reach the machine.

[8] I am prescinding from the possibility that there might someday be a resurrection of the dead.

[9] It might also be objected that when a terror bomber drops his bombs on noncombatants, he does so only intending to *make them dead temporarily* (until the conclusion of the war). But what does it mean to intend to bring about a state of affairs temporarily? I can think of two possibilities. On the most natural interpretation, it is to intend to bring about a state of affairs and also to reverse it after some period of time. For instance, if I say I intend to move to St. Louis for two years, I would normally be taken to mean that I intend to move to St. Louis for two years and then move back to my current location. If the terror bomber is sane, then he cannot intend to bring about noncombatant deaths temporarily in this sense, since he does not have the power to bring them back to life. On another interpretation, an agent might be said to intend to bring about a certain state of affairs temporarily if in order to accomplish her end she only needs that state of affairs to obtain for a certain period of time. This returns us to the point that a terror bomber does not need the noncombatants to be dead permanantly.

applies to *Craniotomy*. I agreed with Hart that a physician performing the procedure need not intend to bring about the child's death. However, the physician does intentionally crush the child's skull as a means to removing it from its mother's birth canal, and a crushed skull is a very grave injury for the child.[10] It is sometimes claimed that what the physician intends is only to reduce the size of the child's head or narrow its cranium (Finnis, Boyle, and Grisez 2001, 29). The problem with this analysis lies in the word "only." The physician does intend to reduce the size of the child's head, for this is what allows it to be removed from the birth canal, but it is not *all* that he intends. He cannot simply "reduce the size of the child's head" – he needs to settle on some more specific means of doing so. Given that he lacks a shrink ray and has at his disposal instruments that can effectively crush the child's skull, the means he adopts to reduce the size of the child's head is to crush it.[11]

Noticing that there are harms short of death also allows proponents of double effect to account for a common intuition about the *Footbridge* trolley dilemma:

> *Footbridge*: A runaway trolley is headed toward five trapped people who will be killed if it continues on its present course. You are standing on a footbridge that spans the tracks, and next to you is a large man. The only way to save the five is to push the man off the bridge and onto the tracks. The man's body will prevent the trolley from reaching the five, but he will be killed when he is struck by it (Thomson 1985, 1409).

Some proponents of the PDE claim that acting to save the five in *Footbridge* involves intentionally killing the large man (e.g., Kaufman 2009, 90). On the Anscombian account of intentional action I endorse this is incorrect. If you decide to save the five, the calculation on which you act is most likely the following: (A) prevent the trolley from killing the five, (B) cause the large man to be hit by the trolley, and (C) throw the large man onto the tracks. Since it is not the large man's death that stops the trolley but its collision with his body, the calculation that determines what you do intentionally need not include bringing about his death. This does not mean that your conduct is in the clear by the lights of the PDE,

[10] Quinn claims that if a miracle occurred and after its removal the child were quickly restored to a healthy condition "we would say that the craniotomy had done no real harm" (1993a, 178). What we ought to say is not that it had done no real harm but that it had done no *lasting* harm. In the real world where crushed skulls are not immediately repaired by miracles, a crushed skull is a very serious harm.

[11] We should also not forget that a craniotomy typically involves making a hole in the child's cranium and evacuating its contents prior to crushing it. This is also a very grave harm.

however, for you do cause the large man *to be hit* by the trolley as a means to saving the five, and this is a form of intentional battery (Mikhail 2011, 133–6; cf. Shaw 2006b).

Battery is an application of force to a person's body that is either harmful or offensive. In his reflection on why battery is prohibited by criminal law, Lord Goff refers to the "fundamental principle . . . that every person's body is inviolate." Since our bodies are inviolate, the law should protect us "not only against physical injury but against any form of physical molestation" (*Collins* v. *Wilcock* [1984] 1 WLR 1172; qtd. in Herring 2018, 318). Lord Goff's remark points us to a certain good, the good of bodily integrity, which includes being free of harmful or offensive trespasses against one's body. Batteries are evils because they deprive us of this good. For purposes of law, even minor transgressions against a person's body, such as unwelcome touching of hair or clothes, sometimes count as battery. Some batteries are surely worse than others, however. I propose that we define *serious* batteries as applications of force to a person's body that result in grave injury or death, and that a serious battery is a serious evil. As such, the constraint against intentional harm includes a constraint against serious battery. This in turn explains (one reason) why you act wrongly in *Footbridge* if you throw the man onto the tracks in order to save the five.[12]

This explanation of how the PDE applies to *Footbridge* avoids an objection by Nelkin and Rickless (2015, 381–2). They claim that the agent in *Footbridge* intends a harmful impact, but they note that the phrase "harmful impact" is ambiguous. It might mean either (1) an impact along with its harmfulness or (2) an impact that, as it happens, is harmful. They then argue that it is plausible that the agent intends (2) rather than (1). I agree that the agent need not intentionally bring about any of the harms that immediately follow from being impacted by the trolley. My claim is, rather, that the agent intentionally causes the large man to be hit by the trolley, and that this is a serious battery because it is a trespass against the man's bodily integrity that causes harm and death. That sort of trespass is a serious harm or evil even if the harms that causally result from it are not intended.[13]

[12] The qualification in parentheses makes room for the possibility that the action in *Footbridge* is wrong on multiple grounds. For instance, it is sometimes suggested that the action is wrong because it violates the Kantian prohibition on using others as mere means to an end (Thomson 1985, 1403; Masek 2018, 124).

[13] Howard Nye says it is "preposterous to claim that the moral barriers to using as a means a 'harm' like mere violent impacting, quite independent of death, are anything like the moral barriers to using death as a means" (2013, 265n13). His grounds for this assertion are that if in *Footbridge* you

5.3.3 Other Wrong-Making Features of Conduct

I have argued that the PDE can explain the wrongfulness of the agent's conduct in *Footbridge*. If I am incorrect about this application, that does not constitute a reason to reject the principle. It merely shows that some other factor explains why the agent acts wrongly. More generally, the fact that conduct that is intuitively wrongful cannot be shown to be wrongful on the grounds that it intentionally brings about serious harm does not show that the constraint against intentional harm is inadequate unless it is supplemented with a criterion of closeness. It shows only that the PDE is best thought of as one element of a pluralistic moral theory, that is, a moral theory that recognizes a multiplicity of wrong-making factors (Shaw 2006a; Liao 2016; Masek 2018, ch. 4). This is significant because it seems to me that some of the cases raised as objections to the PDE in the literature on the closeness problem are not really double effect cases at all. They are cases where the agent acts wrongly, but the wrongfulness is not to be explained by the constraint against intentional harm. In this section, I will illustrate this claim by discussing three scenarios.

5.3.3.1 Guinea Pig

Nelkin and Rickless claim that the closeness problem is an embarrassment for double effect because it shows that agents do not, or need not, intend harm even in scenarios that are supposed to be "paradigmatic instances in which [the PDE] applies to intended harm" (2015, 377). One of these allegedly paradigmatic cases is from Quinn:

> *Guinea Pig*: There is a shortage of resources for the investigation and proper treatment of a new, life-threatening disease. Doctors decide on a crash experimental program in which they deliberately leave the stubborn cases untreated in order to learn more about the nature of the disease. By this strategy, they reasonably expect to do a significant amount of long-term medical good (1993a, 177).

could quickly anesthetize the large man before pushing him, and after the trolley had hit him quickly reassemble his body so he awoke a few minutes later, then you would be required to push him onto the tracks. Even if this is true, it does not support Nye's claim. To see why, consider another case. Suppose it were possible to anesthetize a person, remove all of his healthy limbs in order to prevent a tyrant from killing five people and then reattach them a few minutes later. Grant that in such a situation you ought to remove his limbs to save the five. That hardly shows that in the actual world there are no strong moral barriers against removing a person's healthy limbs. This is a variation of the point I made in Section 5.3.1 in response to an objection that purported to show that death is not an evil.

The intuition is that the doctors act wrongly, or at least in a way that is more difficult to justify than the following contrast case:

> *Direction of Resources*: There is a shortage of resources for the investigation and proper treatment of a new, life-threatening disease. Doctors decide to cope by selectively treating only those who can be cured most easily, leaving the more stubborn cases untreated. This way, the doctors expect to do a significant amount of long-term medical good.

Nelkin and Rickless claim that proponents of the PDE think that our intuitions about these cases should be explained by the fact that whereas the doctors in *Direction of Resources* simply foresee the harm suffered in the stubborn cases, the doctors in *Guinea Pig* intend that harm. They then point out that this putative explanation is unconvincing. Plausibly, what the doctors in *Guinea Pig* intend is that the disease progress sufficiently to allow for the acquisition of additional knowledge, while they foresee that the progression of the disease will harm their patients (2015, 381). It is noteworthy, however, that Nelkin and Rickless do not cite any proponents of double effect who actually believe the PDE handles this case.[14] It is certainly not one of the traditional applications of it, and one wonders why it is supposed to be a *paradigmatic* one.

My view is that the moral difference between *Guinea Pig* and *Direction of Resources* is not best explained by the PDE. The difference can instead be explained by two other moral factors. First, in *Guinea Pig*, the doctors *use* the stubborn cases as means to acquiring medical knowledge, without their consent. It therefore falls under the Kantian prohibition against using others as mere means. By contrast, the doctors in *Direction of Resources* do not use the stubborn cases as means to an end.

A second difference between the two cases emerges when they are considered in relation to the precept of beneficence in its application to medicine. Health care professionals have a duty to care for the health of their patients; this is a special obligation they have to them that is stronger than the general duty of beneficence we have to others as fellow human beings. If they have the ability and resources to treat the illness of their patients, those patients can claim the treatment as their due, and it therefore should not be withheld simply because withholding it is expected to be of some benefit to others in the long run.[15] The doctors' conduct in *Guinea Pig* is wrong, or relatively difficult to justify, because they fail to

[14] Quinn himself was a critic of the PDE who sought to replace it with a different principle, which he confusingly called a version of the PDE. See note 4.

[15] Though this duty may be subject to a threshold.

provide treatment to their patients when they can and ought to do so. In other words, they are guilty of a privation of beneficence.[16] The circumstances in *Direction of Resources* are quite different. Here the doctors have duties of care to many patients but lack the resources to effectively treat them all. They therefore must make a decision about how to utilize the available resources, and it seems reasonable to give priority to cases where they would save the most lives. Hence, the doctors in *Direction of Resources* are not guilty of a privation of beneficence when they treat the easier cases first, assuming they still provide basic care to the more stubborn cases.[17]

5.3.3.2 Ruthless CEO

Another alleged closeness case raised by Alexander Pruss is that of a ruthless CEO:

> *Ruthless CEO*: A ruthless CEO orders her very efficient subordinate: "Do whatever it takes to gain the contract." She has good inductive reason to believe her subordinate will succeed at the task. She also believes that what it would take to gain the contract is lethally bombing the competitor's headquarters and she believes that that is what her subordinate will do. But she does not care about this (2013, 54).

The conduct of the CEO is clearly wrong, but she does not intentionally kill her competitors; indeed, she does not *bring about harm* at all – her subordinate does. Pruss believes this case constitutes a counterexample to the PDE because he thinks the PDE arises from an intuitive rule that we should "work no evil" and the CEO does "work evil" in some sense. However, this conflates one possible *rationale* for the PDE with the principle itself. Moreover, this is not a rationale I think we should adopt. An agent can be said to work evil anytime she engages in wrongdoing and

[16] For the notion of a privation of beneficence, see Section 3.4.2.

[17] Cf. Masek (2018, 167). Nelkin and Rickless argue that the closeness problem also affects the application of the PDE to three other pairs of "paradigmatic" cases: *Terror Bombing/Precision Bombing*, *Craniotomy/Hysterectomy*, and *Footbridge/Switch*. I believe that the PDE can in fact distinguish these cases. Even so, it is worth pointing out that only *Terror Bombing/Precision Bombing* deserves to be counted as a paradigmatic pair of double effect cases. We have seen that *Craniotomy/Hysterectomy* is disputed among proponents of double effect, and Masek shows that that the trolley problem cases were originally due to opponents of the PDE (Masek 2018, ch. 4). If the principle has another canonical application, it is to distinguish euthanasia from cases of palliative care in which a foreseen side effect of administering pain-killing drugs is the hastening of the patient's death. Nelkin and Rickless agree, though, that the intentional structures of euthanasia and palliative care differ in the way that proponents of double effect claim (2015, 385).

there are multiple bases of wrongdoing, including many that do not involve intentionally bringing about serious harm.[18]

There is no need to haul in the PDE to explain the wrongfulness of the CEO's conduct. Its wrongfulness is better explained on other grounds. Specifically, her conduct is wrong because she authorizes her subordinate to do "whatever it takes" to gain the contract. She has no authority to authorize this, especially since she knows the subordinate will carry out her order by lethally bombing the opposing company's headquarters.

5.3.3.3 Returning Population

The final case is due to FitzPatrick:

> *Returning Population*: A pilot wishes to demoralize the enemy government during a war and knows he could do so by creating the belief that large numbers of civilians have been killed. He is reluctant to bring this about by deliberately killing civilians but thinks he sees a way around this. It turns out that a major population center has been evacuated unbeknownst to the central government so that if it is bombed, they will believe that there have been massive civilian casualties, simply viewing it from afar. He thus plans to go ahead and bomb the empty city. At the last minute, however, he discovers that the population has returned. He goes ahead with the mission anyway (2006, 612).

The Anscombian account classifies the noncombatant deaths in *Returning Population* as being incidental rather than intentional. But FitzPatrick believes the case should be grouped with terror bombing rather than precision bombing, and he therefore takes it to show that we need a criterion of closeness that will enable us to classify the noncombatant deaths as intentional. However, even if the case is in some respects similar to terror bombing, it is hasty to conclude that the two cases must have the same intentional structures. *Returning Population* is different in important respects from both ordinary terror bombing and ordinary precision bombing and should not be assimilated to either.

The pilot's conduct is physically similar to – perhaps even indistinguishable from – a terror bomber's, and because of this, third-party observers might justifiably believe that he is engaged in terror bombing. But actions that are behaviorally identical can embody different calculations. The action of the pilot in *Returning Population* is different from that of a terror bomber in just this respect. That noncombatants should be seriously injured and/or killed is an essential part of a terror bomber's calculation,

[18] See the distinction between moral evil and natural evil in Section 1.2.2.

for it is seeing the wounded and dead bodies that is supposed to reduce morale, and thus help secure victory. On the other hand, harm to noncombatants does not figure in the calculation on which the pilot in *Returning Population* acts: His idea is to end the war by demoralizing the government officials, which is done by causing them to form the belief that there have been massive civilian casualties, which is to be accomplished by dropping bombs on the city. This difference in the bombers' calculations underwrites a difference in the intentional structures of their conduct.

However, while *Returning Population* is like precision bombing insofar as the bomber does not intentionally kill the noncombatants, it also differs from ordinary precision bombing in three important ways. First, there is one respect in which its intentional structure is more like terror bombing than precision bombing, namely, the bomber intends to end the war by demoralizing certain people, and he intends to do this by causing the perception of massive civilian harm rather than by destroying the adversary's military capabilities. Second, unlike an ordinary precision bomber, the bomber in *Returning Population* makes no attempt to discriminate between civilian and military objects, and he intentionally destroys civilian objects and property. Even if the constraint against intentionally destroying civilian objects and property lacks the same stringency as the constraint against intentionally harming civilian persons, such destruction is still typically wrong and is prohibited by international law (Section 1.5.2). Finally, *Returning Population* is also unlike ordinary precision bombing in terms of the massive scale of incidental damage the bomber causes. This is significant because the quantity of incidental harm means that the bomber's conduct almost certainly violates the Principle of Proportionality.[19] The mere fact that the noncombatant deaths are incidental does not mean that he acts permissibly.

5.4 A Fine Challenge

In the previous section, I argued that proponents of double effect have several resources that can be used to deal with cases that allegedly show the need for a criterion of closeness. In this section, I raise a class of cases that cannot be dealt with by any of the strategies employed so far. These cases seem to pose a difficulty for combining the PDE with the Anscombian

[19] The bombing may also violate the Principle of Due Care. Why not delay the bombing until the city can be re-evacuated, or pursue a different strategy that involves less incidental harm to noncombatants?

account of intentional action by exploiting a certain feature of the Anscombian account, namely, that according to it the contents of an agent's intentions in acting are sufficiently fine-grained as to exclude even *aspects* of actions or effects.

This feature is illustrated by a scenario that Anscombe employs to elucidate the distinction between intention and foresight in *Intention.* As in the scenario discussed in Section 4.2, a gardener is replenishing a house's water supply. He knows that someone who wants to kill the house's inhabitants has poisoned the water he is pumping into the cistern. He is not pumping the water *in order to* poison the inhabitants, however, but only in order to earn his usual pay as a gardener. A conversation with us, his confidants, might therefore proceed as follows:

Why are you moving your arm up and down on the pump handle?
– I'm operating the pump.

Why are you operating the pump?
– I'm replenishing the house's water supply.

Why are you replenishing the house's water supply?
– In order to earn my pay.

Suppose we then ask "But why are you replenishing the water supply with *poisoned* water?" and his answer is not "To kill the house's inhabitants" or even "To poison them" but "I don't care about that. I just want to earn my pay." Suppose, that is, that he refuses the "Why?" question application to his action under the description "replenishing the house's water supply with poisoned water." In that case, writes Anscombe,

> although he knows concerning an intentional act of his – for it, namely replenishing the house water-supply, is intentional by our criteria – that it is *also* an act of replenishing the house water-supply with *poisoned* water, it would be incorrect, by our criteria, to say that his act of replenishing the house supply with poisoned water was intentional. (1963, §25)

The calculation that is embodied by the man's pumping activity is (A) earn my usual pay, (B) replenish the house's water supply with *this* water, (C) operate the pump, and (D) move my arm up and down on the pump handle. That the water he is pumping is poisoned is entirely incidental to this calculation. Thus, the man's intentions in moving his arm up and down include replenishing the water supply with *this* water but not replenishing the water supply with *poisoned* water, even though replenishing the water supply with *this* water is, in some sense, the same action as replenishing the water supply with poisoned water. And he intends to bring it about that the water supply is replenished with *this* water, but he does not intend to bring it about that the water supply is replenished with *poisoned* water, even though the water supply's being replenished with *this* water is in some sense the same state of affairs as it's being replenished with poisoned water.[20]

If the contents of intentions are this fine-grained, then it seems possible to construct scenarios in which conduct that surely ought to be prohibited by the constraint against intentional harm will not be caught by the constraint. For example, consider the following case by Pruss:

> *Zookeeper*: An eccentric, literalistic but always truthful magnate tells Sam he will donate to famine relief, saving a hundred lives, if and only if Sam follows his directions to the iota. Sam is to purchase a gun, sneak at night into a zoo owned by the magnate, and kill the first mammal he sees. Sam sneaks into the zoo, sees a mammal in the distance, and forms the intention to shoot it. Then he notices that the mammal is human but shoots nonetheless on utilitarian grounds (2013, 53–4).

Pruss says that when Sam is charged with murdering the zookeeper, he argues that he did not intentionally kill the *human being* there but only the *mammal* there. Of course, he knew that the mammal there was a human being. But its being human was irrelevant to his calculation. That calculation was (A) procure a donation to famine relief, (B) follow the magnate's instructions, (C) kill the first mammal I see, (D) kill *that* mammal, and (E) shoot *that* mammal. Thus, if someone had asked Sam during the shooting "Why are you killing that *human being*?" he would have honestly refused the question application, just as he would have refused application to the question "Why are you killing that *brown-haired animal*?" On the Anscombian account, it follows that Sam's conduct was intentional under the description "killing that mammal" but not intentional under the description "killing that human being." But if Sam did not intentionally kill a human being, then it seems he did not violate the constraint against intentional harm, given that what it constrains against is intentionally killing *human beings* and not mammals more generally.

Pruss believes that *Zookeeper* demonstrates that the PDE needs to be replaced with a different principle, one that is not formulated in terms of

[20] It is important to distinguish this scenario from one in which the gardener is acting on a calculation that involves pumping water in order to poison the inhabitants of the house but tells himself that he is "directing his intention" away from replenishing the house's water supply with poisoned water and toward earning his pay. This gardener deceives himself if he thinks this inner speech makes it the case that his replenishing the water supply with poisoned water is not intentional (Section 4.4.1).

the concept of intention. But it might rather be thought that it shows the need for a criterion of excessive closeness. For it seems absurd that Sam should get off the hook for intentionally killing an innocent human being.

Similar reasoning can also be used to pose an objection to my analysis of *Potholer*. We can put this objection into the mouths of the trapped explorers, who argue as follows:

> You were too quick to condemn us earlier (Section 5.3.2). You accused us of intentionally blowing up a man, but really, our intention was to blow up *the thing that was blocking the cave entrance*. Obviously, we knew that that thing was a member of our party and we knew that being blown up is a serious harm, but none of that was intentional. His being human was incidental, for we would have blown up the thing blocking the entrance even if it had been an inanimate object. And though his being blown to bits was a harm for him, its *character* as a harm was incidental, for we would have acted in the same way even if the man were already dead or an inanimate object. Since corpses and inanimate objects do not have a good, blowing them to bits is not a harm for them.

If this seems bizarre, consider the three *intention trees* in Figure 5.1 (Levine, Leslie, and Mikhail 2018, 1250). An intention tree is an act tree in which the nodes that lie on the main branch represent intentional action descriptions, while the nodes connected to the main branch by diagonal lines represent incidental action descriptions.[21]

In a recent empirical study, Levine, Leslie, and Mikhail found that "The act tree that presupposed that the cavers [in *Potholer*] intended to act on an impersonal entity ('the thing blocking the exit') rather than 'a man' best predicted subjects' judgments of the caver's [sic] intention. The 'thing' that is to be harmed is a person and we do not doubt that subjects are aware of this" (2018, 1253). In other words, the researchers found that their subjects' judgments about the explorers' intentions were best predicted by intention tree (c). Their sample size was small, but my point in referencing the study is that the argument I put into the explorers' mouths should not be immediately dismissed.

Relatedly, Finnis would object to my analysis of *Craniotomy*. He not only denies that the physician necessarily intends to kill the unborn child, he also denies that the physician need even intend *harm* for it. And he defends this conclusion on Anscombian grounds. He writes that a physician who performs a craniotomy as a last resort

[21] For the concept of an act tree, see Goldman (1970, ch. 2).

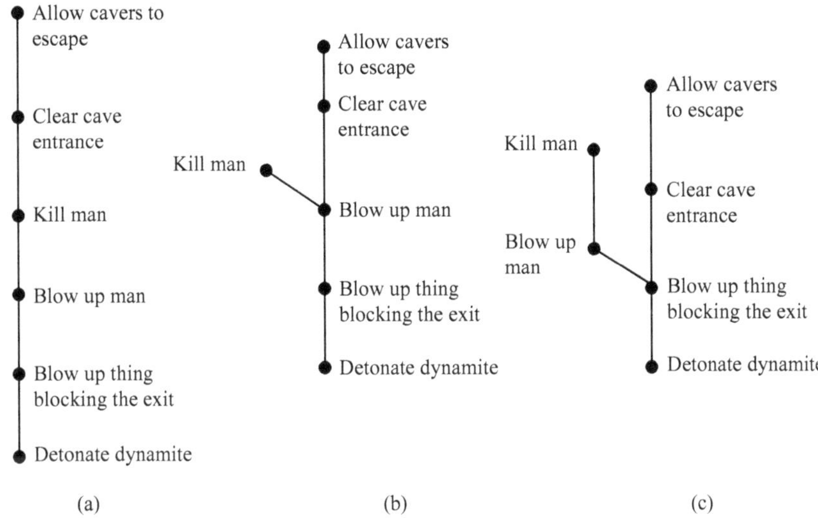

Figure 5.1 The *Potholer* case: (a–c) three intention trees

> would be choosing each step not for its lethality or harmfulness but for its efficacy in reducing the size of the baby, just as *Intention*'s Y [the gardener who replenishes the house's water supply simply to earn his usual pay] chooses to pump water (*known by him* to be poisoned water) not for its character as poisoned or not poisoned but for its replenishing of the cistern with water ... (2013, 484)

Finnis's argument is that the physician intends to crush the child's skull not because it is a *harm* but because it is efficacious in altering the dimensions of the child's body considered as a physical object. Therefore, the crushed skull's character as a harm is incidental.[22] Many proponents of double effect do not share Finnis's opinion that the PDE permits craniotomy, but if one holds an Anscombian account of intentional action, as I do, then one must explain where his analysis goes wrong.

[22] Compare Grisez, who says that the physician's proposal in performing a craniotomy can be simply "to alter the child's physical dimensions and remove him or her, because, *as a physical object*, this body cannot remain where it is without ending in both the baby's and the mother's deaths." (1993, 502; italics added). A similar view is expressed by Quinn: "It is not death itself, or even harm itself, that is strictly intended, but rather an immediately physical effect on the fetus that will allow its removal" (1993a, 178).

I add a final case, which is similar to the ones already considered but targets the fact that the constraint against intentional harm is restricted to *innocent* human beings:

> *Sniper*: A sniper is attempting to pick off enemy combatants on the other side of a large plaza, but he is unable to get a clean shot because there is someone running around in the line of fire. The sniper thinks the man is an enemy solider and prepares to shoot him but then notices that he is not a combatant – a detail of his clothing that reliably indicates this comes into view. The sniper kills the man anyway, in order to get a clear shot at the combatants.

At the sniper's court-martial, he argues, using reasoning similar to Sam's in *Zookeeper*, that he did not intentionally kill an *innocent* human being. He shot the man in the line of fire not because he was innocent but because he was an obstacle to having a clean shot. He claims that he therefore did not violate the prohibition on intentionally killing the innocent.

Let us call these four cases "the problem cases." In each case, it is claimed that the agent or agents can evade the charge they violated the constraint against intentionally bringing about serious harm to an innocent human being. The agents all acknowledge that they harm something that is an innocent human being, but they deny either intent to harm a *human being*, or intent to *harm* a human being, or intent to harm an *innocent* human being. In each case, the evasion seems sophistical and the challenge is to explain why. Do the problem cases show we need a criterion of closeness after all?

5.5 Failure to Transfer

Charles Fried writes, "[I]t is inadmissible to say that one intends to put a bullet through a man, stab him, crush him, or blow him to atoms but does not intend to harm him. All of these things just *are* harming him" (1978, 44). In Fried's view, a physician who performs a craniotomy cannot legitimately affirm that he intends to crush the child's skull but deny that he intends harm, for since a crushed skull is a harm for the child, bringing it about that the child's skull is crushed *just is* bringing about a harm.

This suggests a possible criterion of closeness. The basic idea is that sometimes B is not the effect of A; rather doing or bringing about A *just is* doing or bringing about B. When doing/bringing about A is doing/bringing about B, then B is too close to A for the line between intention and foresight to fall between them: If one aims at A as one's goal or purpose, then one thereby also aims at B. In other words, intentions are "transferred" from A to B across the "just is" relation. Adopting the convention of using square brackets to specify the contents of an intention, we can put the proposed criterion as follows:

> *Transfer*: If S intends [to do/bring about A] and in S's circumstances doing/bringing about A just is doing/bringing about B, then S intends [to do/bring about B].

In speaking of "doing X" or "bringing about X," *Transfer* is not referring to events.[23] Events are temporal particulars, and as such are dated and unrepeatable. They are standardly picked out by nominalized phrases such as "Lisa's pulling weeds in her garden" or "Clark's walk to the store." But the variables "doing X" and "bringing about X" do not stand for temporal particulars. Rather, they stand for things like *pulling weeds in Lisa's garden* and *walking to the store*, and these are not particulars: We could both pull weeds in Lisa's garden together and you might walk to the store on multiple occasions. They are *things that people do* rather than their *doings* of those things (Hornsby 1980, ch. 1). What *Transfer* assumes is that sometimes doing one thing *amounts to* doing another. For instance, if yellow is Aunt Rita's favorite color, then painting a wall yellow just is (amounts to) painting it Aunt Rita's favorite color, and if Jocasta is the mother of Oedipus, then marrying Jocasta just is (amounts to) marrying the mother of Oedipus.[24]

The final illustration also makes it clear, however, that in order to be even initially plausible *Transfer* stands in need of a refinement. Oedipus intended [to marry Jocasta], yet he did not intend [to marry his mother], for he had no idea that Jocasta was his mother. So whether intentions are transferred across the "just is" relation will depend on what the agent knows or believes:

> *Transfer$_I$*: If S intends [to do/bring about A] and in S's circumstances doing/bringing about A just is doing/bringing about B, and if S *knows* or *believes* that doing/bringing about A just is doing/bringing about B in her circumstances, then S intends [to do/bring about B].[25]

If *Transfer$_I$* is correct, it enables proponents of the PDE to say that the agents in the problem cases violate the constraint against intentional harm,

[23] I am using the term "event" in a broad way, as a term for the genus of temporal particulars that includes activities/processes, accomplishments/developments, and achievements/punctual occurrences. It thus corresponds to what Mourelatos calls "occurrences" (1978, 423).

[24] Proponents of *Transfer* need to say more about what it is for doing A to amount to doing B, but for our purposes I do not think it is necessary to give a precise account.

[25] FitzPatrick (2006) and Jensen (2014) endorse theories that are, if not identical to *Transfer$_I$*, at least in the same spirit. They tend to speak specifically about what an agent *knows* about her circumstances, but I think they would want to include belief as well.

for the reason that they do in fact intend [to bring about harm to an innocent human being]:

> *Zookeeper*: Sam intends [to kill *that* mammal]. Killing *that* mammal just is killing *that* human being, and Sam knows it; so he intends [to kill *that* human being].
>
> *Sniper*: The sniper intends [to kill *that* man]. Killing *that* man is killing an innocent man, and he is aware of this fact. Hence, the sniper intends [to kill *that* innocent man].
>
> *Potholer*: The explorers intend [to blow up the thing blocking the exit]. Blowing up that thing is blowing up a man, and they know it. So they intend [to blow up a man]. Furthermore, blowing up a man is harming him, and they know this, so they intend [to bring about harm].
>
> *Craniotomy*: The physician intends [to bring it about that the child's skull is crushed]. To bring this about is to bring about a serious harm for the child, and the physician knows it. So he intends [to bring about harm].

Transfer$_I$ has congenial results. But why should we believe it? One might appeal to ordinary language. Steven Jensen claims that according to our ordinary practices of ascribing intentions, when a change falls within an agent's intention, then so too do all the descriptions of it of which the agent is aware (2014, 283). For instance,

(1) A thief intends to steal a car. If he knows the car is red, then it would not be incorrect to say that he intends to steal a red car. This is so even if he is indifferent to the car's color and it plays no role in his motivation for stealing it.
(2) If I intend to play golf and I know the regime has passed a law that outlaws playing golf, then it would not be incorrect if I were to say to myself that I intend to break the law. This is the case even if I am only playing golf to have fun.

The problem with this argument is that these linguistic intuitions do not support *Transfer*$_I$. The contention that they do rests on a certain ambiguity in statements about peoples' intentions. Suppose I make the following statement:

(3) Dennis intends to have sexual intercourse with a nonconsenting woman.

This statement could mean either (3a) or (3b):

(3a) Dennis intends [to have sexual intercourse with a woman without her consent].
(3b) Dennis intends [to have sexual intercourse with a woman] without her consent.

These statements are importantly different. Statement (3a) asserts that part of Dennis's purpose in having sex is to have sex with an unconsenting woman. Statement (3b) asserts that Dennis intends to have sex with a woman and that, as a matter of fact, she has not consented to it, but it is no part of his purpose to have sex with an unconsenting partner. In the second case, the fact that the woman does not consent to sex does not figure in the *content* of Dennis's intention; it is rather part of the *context* in which he executes it (Duff 1996, 6).

(1) and (2) are affected by a similar ambiguity. For example, in asserting that the thief intends to steal a red car, we may mean to be conveying either (1a) or (1b):

(1a) The thief intends [to steal a red car].
(1b) The thief intends [to steal a car] and that car is red.

Our willingness to assert that the thief intends to steal a red car in the circumstances described in (1) therefore does not show that we hold that the thief [intends to steal a red car], which is what is required if that willingness is to count as evidence for *Transfer*$_I$. For, we might mean to be asserting (1b) rather than (1a).[26]

The observation about our ordinary practices of ascribing intentions does not support *Tranfer*$_I$. The study by Levine, Leslie, and Mikhail cited earlier (Section 5.4) also constitutes one piece of empirical evidence against it. There is another, stronger reason for thinking that the principle is false, however. *Transfer*$_I$ is inconsistent with the notion that an agent's intentions in acting define the success conditions for her actions (Section 4.5.1).

This is easiest to see in a situation in which the agent intends [to do A] and mistakenly believes that doing A amounts to doing B. Suppose I know the regime has passed a law making it illegal to play golf. Undeterred, I set out to play a round of golf in order to relax and exercise. However, right before I tee off the regime succumbs to pressure from unhappy citizens and repeals the law. I still believe, and reasonably so, that playing golf is illegal, so according to *Transfer*$_I$, I intend [to do something illegal]. If that is so, then afterward – when I learn that the law prohibiting golf was

[26] We might be willing to say that the thief intends to steal a red car even if it is clear to us that he does not intend [to steal a red car]. Suppose I see a thief attempting to steal a car in the parking lot. I know that he cannot tell what color it is – it is too dark to tell the colors of things by looking at them – but I also know that the car is red (I recognize it is my colleague's new Prius). In that case, I might give a hint to another colleague about which car the thief is trying to steal by saying, "The thief intends to steal a red car." In this case, I clearly do not mean to say that the thief intends [to steal a red car], for I know that he does not have an intention with that content.

repealed – I must see my actions on the golf course as having been in part a failure. Not a total failure, since I still played golf and got some relaxation and exercise, but a partial failure, since my alleged intention [to do something illegal] was not satisfied. But this conclusion seems plainly false: If I really was playing golf simply in order to relax and exercise, then I need not regard my golfing activities as having been even in part a failure. Thus, in playing golf I did not intend [to do something illegal], even though I mistakenly believed that playing golf was engaging in an illegal activity.

In the scenario above, I have a mistaken belief about whether doing A (playing golf) in my circumstances is doing B (doing something illegal). But that feature is not essential. My mistaken belief that playing golf is illegal simply serves to highlight the point that being against the law is not part of what *makes* my golfing activity successful. We can vary the scenario so that the regime has not changed the law and I *know* that playing golf is illegal. Even in this case it is true that if I am playing golf only in order to relax and exercise, my conduct is not successful *in virtue of* being against the law, so that being against the law is not among its success conditions.

What makes it the case that playing golf just is breaking the law is the existence of a positive law, which might be regarded as a sort of convention. But the argument against *Transfer*$_I$ works equally well when doing A just is doing B as a matter of natural fact.[27] Anscombe's example of the gardener who pumps poisoned water simply in order to earn his usual pay illustrates the point (Section 5.4). The man intentionally replenishes the house's water supply with a certain quantity of water and he knows that replenishing the water supply with that quantity of water just is replenishing it with poisoned water. Nonetheless, it is very plausible that in operating the pump he does not intend [to replenish the water supply with poisoned water], for whether or not the water is poisoned is irrelevant to the success of his action. As evidence for this, we can note that if his belief that the water is poisoned should turn out to be false and the cistern is replenished with water that is clean and wholesome, the gardener would not count his action as being in any way a failure. A similar point applies to the thief who intends to steal a car which he knows is red. If he is indifferent to its color but steals it only because it is a car and any car will do, then its color does not enter into the success conditions of his action. His action is not successful in virtue of the fact that the thing he steals is

[27] FitzPatrick proposes that if the relation between two states of affairs is known to the agent, natural (as opposed to conventional), and constitutive rather than causal, then the agent cannot intend to bring about one while merely foreseeing the other (2006, 603).

red, but simply in virtue of the fact that it is a car. This supports the claim that he does not intend [to steal a red car] but rather [to steal a car] that he knows is red.

In this section, I have argued that the attempt to deal with the problem cases with a criterion of closeness along the lines of *Tranfer*$_I$ fails. In the next section, I argue that what we need to resolve the problem cases is not a criterion of closeness but a clarification of the *content* of the constraint against intentional harm.

5.6 Clarifying the Constraint against Intentional Harm

According to the PDE, there is a strict constraint against intentionally bringing about serious harm to the innocent. But there are two different ways we might interpret the content of this constraint.

On the first interpretation, the constraint against intentional harm is to be understood as a constraint against successfully executing an intention [to bring about a serious harm for an innocent human being]. Call this interpretation PDE$_1$. On this understanding, in order for an agent's conduct to run afoul of the constraint, the concepts *harm*, *human being*, and *innocence* must figure in the content of her intentions. The objection to the PDE based on the problem cases from Section 5.4 presupposes that the constraint should be read as PDE$_1$. For instance, Pruss argues that Sam killed the zookeeper but he did not intend [to kill a human being], and from this he infers that there is something wrong with the PDE. This inference is only valid, however, on the assumption that violating the constraint against intentional harm requires successfully executing an intention with a content that includes the concept *human being*. Likewise, *Sniper* makes trouble for the PDE only if we assume that the fact that the sniper does not intend [to kill an innocent human being] entails that he does not violate the constraint. And the objections stemming from *Potholer* and *Craniotomy* assume that the PDE does not catch agents who do not intend the *harmfulness* of a state that is, in fact, a harm (being blown up and having a crushed skull, respectively).

The problem cases are indeed problematic if we interpret the constraint against intentional harm as PDE$_1$. There is a better way to understand the constraint, however. On this interpretation – call it PDE$_2$ – it should be read as a constraint against successfully executing an intention [to bring about E], where E is, as a matter of fact, a serious harm or evil for an innocent human being. On this understanding, an agent's conduct can violate the constraint even if the concepts *harm*, *human being*, and *innocence* do not figure in the content of her intentions. It is sufficient that in the *context* E is in fact a serious harm for an innocent human being.[28]

If we interpret the constraint against intentional harm as PDE_2, then the problem cases are no longer problematic. Sam intends [to kill] the zookeeper, and Sam knows that the zookeeper is an innocent human being. In virtue of this, Sam violates PDE_2 and acts wrongly. His plea that it was irrelevant to his calculation that the thing he killed was a human being does not exonerate him. Similarly, the sniper intends [to kill] a man whom he knows is a noncombatant, so he violates the constraint against intentional harm. The trapped explorers intend [to blow up the obstacle blocking the exit], and they are fully aware that this obstacle is a man and that being blown to bits is a serious injury for him. Finally, the physician who performs a craniotomy intends [to crush the skull] of the child, and he knows that having a crushed skull is a grave harm for a human being. Finnis's point that the physician need not intend the harmfulness of what he does is not relevant. What matters is that he intends to bring about a state, a crushed skull, which in the circumstances is a serious harm, and he is aware of this fact.[29]

Although PDE_2 explains why the agents in the problem cases act wrongly, it may seem to run into another difficulty. The problem arises in cases in which the agent acts in a way that conflicts with the constraint

[28] Pruss seeks to handle *Zookeeper* by arguing that a moral analysis of the case should focus not on what Sam intended but what he accomplished. He argues that even though Sam did not intend to kill *a human being*, nonetheless, in carrying out his intentions he accomplished the death of a human being, and this makes his action wrong (2013, 56–7). This is not so different from the account I am putting forward. Pruss understands his proposal as a *revision* of double effect because he assumes that the PDE must be understood along the lines of PDE_1.

[29] Luke Gormally has published a hand-written note by Anscombe, which includes the following passage:

> [I]f your purpose in shooting [an] arrow is one that can only be attained *by transfixing* a man, so that transfixing a man is your means to the accomplishment of the purpose, *then* you could not argue that you were only *transfixing* him with the arrow, not damaging him with the arrow, on the ground that your purpose would be attained by transfixing without damage, were that possible. For *if* transfixing a man with an arrow is certainly damaging him, and *if* you may absolutely not try to damage him, you may not try to transfix him. (qtd. in Gormally 2013, 96)

Both Gormally and Finnis (Finnis 2013, 482) take Anscombe to be asserting that if you try [to transfix] a man, then you necessarily try [to damage] him. There is another way to read the text, however, on which Anscombe is making a point that coheres with PDE_2. That is, suppose there is a prohibition on trying to damage someone. Then, given that transfixing a man is a way of damaging him, the prohibition prohibits trying to transfix him. It cannot be evaded by claiming that one transfixed a man with intent [to transfix him] but not [to damage him].

against intentional harm but is unaware that she is harming an innocent human being. Consider a variation of the *Potholer* scenario:

> *Ignorant Killing*: Similar to *Potholer*, but the man stuck in the cave entrance appears to be dead. The trapped explorers do reasonable checks and form the justified belief that he is dead before blowing up what they take to be his corpse. Their belief is mistaken, however: The man is alive, but his vital signs are so faint that they cannot be detected without sensitive medical equipment.

It seems that the explorers violate the constraint against intentional harm, interpreted along the lines of PDE_2, and so act wrongly. That verdict seems counterintuitive, however. If we know all the relevant facts, we certainly will not want to see them prosecuted for murder.

There are two lines of response to this objection open to proponents of double effect. The first relies on the distinction between wrongdoing and blameworthiness.[30] Wrongdoing and blameworthiness normally go together, but it is possible for them to come apart, for there can be factors present that make it the case that the agent is excused from blame for engaging in wrongdoing. A classic example is duress. If a person cooperates with someone else's wrongdoing but does so only because his life has been threatened, we may believe that he should not have acceded to the threat but that it is understandable that he did. Refusing to cooperate would have taken an unusually high degree of courage, and so we do not blame or punish the person for his cooperation, though we still judge that it was wrongful.

According to the response at issue, *Ignorant Killing* is an atypical case of wrongdoing in a different way. It is an example of what Duff calls warranted wrongdoing (2007, 275–6). The explorers' conduct is wrong because it conflicts with the constraint against intentional harm, but it is warranted because if things were as they believed them to be, their conduct would have been permissible and their mistake about the facts was a reasonable one. The fact that their conduct was wrong means that if the explorers later found out that the man was still alive when they blew him up, they would have reason to regret their action. But the fact that it was *warranted* means they were acting reasonably in response to the evidence they possessed at the time, and they therefore do not deserve condemnation for it. This response retains the claim that the explorers act wrongly in blowing up the man. But it takes the bite out of the objection, for it

[30] I utilized this distinction in responding to the present objection in Stuchlik (2017).

enables us to agree with the intuition that they should not be blamed or punished for their conduct.

Alternatively, a second response makes use of a different distinction, the distinction between *infringing* a constraint and *violating* it. An agent infringes a constraint when she does what it says not to do, but an agent violates a constraint when she infringes it in such a way that she acts wrongly in doing so. One way it can happen that a person infringes a constraint without violating it is if the constraint is defeasible and the agent infringes it in circumstances in which it is overridden. Nonabsolutists about the constraint against intentional harm, for instance, hold that if a great enough good is at stake, a person may permissibly infringe it (Section 1.3). On the view under discussion, there is a different way that an agent might infringe a constraint without violating it, for according to it an agent violates a constraint only if her infringement of it is *voluntary*, so that the infringement can be imputed to her as a rational agent.[31]

The idea can be illustrated by an example involving force. Suppose I place a sign on my property that reads "Keep off the lawn." You are walking by on the sidewalk when a person – or a powerful gust of wind – pushes you onto the grass. We might say that this is a case of blameless wrongdoing. However, I find it more plausible to say that it is not a case of wrongdoing at all (supposing that you do not linger). The reason is that while you have infringed the rule, your infringement of it was involuntary. Therefore, you are not responsible for your infringement qua rational agent and you are exonerated of any wrongdoing.

Now, as Aristotle observed, force is not the only factor that negates voluntariness; ignorance of the circumstances sometimes does so as well.[32] For instance, a man who unwittingly has sexual intercourse with a woman he has every reason to believe is his wife but who is really her twin sister posing as her has not voluntarily slept with someone who is not his spouse. So on the present view, he has infringed the constraint against adultery, but he has not violated it. We can say something similar about *Ignorant Killing*. The explorers are ignorant of the fact that the thing they are blowing up is a man rather than a corpse and their mistake, we have said, is a reasonable one. They therefore do not violate the constraint against

[31] Anscombe observes that when moral constraints are framed as rules to be considered in practical deliberation, they are not formulated as stating "do not *voluntarily* do such-and-such," for one cannot consider whether or not to do such-and-such voluntarily. Rather, the voluntariness that is necessary for the notion of violating the rule to apply is *presupposed* in one's considering whether to do such-and-such (1981d, 8).

[32] *NE* 3.1, 1110b18–1111a20.

intentional harm, and since they do not violate it, they do not deserve blame for their lethal conduct. If the explorers later learn that the man was actually still alive, it may nonetheless be appropriate for them to feel regret, however. After all, they did infringe the constraint against intentional harm, even if they did not do so voluntarily, and they intentionally blew the man up even though he was not a suitable object for this sort of treatment, being neither deserving of nor liable to it.

The view is not that ignorance or mistake about the circumstances *always* exonerates the agent. Let us alter the details of *Ignorant Killing* and suppose that the explorers assume their comrade is dead, but that if they were to check his vital signs, they would easily discover that he is still alive. They omit to do so, however, either through sheer carelessness or because they do not want to know whether he is alive (call this variation *Negligent Killing*). Given that they do not take reasonable steps to find out whether the stuck man is alive, their ignorance of that fact is voluntary.[33] And since their ignorance is voluntary, what they do as a result of it is also not outside the realm of the voluntary and they are responsible for it as rational agents. If they were to respond to an accusation of wrongdoing by saying "We did not know the thing we blew up was a living human being, we mistakenly thought he was a corpse," the proper reply would be "That does not get you off the hook, for you should have known better."

I have indicated two possible replies to an objection that arises if we interpret the constraint against intentional harm as PDE_2. It is significant for both replies that the explorers' ignorance that the man they blow up in *Ignorant Killing* is reasonable ignorance. But it matters in slightly different ways. On the first response, the reasonableness of the explorers' ignorance makes their conduct a case of *warranted* wrongdoing. On the other hand, on the second response, the reasonableness of the explorers' ignorance makes it the case that their infringement of the constraint against intentional harm is not a *violation* of the constraint, and so not a case of

33 The explanation of why their ignorance is voluntary depends on the idea that people are sometimes responsible for things that occur as the result of their omissions. For example, a ship's pilot omits to steer it and it sinks as a result. The loss of the ship can be ascribed to the pilot as its cause. Or, to borrow Anscombe's example, a cook is the cause of the spoiling of the potatoes when he fails to put salt in them (1981d, 8). The loss of the ship and the spoiling of the potatoes can be imputed to the pilot and the cook because (1) there is something they could have done to prevent these events (steering and putting salt in the potatoes), and (2) they ought to have done those things, insofar as doing them was part of their professional responsibilities. In a similar way, ignorance of some fact can be ascribed to a person's will as cause when the person could have known that fact, had she undertaken the appropriate inquiry, and she ought to have undertaken the inquiry (see *ST* I-II 6.8).

wrongdoing. Both responses enable a proponent of double effect to evade the objection that if we accept PDE_2, then we must hold that the explorers should be blamed or punished for their conduct.

Understanding the constraint against intentional harm along the lines of PDE_2 also coheres with the solidarity rationale from Chapter 3 (Section 3.5). The main idea, recall, is that agents who intentionally harm innocent people engage in conduct that grossly deviates from the standard of solidarity that measures their conduct in relation to others. Conduct that intentionally brings about intentional harm deviates from this standard because it successfully manifests or expresses a desire for an evil for a fellow human being rather than a good. Since, e.g., being killed, crushed, or blown up are evils, an agent who intentionally kills, crushes, or blows up someone engages in conduct that expresses a desire for an evil, whether or not he intends [to bring about an evil]. In the terminology I adopted from Foot, a person who intentionally [brings about evil] *comes out against* the patient, but so too does a person who intentionally kills, crushes, or blows up another, even if he does not intend [evil] or [evil for a human being]. In typical circumstances, the agent knows or is aware of the relevant contextual factors. In these circumstances, an agent of intentional harm both acts wrongly and is blameworthy for his wrongful conduct. I have argued, however, that in unusual circumstances the agent does not deserve blame for intentional harm, either because his reasonable ignorance of the facts means that his wrongdoing is warranted or because it means his infringement of the constraint against intentional harm does not constitute a violation of it.

5.7 Conclusion

The closeness problem poses a dilemma for proponents of double effect: either provide a criterion of excessive closeness or be stuck with consequences that are absurd and render the PDE unable to do the moral work it is supposed to do. In this chapter, I have argued that the second horn of the dilemma is less troubling than critics of the PDE contend. I do not deny that the principle sometimes distinguishes between cases in a way that some people find artificial, nor do I deny that there are cases where it returns counterintuitive verdicts (Section 2.3). There is no substantive moral principle that perfectly fits everyone's case-based intuitions, and the costs that the PDE incurs on this score must be weighed against its merits. Rather, my purpose has been to argue against the strong claims that are often made about the closeness problem, such as the contention that it poses "intractable difficulties" for double effect (Nelkin and Rickless 2015, 377) or that without a criterion of closeness the PDE is "nonsense from the beginning" (Foot 2002, 21). These claims suggest that the PDE suffers from a fundamental defect, one that renders it totally unworkable. My review of a large segment of the literature has found that this conclusion is not warranted. Friends of the PDE have a variety of resources to handle cases that allegedly show the need for a criterion of closeness.

CHAPTER 6

The Irrelevance Theory and More Objections

6.1 Introduction

It is common to distinguish between normative and motivating reasons for action. A *normative reason* for ϕ-ing is a consideration that counts in favor of ϕ-ing. This reason may not be decisive, but the existence of the reason means there is something to be said for ϕ-ing. On the other hand, a *motivating reason* is a consideration on which, or in the light of which, an agent acts.

Motivating reasons help explain action. There is a close connection between an agent's motivating reasons and her intentions in acting. An action is intentional under a certain description just in case the question "Why?" has application to it under that description, where the question asks for a reason for acting (Anscombe 1963, §5). The question "Why?" is not refused application by answers in the range of "No reason," and this means that it is possible to act intentionally but without a motivating reason. But when a person acts intentionally, she typically acts for the sake of achieving an end or goal, and when she does, she both acts with the intention of achieving the end and in light of the considerations that make the goal seem desirable, and these considerations are among her motivating reasons (see 4.3.2 and Alvarez 2010, ch. 5).

According to the moral theory I presented in Chapter 3, an agent's intentions and motivating reasons are sometimes relevant to the moral permissibility of her conduct. This is evident in the case of the PDE, but I argued that the morality of solidarity also grounds a precept of beneficence. When this precept imposes a moral requirement, fulfilling it requires acting for the right sort of reason. If someone is in need of urgent assistance, then one acts beneficently only if one assists the person in need for her sake; one does not act beneficently if one helps only because, say, doing so is likely to get one's name in the local newspaper (Section 3.4.2).

Many philosophers disagree with these claims. They hold that intentions and motivating reasons are not relevant to questions of moral permissibility, at least at the fundamental level.[1] Call this the Irrelevance Theory.[2] Consequentialists are committed to the Irrelevance Theory, inasmuch as they hold that the only thing that is fundamentally relevant to the permissibility of an agent's conduct is its consequences.[3] But many nonconsequentialists, including T. M. Scanlon, Judith Jarvis Thomson, and Frances Kamm, also hold the Irrelevance Theory.

Proponents of the Irrelevance Theory do not hold that intentions and motivating reasons are irrelevant to all forms of moral assessment. They think we should distinguish between assessments of whether an agent's conduct is morally permissible and other sorts of moral assessment, such as whether the agent has a good or bad character, whether the agent is praiseworthy or blameworthy for acting as she did, and whether she deserves criticism for the decision-making that led to her action. Even if intentions and motivating reasons are not relevant to permissibility, they may be relevant to these other sorts of assessment.[4] Proponents of the Irrelevance Theory often suggest that their opponents mistakenly hold that intentions and/or motivating reasons are relevant to permissibility because they confuse appraisals of permissibility with these other sorts of moral appraisal.

Those of us on the other side of the debate deny we are guilty of any such confusion. The morality of solidarity follows Strawson in holding that a fundamental moral demand is the demand for "the manifestation of a certain degree of goodwill or regard" on the part of human beings toward others (1974, 14). Whether an agent's conduct flouts this demand, and so is wrong, is determined in part by the agent's intentions and motivating

[1] On Scanlon's (2008) sophisticated version of the Irrelevance Theory, intentions and motivating reasons are not fundamentally relevant to moral permissibility, but they sometimes possess derivative relevance. This means, roughly, that when they are relevant, they are so only in virtue of some more basic moral requirement whose specification does not make reference to intentions or motivating reasons.

[2] Since the moral permissibility of acting in a certain way depends on the normative reasons for or against acting in that way, another way to frame the debate is as one over whether there can be normative reasons to act (or not act) with certain intentions or for certain reasons. For this way of framing the debate, see Heuer (2015).

[3] Sverdlik (2011) argues that consequentialists should hold that intentions and motivating reasons have derivative relevance to moral permissibility.

[4] This point is sometimes formulated in terms of a distinction between "first-order" and "second-order" moral judgments. First-order moral judgments are judgments about whether an agent's conduct is permissible or impermissible; second-order judgments include various other sorts of moral assessment (Bennett 1995, 46–7; McCarthy 2002, 622–3).

reasons, and reactive attitudes such as resentment and indignation are responses to violations of the same demand. Nonetheless, rejecting the Irrelevance Theory is compatible with holding that wrongdoing and blameworthiness can come apart. The gap is made possible by the concept of an excuse. Excuses are distinct from justifications. The function of a justification is to show that while the agent acted in a way that is presumptively wrong, her action was not wrongful all things considered, e.g., because it was part of a proportionate defense to unjustified aggression. Excuses, on the other hand, admit that the agent's conduct was wrong but claim that certain features of the agent, or her circumstances, make it such that she should not be blamed for it, or that the amount of blame she deserves should be mitigated.[5]

Philosophers who hold the Irrelevance Theory often attack the PDE. Part of their strategy involves raising counterexamples. I addressed some of these in Chapter 2, where I discussed the intuitive case for the PDE. This chapter is devoted to responding to further objections to double effect.[6] In Section 6.2, I address the objection that it is difficult to understand why the moral permissibility of an agent's conduct should depend on facts about her intentions in acting, insofar as these seem to be facts about her mental states rather than facts about what happens in the world. In Section 6.3, I reply to the objection that the PDE entails judgments about cases that violate the rational norm of consistency. The next topic is an argument from Judith Jarvis Thomson, the deliberative perspective objection. Although this objection is frequently cited in the literature, the precise nature of the argument is unclear. I offer an interpretation and critique of the argument in Section 6.4. In Section 6.5, I then consider an alternative interpretation of Thomson's objection, which says that if the PDE is true, then agents must focus their attention inward on their own intentions when deciding how to act in a way that is implausibly narcissistic. Finally, in Section 6.6, I present two arguments contending that the PDE sometimes has absurd implications for how we should respond to agents with bad intentions. My conclusion will be that none of these objections seriously damage the PDE.

[5] For more on the distinction between justifications and excuses, see Baron (2005) and Duff (2007, ch. 11).

[6] Scanlon also attacks the view that people can be required to aid others for the right (benevolent) reason (2008, 56–62). I will not address Scanlon's objection here because the focus of this book is the PDE (but see Lillehammer 2010 and Kolodny 2011, §3).

6.2 All in the Head?

In the course of criticizing the PDE, Gerhard Øverland asks, "Why should what goes on in the mind of the agent be relevant to determining whether killing a person is permissible?" (2014, 482). The question is rhetorical, but I think it reveals one of the basic motivations for rejecting the PDE. We can articulate the sentiment that underlies Øverland's question as follows. It is unproblematic to think that the permissibility of an agent's conduct depends on what happens in the world because of it. However, whether the agent does something (e.g., kill a person) *intentionally*, as opposed to incidentally, is a fact about her state of mind rather than a fact about what happens in the world. And it seems mysterious why moral permissibility should turn on the agent's state of mind in acting. Aren't thoughts one thing and actions another?

One might question the assumption that only overt actions can be morally wrong. Some thoughts present themselves in a way that bypasses one's agency, as when one spontaneously thinks "What a beautiful tablecloth" upon entering a dining room, and it is implausible to think that one should be morally responsible merely for having thoughts of this sort. But a person can also consent to thoughts of wicked things by dwelling on them, and it is not absurd to think that one acts wrongly in doing so. As a response to the present objection, this response misses the mark, however, for what the critic finds mysterious is not the idea that mental acts are sometimes wrongful, but the idea that when an agent acts *on the world*, her state of mind should affect the moral status of her action.

There is no need to deny that an agent's intentions in acting are, in some sense, states of mind. Accepting this does not commit one to the philosophical theory of human action according to which actions are bodily movements that are caused by intentions conceived as purely "inner" entities, entities that literally exist inside the agent's head. Rather, it simply acknowledges the truism that a rational agent's intellect and will are at work in her intentional activity.[7] The part of the objection that we should take issue with is its contention that whether an agent does something intentionally is a fact about her mental state *rather than* a fact about what happens in the world.

The falsity of this assumption is one of the main upshots of *Intention*. We can see why by returning to the story of the gardener at the pump

[7] For this reason, it is perfectly intelligible that penal codes that make an analytical distinction between *mens rea* and *actus reus* place intention on the *mens rea* side of the divide.

(Section 4.2). Recall that we are the confidants of a man who is pumping poisoned water into the cistern of a house that is inhabited by some Nazi party chiefs. We see him moving his arm up and down on the pump handle and ask him, "Why are you doing that?":

Why are you moving your arm up and down on the pump handle?
– I'm operating the pump.

Why are you operating the pump?
– I'm replenishing the house's water supply.

Why are you replenishing the house's water supply?
– I'm poisoning the inhabitants.

Our successive applications of the question "Why?" reveal an order that is present in the man's will as he moves his arm up and down on the pump handle: He is moving his arm with the intention of (i) operating the pump, (ii) replenishing the house's water supply, and (iii) poisoning the Nazis. But the man's answers do not only identify an order that is present in his will. They also reveal an order that is present in the world, in *what he is doing* as he moves his arm up and down. The order in question is an explanatory and teleological one: The man is moving his arm up and down on the pump handle *because* he is operating the pump and *in order to* operate it, he is operating the pump *because* he is replenishing the house's water supply and *in order to* replenish it, and he is replenishing the water supply *because* he is poisoning the Nazis and *in order to* poison them.

Evidently, the gardener believes that ridding the world of the Nazis will somehow usher in the eschaton, for when we ask him why he is poisoning them he replies, "To inaugurate the Kingdom of Heaven on earth." As we noted in Section 4.2, this answer differs from the previous ones, insofar as inaugurating the Kingdom of Heaven on earth is too far removed from poisoning the Nazis to be properly describable as something the gardener is doing: Inaugurating the Kingdom of Heaven is not something he *is doing* but a goal he is aiming *to* achieve by poisoning them. Nonetheless, in virtue of the man's eschatological intention, it is still a fact about his present conduct that it is *ordered to* and *directed at* realizing this goal.

The gardener's answers to the question "Why?" identify a teleological order that is present in his activity at the pump. This order differs in an important respect, however, from other sorts of teleological order. Consider nonrational vital processes, such as the processes that occur as an acorn matures into an oak tree or those that occur when the heart pumps blood in order to nourish the body's organs. These processes are also teleologically ordered, but the order obtains independently of anyone's knowledge of them. By contrast, the teleological order of the gardener's intentional activity is internally related to his knowledge or awareness of it, for that order is determined by his own calculation about how to realize his end of inaugurating the Kingdom of Heaven on earth (Section 4.3.3).

The story of the gardener at the pump shows that the objection currently under consideration is incorrect in its assumption that whether someone does or brings about something intentionally is a fact about what goes on in her mind *rather than* a fact about what happens in the world. Intentional descriptions of what the agent is doing or bringing about are elements of a self-conscious teleological and explanatory order that is present in her conduct. By contrast, incidental descriptions do not fit within any such teleological order. The agent's conduct is not directed at or ordered to incidental effects or aspects of it, though she is aware of them.

We can apply this point to the distinction between precision bombing and terror bombing (Section 2.2.1):

> *Precision Bombing:* A bomber pilot's end is to help his country win a just war, and he pursues this end by targeting a munitions factory, though he foresees that a number of nearby noncombatants will be killed or injured from the explosions of his bombs.
>
> *Terror Bombing:* A bomber pilot's end is to help his country win a just war, and he pursues this end by dropping his bombs over the built-up area of a city in order to kill and injure noncombatants. He does this because he believes that the terror that results from the casualties will demoralize the enemy population and lead them to pressure their leaders to surrender.

We can imagine that in both cases a pilot flies over a section of a city, bombs fall out of his aircraft, some buildings are damaged and destroyed, and some human bodies cease to move. Moreover, both pilots have the same ultimate end in view: to help their respective countries win a war. But these similarities should not obscure the fact that the activities of the two pilots embody very different teleological-explanatory orders.

The precision bomber is making certain movements in his plane *because* he is dropping his bombs and *in order to* drop his bombs, and he is dropping his bombs *because* he is destroying a military facility and *in order to* destroy a military facility. The movements he makes with his body, the movements of his plane, and the falling of his bombs are all events that are *ordered to* and *directed at* the destruction of this object and not at harm to innocent people, though the bomber knows that the explosions of his bombs will cause them harm. On the other hand, the terror bomber is releasing his bombs *because* he is engaged in killing and injuring noncombatants and *in order to* kill and injure noncombatants, and the movements of his body, his plane, and his bombs are all ordered to and directed at harming them. These facts about the teleological orders of the two pilots' actions are facts about what is going on in the world just as much as the fact that their hearts are pumping blood *in order to* nourish their vital organs. And in light of the conclusions of Chapter 3 (Section 3.5), we can add that it is equally a fact about what is going on in the world that the terror bomber, but not the precision bomber, is *attacking* noncombatants, that his conduct is successfully *expressing a malevolent desire* to kill and injure noncombatants, and that he is *coming out against* them in it in the sense we have given that phrase. All this is so even though these facts about what is happening depend on facts about the calculations the pilots have adopted about how to contribute to their countries' war efforts.

6.3 The Inconsistency Objection

James Rachels argues that people who hold that intentions are relevant to determining the permissibility of actions are committed to making inconsistent judgments about cases. Since consistency is one of the basic norms of rationality, he concludes that intentions are irrelevant to assessments of permissibility. To illustrate the problem, Rachels asks us to consider the following case:

> *Jack and Jill*: Jack visits his sick and lonely grandmother and entertains her for the afternoon. He loves her, and his only intention is to cheer her up. Jill also visits the grandmother and provides an afternoon's cheer. But Jill's only concern is that the old lady will soon be making her will; Jill wants to be included among the heirs. Jack also knows that his visit might influence the making of the will in his favor, but that is no part of his plan (1986, 93).

Rachels comments:

> Jack and Jill do the very same thing – they both spend an afternoon cheering up their sick grandmother – and what they do may have the same consequences, namely influencing the will. But their intentions are quite different.
>
> Jack's intention was honourable and Jill's was not. Could we say on that account that what Jack did was right, but what Jill did was wrong? No; for Jack and Jill did the very same thing, and if they did the same thing, in the same circumstances, we cannot say that one acted rightly and one acted wrongly. Consistency requires that we assess similar actions similarly. Thus

> if we are trying to evaluate their *actions*, we must say about one what we say about the other. (1986)

The argument is that if we believe that an agent's bad intention makes her action wrong, then we will judge that Jack acted rightly and Jill acted wrongly. But Jack and Jill did the very same thing – spend the day with their sick grandmother. Therefore, we are committed to judging similar actions differently, and this violates the norm of consistency.

Rachels believes, however, that matters are different if we hold instead that the agent's intentions are relevant to assessing her character:

> Even though their actions were similar, Jack seems admirable for what he did, while Jill does not. What Jill did – comforting an elderly sick relative – was a morally good thing, but we would not think well of her for it because she was only scheming after the money. Jack, on the other hand, did a good thing *and* he did it with an admirable intention. Thus we think well, not only of what Jack did, but of Jack. (1986, 93–4)

The *Jack and Jill* scenario is not a double effect case since Jill does not intentionally harm her sick grandmother. However, Robert Holmes applies similar reasoning to the distinction between precision bombing and terror bombing (1989, 197). He imagines two pilots who fly over a military facility surrounded by civilian structures. The first pilot drops his bombs intending to destroy the military facility while the second drops his bombs intending to kill noncombatants. Holmes claims that both bomber pilots perform "virtually identical acts," insofar as they both drop their bombs on the same target area. But the PDE judges that the terror bomber acts wrongly while the precision bomber may act permissibly depending on the circumstances. Therefore, Holmes concludes, the PDE judges similar actions differently. Like Rachels, Holmes believes that intentions are relevant to assessing persons and not actions.

It would be a devastating objection to the PDE if it could be shown that it entails inconsistent judgments. Fortunately, it does not violate the norm of consistency. In order to see why we must make two distinctions.

6.3.1 Two Distinctions

6.3.1.1 Deeds vs. Concrete Actions

There is an ambiguity in the word "action." It can refer either to something that a person does or to her doing of it.[8] Suppose Anna is singing the

[8] See Hornsby (1980, ch. 1). The distinction is also present in Ross (1930).

National Anthem. We can distinguish what Anna is doing (singing the National Anthem) from her doing it (her singing the National Anthem). Anna's singing the National Anthem is an event, and it takes place at a particular location and over a particular interval of time. However, *singing the National Anthem* is not a particular but a repeatable: Anna might also have sung the National Anthem yesterday, and during her performance other people in the crowd might join in and sing it with her. In the philosophy of action, it is often said that actions are events. But it is also perfectly appropriate to speak of the things people do as their actions. For instance, instead of asking "What is Anna doing?" we could ask "What action is she performing?" And the answer to both questions is, "She is singing the National Anthem."

Let us call things that people do *deeds*, and their doing of those things their *concrete actions*. Deeds are specified by descriptions of actions or act-types, while concrete actions are sometimes referred to as "act-tokens" (Goldman 1970). There is no objection to speaking of both deeds and concrete actions as actions so long as we do not confuse them. So if we say that actions are events, then we speak truly only if we are speaking of concrete actions. And if we say that people do actions, then we must have in mind actions in the sense of deeds, for people do not do their concrete actions; rather, they do things like sing the National Anthem and walk to the store, and these are deeds.

Both concrete actions and deeds are objects of moral evaluation. On August 21, 1911, Vicenzo Peruggia stole the Mona Lisa from the Louvre. His concrete action – his stealing the Mona Lisa, which occurred in a certain region of space and over a certain duration of time – was wrong: It was an instance of wrongdoing. Assessments of concrete actions do not exhaust the range of our moral judgments, however. We judge not only that *Peruggia's theft of the Mona Lisa* was wrong, but that *stealing* is wrong (at least prima facie). And we judge that Peruggia's concrete action was wrong in virtue of the fact that it is describable as stealing.

The distinction between concrete actions and deeds is related to a distinction between two different grammatical forms of permissibility judgment. Matthew Hanser (2005) draws attention to the fact that permissibility judgments can take either an adverbial or adjectival form. Adverbial permissibility judgments include judgments such as S is acting (im)permissibly, S acted rightly, or S acted wrongly. These are judgments of concrete actions, either actual or hypothetical. For example, if I say that John acted wrongly on a certain occasion, then I am making an assessment of John's concrete action. Adverbial permissibility judgments can also be used to specify in virtue of what John acted wrongly; for instance, it may be that he acted wrongly in virtue of driving his neighbor's car without her permission. Adjectival permissibility judgments include judgments such as ϕ-ing is (im)permissible or obligatory, ϕ-ing is (im)permissible or obligatory in circumstances C, and it is (im)permissible or obligatory to ϕ in C. Hanser seems to think that adjectival permissibility judgments always evaluate deeds, but the adjectival form can also be used in making assessments of concrete actions. For instance, one might judge that John's drive to the store is permissible or that Lucy's conduct in the office last Tuesday morning was seriously wrong. The distinction between adverbial and adjectival permissibility judgments is helpful because it enables us to see that we can assess both concrete actions and types of action considered in the abstract, but it is the distinction between these two *objects* of assessment, rather than the grammatical distinction per se, which is of philosophical interest.

6.3.1.2 Act-Types vs. Conduct-Types

The second distinction is one within the category of action descriptions. Wedgwood (2011a) notes that some act-types are more specific than others. One way that one act-type can be more specific than another is if the more specific act-type includes reference to a specific intention. Wedgwood calls act-types that do not include an intention (or we might add, a motivating reason) *thin act-types* and act-types that do include an intention (or motivating reason) *thick act-types*. So on this classification, *giving alms* is a thin act-type while *giving alms with the intention of earning praise*, *giving alms in order to earn praise*, and *giving alms for the reason that one will thereby earn praise* are thick act-types.

One might wonder whether thick act-types really describe a type of deed. Audi distinguishes two questions that appear to be quite different: What is the agent doing? and Why is she doing it? (2016, 51). Insofar as act-types specify things that people do, they answer the first question. But thick act-types answer both questions simultaneously: They tell us both what the agent is dong and provide an explanation of why she is doing it. Audi recognizes, however, that when we act, we do not simply instantiate act-types: We typically *do* certain things in a certain *manner* and *for* certain reasons (or *with* certain intentions). In this book, I have followed Audi's proposal that we use the term "conduct" to pick out an agent's doing something in a certain manner and for a certain reason or with a certain intention. Speaking of an agent's conduct serves as a reminder that our concrete actions have multiple dimensions, including an intentional dimension. I will use the term "conduct-type" to pick out action descriptions that give information about two or more dimensions of a person's conduct. On this terminology, "act-type" is reserved for what Wedgwood calls "thin act-types" and Wedgwood's thick act-types are a kind of conduct-type.

It would be wrong to suppose that the distinction between act-types and conduct-types is a sharp one. Many action descriptions that superficially appear to be one-dimensional actually provide information about two or more dimensions of the agent's conduct. For instance, a person can answer the question "What are you doing?" by replying, "Yelling," and yelling is something that can be done in various manners, such as shrilly or nervously. Yet the act-type "yelling" itself has a certain manner built into it since what it is to yell is to speak loudly (Audi 2016, 54). Other act-types are such that a certain answer to the question "Why?" is built into them. For instance, in criminal law, burglary is defined as entering a building of another *with the intention of* committing a crime therein, bribery is giving an official a gift *in order to* influence his or her judgment, and treason is not merely giving assistance to the enemy, but assisting the enemy *with the intention of* betraying one's country (Husak 2009). Therefore, describing a person as engaging in burglary, bribery, or treason gives us some information about her intentions in acting. Even so, different agents can engage in these sorts of conduct for a variety of further reasons. For instance, one person might commit treason for financial gain while another does so in order to avenge what he sees as a wrong his country has done him.

Although the distinction between act-types and conduct-types is not sharp, it has a useful analytical function. It helps explain how it is possible for an agent to do a deed K that has a certain moral status and yet it also be the case that her K-instantiating concrete action or conduct has a different moral status. For instance, according to Aquinas, giving alms is good and admirable, but if on a certain occasion a person gives alms in order to earn praise, then his concrete action is wrong (*malum*) (*ST* I-II 20.1). It is not that *giving alms* has somehow become wrongful; "giving alms" names a type of deed that is admirable when considered in the abstract. What is wrong is rather the conduct-type *giving alms in order to earn praise*. The agent's concrete action or conduct – his giving alms here and now, which is his giving alms with the intention of earning praise – is wrongful, but it is not wrongful in virtue of the fact that he gives alms but in virtue of his vainglorious intention.

6.3.2 Response

With these distinctions in hand, let us return to the inconsistency objection. Recall Rachels's argument:

1. The view that an agent's bad intention makes her action wrong judges that Jack acted rightly and Jill acted wrongly.
2. Jack and Jill did the same thing, viz., spend the day with their sick grandmother.
3. Therefore, the view that an agent's bad intention makes her action wrong judges similar actions differently.

The argument's conclusion does not follow from its premises. Jack and Jill's concrete actions both instantiated the act-type *spend the day with my sick grandmother.* But it does not follow that if we judge that Jack acted rightly and Jill wrongly, then we are judging similar actions differently. As we have seen, adverbial permissibility judgments are judgments of concrete actions. But it does not follow from the fact that two concrete actions instantiate act-type K that they must be assessed the same, for concrete actions can have morally significant properties that are not included in K. It is therefore not inconsistent to judge that Jill's concrete action or conduct has a wrong-making feature that Jack's does not, namely her bad intention.[9]

We can also frame what amounts to the same response at the level of conduct-types. Both Jack and Jill instantiate the same act-type: *spend the day with my sick grandmother.* But they also instantiate different conduct-types. Jack instantiates V_1: *spend the day with my sick grandmother in order to cheer her up*, while Jill instantiates V_2: *spend the day with my sick grandmother in order to influence her will.* It is not inconsistent, however, to judge that one acts permissibly if one instantiates V_1 but impermissibly if one instantiates V_2.

Holmes's argument, which brings the inconsistency objection to bear directly on the PDE, can be handled in a similar way. We can agree that in Holmes's example, both the precision bomber and the terror bomber perform similar deeds, insofar as they both drop their bombs on a target area containing both a military facility and civilian structures. But someone who holds the PDE also holds that the bombers' concrete actions

[9] Similarly, suppose that Jack disciplines his child firmly yet gently while Jill disciplines her child harshly. Jack and Jill do the same thing, namely, discipline their children. Yet, it is not inconsistent to judge that Jack acts rightly while Jill acts wrongly because of the harsh *manner* in which Jill disciplines her child.

differ morally. The terror bomber acts wrongly insofar as he intentionally kills noncombatants, while the precision bomber's conduct does not have this wrong-making feature. Or, at the level of conduct-types, the precision bomber instantiates the conduct-type V_1: *drop bombs on the target area with the intention of destroying the military facility*, while the terror bomber instantiates the conduct-type V_2: *drop bombs on the target area with the intention of killing noncombatants.* It is not inconsistent to judge that the terror bomber acts wrongly in virtue of instantiating V_2 and succeeding in his goal of harming noncombatants, while the precision bomber acts permissibly in instantiating V_1.

The inconsistency objection therefore fails. If it did succeed, however, then it seems a parallel argument would undermine Rachels's and Holmes's view that an agent's intentions in acting are relevant to assessments of her character. Rachels claims that although their actions are similar, Jack seems admirable for what he did while Jill does not. But consider the following rejoinder: Jack and Jill did the very same thing; therefore, it would be inconsistent to judge that Jack is admirable for what he did while Jill is not. It is not difficult to see how Rachels would likely respond to this objection. He would say that it is admirable to do a good thing such as visiting a sick relative with a good intention but that it is not admirable to do a good thing with a bad intention. Rachels's opponents will simply add that it is also permissible to do a good thing with a good intention and wrong to do a good thing with a bad intention.

6.4 The Deliberative Perspective Objection

One of the most influential objections to the PDE is due to Thomson.[10] Kasper Lippert-Rasmussen (2014) dubs it the "deliberative perspective objection" because it purports to support the Irrelevance Theory by asking us to consider the point of view of a deliberating agent. The most oft-cited presentation of the objection is from Thomson's article "Self-Defense."[11] There she asks us to imagine that we are the moral advisor to a bomber pilot who comes to us before embarking on a mission:

> Suppose a pilot comes to us with a request for advice: "See, we're at war with a villainous country called Bad, and my superiors have ordered me to drop some bombs at Placetown in Bad. Now there's a munitions factory at Placetown, but there's a children's hospital there too. Is it permissible for me to drop the bombs?" And suppose we make the following reply: "Well, it all depends on what your intentions would be in dropping the bombs.

[10] Thomson's argument is endorsed by Scanlon (2008, ch. 1).
[11] The argument also appears in Thomson (1999) and Thomson (2008).

> If you would be intending to destroy the munitions factory and thereby win the war, merely foreseeing, though not intending the deaths of the children, then yes, you may drop the bombs. On the other hand, if you would be intending to destroy the children and thereby terrorize the Bads and thereby win the war, merely foreseeing, though not intending, the destruction of the munitions factory, then no, you may not drop the bombs." What a queer performance this would be! Can anyone really think that the pilot should decide whether he may drop the bombs by looking inward for the intention with which he would be dropping them if he dropped them? (1991, 293)

Despite the fact that this passage is often invoked against the PDE, it is not immediately obvious what the objection is. The pilot asks us whether it would be permissible for him to drop his bombs on a certain target area. It is then imagined that you reply "It depends" followed by two conditional statements: "If your intention in dropping your bombs would be to ϕ, then yes, you may drop your bombs. If your intention in dropping your bombs would be to ψ, then no, you may not drop your bombs." It is then claimed that this is a "queer performance."

This raises a number of questions: Is your reply really queer? If so, what makes it queer? Does the best explanation of its queerness (if indeed it is queer) have anything to do with the relevance of intentions to permissibility, or is it best explained in some other way? To answer these questions, we must get clearer about what the objection is supposed to be.

6.4.1 An Interpretive Hypothesis

My hypothesis is that Thomson's objection is best interpreted in light of an argument originally due to Rachels (1986, ch. 6).[12] Rachels is explicit that his argument is posed from the point of view of a deliberating agent. He brings up a case in which an infant is born with an out-of-control necrotic bowel condition. The question is whether you, the infant's doctor, should submit it to further treatment:

> Suppose you are trying to decide ... whether to continue the infant's treatment. Remember that *the rightness or wrongness of an act is determined by the reasons for and against it.* You will, therefore, want to consider the reasons for and against this particular act. What are those reasons? On the one hand, if treatment is ceased the baby will die very soon. On the other hand, the baby will die eventually anyway, even if treatment is continued. It has no chance of growing up. Moreover, if its life is prolonged, its suffering

[12] Thomson cites Rachels's chapter approvingly in the course of criticizing the PDE (1999, 516n18).

> will be prolonged as well, and the medical resources used will be unavailable to others who would have a better chance of a satisfactory cure. In light of all this, you may well decide against continued treatment. But notice that there is no mention here of anyone's intentions. *The intention you would have, if you decided to cease treatment, is not one of the things you need to consider. It is not among the reasons for or against the action.* That is why it is irrelevant to determining whether the action is right. (1986, 95; italics in original)

Rachels's argument is straightforward:

Rachels's Argument:

1. Whether it is right or wrong to continue the infant's treatment is determined by the reasons for and against continuing treatment.
2. Your intentions are not among the reasons for or against continuing treatment.
3. So, your intentions are not relevant to the question of whether it is right or wrong to continue treatment.

In defense of premise (2), Rachels considers the various factors that would count for or against continuing treatment. He claims that you would not include among a list of pro and con factors information about the intention with which you would be continuing to treat the infant if you decide to continue treatment. Thus, whether or not it is right to continue treatment depends on "objective" factors (or perhaps expectations about objective factors) such as whether continuing treatment will increase the infant's lifespan by an appreciable amount and whether doing so will ease its suffering. It does not depend on the intention with which you would continue or discontinue treatment.

As I interpret her, Thomson means to apply similar reasoning to the bombing cases that are dear to proponents of double effect. The passage quoted earlier is best understood in the context of an implicit background argument that can be formulated as follows:

Thomson's Background Argument:

1. Whether it is permissible for the pilot to drop his bombs on the target area is determined by the reasons for and against doing so.
2. The pilot's intentions are not among the reasons for or against dropping bombs on the target area.
3. So, the pilot's intentions are not relevant to the question of whether it is permissible for him to drop his bombs on the target area.

According to my interpretative hypothesis, the aim of the quoted passage is to support premise (2). It plays the same role in *Thomson's Background Argument* that Rachels's list of pro and con factors plays in *Rachels's Argument*. If the pilot asks us for advice about whether he should drop his bombs on the target area, we would be expected to bring up reasons for and against dropping them there. Presumably, Thomson doesn't think it would be queer for us to say, "Well, it depends on how many civilians will likely be killed," or "It depends on how important the factory is to our overall strategy for winning the war." On the other hand, the oddity of saying "It depends" followed by the two conditional statements about the pilot's intentions is supposed to constitute evidence that they are not among the factors that count for or against dropping bombs on the target area. And this in turn is supposed to support the claim that whether or not it is permissible for the pilot to drop his bombs depends on objective factors (or expectations about objective factors) rather than his intentions.

Thomson's compact presentation of the deliberative perspective objection in Thomson (2008) supports this interpretation. There she writes,

> It is . . . silly to suppose that if A asks us whether it is morally permissible for him to V_{act}, then we should reply, "We can't tell unless you first tell us what you would be intending, as opposed to merely foreseeing, if you V_{act}-ed."
>
> That means that anyone who wants to justify the claim that Alan [who has been ordered to bomb a munitions factory] may drop his bombs whereas Arthur [who has been ordered to bomb a city] may not must find grounds for it lying, not in subjective facts about their intentions and beliefs, but rather in objective facts about the circumstances in which they would be acting. (220–1)

Thomson is explicit here that the objection is supposed to support the conclusion that what justifies claims about the permissibility or impermissibility of doing something like dropping bombs are not "subjective" facts about the intentions with which the agent would act, but objective facts about the circumstances.

If this interpretation is correct, then the fact that in the passage from "Self-Defense" Thomson presents the objection as a dialogue between an advisor and advisee is not essential to it. The relevant points can all be made if we imagine instead that the pilot is asking himself whether it would be morally permissible for him to drop his bombs.

6.4.2 *Response*

If my interpretation of the deliberative perspective objection is correct, then it fails to make contact with the PDE. Friends of double effect can even agree that *Thomson's Background Argument* is sound.[13]

[13] Likewise for *Rachels's Argument*.

The reason the objection fails to make contact with the PDE is that the principle does not say that the pilot's intention to kill noncombatants, or the fact that if he were to drop his bombs he would be dropping them with the intention of killing noncombatants, is a reason against *dropping his bombs on the target area*, or that the bad intention makes it the case that it is impermissible for him to *drop his bombs*. We can agree that the permissibility of dropping bombs on the target area depends on facts about the circumstances, such as the number of noncombatants that will likely be killed, the probability that the factory will be destroyed, and the factory's military value. But the content of morality is not exhausted by assessments of the act-types that agents instantiate. Morality is concerned with assessing human conduct, and human conduct also includes a motivational or intentional dimension. The PDE is concerned with this latter dimension of our conduct, and it *adds* that whether or not there is sufficient reason for the pilot to drop his bombs *there is also* a decisive reason for him not to intentionally kill, or otherwise seriously harm, noncombatants.[14] Thus, there is a decisive reason for the pilot not to drop his bombs *in order to* kill the noncombatants, for if he does, he will kill them intentionally.

Why is there a decisive reason against intentionally killing noncombatants? The answer to that question is provided by the rationale for the PDE. According to the solidarity rationale (Section 3.5), the reason against intentionally killing noncombatants is that doing so grossly deviates from the standard of human solidarity that measures one's conduct in relation to them.

If the PDE is correct, then if the pilot asks you whether it is permissible for him to drop his bombs on the target area, your answer should be not "It depends, if you would drop the bombs with the intention of killing the noncombatants, then no, you may not drop your bombs; but if you would drop them with the intention of destroying the munitions factory, then yes, you may drop your bombs." Rather, supposing that the expected number of noncombatant casualties is not disproportionate, etc., one thing you could truly say in response to his question is, "Yes, dropping your bombs is permissible, but you may not drop them in order to kill the noncombatants."[15]

It might be claimed, however, that the qualified affirmative answer also sounds queer, and that even if I have correctly diagnosed Thomson's

[14] Assuming we are not in circumstances in which the constraint against intentional harm may be permissibly infringed (Section 1.3).

[15] Cf. Wedgwood (2011b, 468).

argument, the queerness of the answer still counts against the PDE. This would be too quick, however, for the best explanation of the queerness may not be that it is false but lie in some other feature of the scenario.

I think this is indeed the case: If the qualified answer sounds queer, it is due to the context in which it is being uttered. In particular, although the answer is true, it violates a conversational norm, Grice's maxim of relation or relevance (1975). We normally assume that bomber pilots are decent human beings and that they do not possess a desire to kill noncombatants that they long to satisfy in their work. Moreover, given that the Principle of Noncombatant Immunity is a well-known part of international law (Section 1.5.2), the pilot presumably already knows that he ought not to make killing noncombatants the object of his attack.[16] In asking for your advice, the pilot probably wants to know whether you think there are sufficiently weighty reasons for destroying the munitions factory, given that the explosions of his bombs will cause incidental harm to nearby civilians. Given this conversational background, it would be highly impertinent to remind him that that intentionally killing noncombatants is wrong.

This explanation is supported by the fact that things would be quite different if we stipulate that you know the bomber pilot is a sadistic agent who harbors an unusual hatred for the adversary's people. In that case, it would not sound queer to me in the least if you answered his question "May I drop my bombs on the target area?" by replying "Yes, but you may not drop them in order to kill innocent people!"[17]

6.5 Looking Inward?

Thomson concludes the passage quoted in Section 6.4 with a question: "Can anyone really think that the pilot should decide whether he may drop the bombs by looking inward for the intention with which he would be dropping them if he dropped them?" On my reconstruction of the deliberative perspective objection, the phrase "looking inward" is not essential to it. It is simply a rhetorically loaded way of indicating that intentions are a "subjective" factor rather than an "objective" one. And it is

[16] This holds a fortiori for Scanlon's version of the case, in which you are the prime minister and it is the commander of your country's air force that has come to you for advice.

[17] I return to the case of the vicious bomber pilot in Section 6.6.2.

noteworthy that in Thomson's other presentations of the objection the phrase does not appear. Nonetheless, the passage is often read in such a way that the phrase is essential (Hanser 2005; Tadros 2011, ch. 7; Wedgwood 2011b). On this interpretation, Thomson's objection to the PDE is that if it were true, then in scenarios like the bombing case moral deliberation would have to take the form of a self-investigation, for the agent would have to explicitly consider her own intentions in deciding how she may act. It would be objectionably narcissistic for moral deliberation to take such a form, however.

Whether or not this argument is a good interpretation of the deliberative perspective objection, it is not clear how much force it has. There are some contexts in which it seems unobjectionable for the agent to turn inward in the course of moral deliberation (Kolodny 2011, 119). For instance, suppose that the landlord of a rental property is trying to decide whether to turn down an applicant with a prior eviction. The applicant is a member of a minority religion, and it would be illegal to turn him down on the basis of his religious beliefs. The landlord also recognizes that he may have a lingering prejudice against members of the minority religion. In this case, it seems perfectly in order for him to reflect on whether his inclination to turn down the applicant is a result of the applicant's prior eviction or whether it is motivated by the fact that he is a member of the minority religion.

Let us grant for the sake of argument, however, that it would be narcissistic for an agent to deliberate about her own intentions in deciding how to act in scenarios like the bombing case. Even granting that assumption, the objection misses the mark. For even if the agent's intentions in acting are relevant to moral permissibility in the way specified by the PDE, a deliberating agent concerned with acting permissibly need not focus her attention on her own intentions.

According to the account I presented in Chapter 4 (Section 4.3.1), practical deliberation is a search for effective and acceptable means to an end that the agent wants to achieve. The question that is addressed in deliberation is therefore the question "How?," where the question is understood as asking after possible means to an end. Now, the means that will be effective in bringing about the deliberating agent's end are typically things in the world rather than things in her mind. So, in trying to answer the question "How?" the agent will ordinarily be focused on things in her environment rather than on her own mental life.

Imagine, for example, that my son needs a bed and I decide to build him one. In thinking about how to build the bed, I first need to determine what its parameters should be and the materials out of which it should be constructed. How large will the bed need to be if he is not going to outgrow it in a year or two? How will it fit in his room with the other furniture? What sort of wood should I use and what kind of finish will look best? I then need to think about how I will assemble the materials and the tools that I will need to assemble them. Will I use hammer and nails or a screwdriver and screws? Finally, I must deliberate about how to acquire the materials I need to build the bed. This may involve cutting to size boards I already possess or going to the store and purchasing them. The point is that in posing and answering questions like these my practical thought is focused on the bed and the question *how to construct it* and not on my intentions or my other mental states.

I will define a sort of rule that I will call a *deliberative rule*. Deliberative rules take the form "Do X" or "Do not do X," where these are to be understood as fit for guiding the ends one adopts for deliberation and one's answers to the deliberative question "How?" Many rules that are employed in games and technical contexts are plausibly understood as being deliberative rules. Consider, for example, the chess rules "Castle early on the king's side" and "Do not trade a queen for a pawn," or the rules for writing philosophy papers "Begin by formulating a clear thesis" and "Do not begin with hackneyed phrases like 'Since the dawn of time . . .'." These rules are addressed to people who are asking themselves *how* to play chess well or *how* to write a good philosophy paper. The examples also illustrate that, like other sorts of rule, deliberative rules can range in stringency from mere rules of thumb ("Castle early on the king's side") to prohibitions that are absolute or nearly absolute ("Do not begin philosophy papers with hackneyed phrases").

Consider the deliberative rule "Do not kill or seriously harm innocent people." A deliberating agent who is concerned with avoiding wrongdoing need not think explicitly about his own intentions to comply with the PDE. He need only follow this deliberative rule. For instance, let us imagine that a bomber pilot has the objective of contributing to his country's war effort and that he has calculated a set of possible means to his end, a set of means which can be represented by the following practical syllogism:[18]

[18] This practical syllogism is in what I termed the Pattern 1 form in Section 4.3.2.

(a) End: Advance my country's war effort.
If I weaken enemy morale, that will advance the war effort.
If I terrorize the enemy population, that will weaken their morale.
If I kill and injure lots of noncombatants, it will terrorize the enemy population.
If I drop bombs on the residential districts of city X, I will kill and injure lots of noncombatants.[19]

The calculative order that the pilot has hit on for realizing his end of advancing the war effort is therefore as follows:

(b) Weaken enemy morale [D]
Terrorize the enemy population [C]
Kill and injure noncombatants [B]
Drop bombs on the residential districts of city X [A]

Reading these answers from top to bottom (D–A) gives us the pilot's answers to the question "How?" asked in regard to advancing the war effort. If the pilot follows the deliberative rule "Do not kill or seriously harm innocent people," he will refrain from acting on this calculation, for B violates it. On the other hand, if he does not follow the deliberative rule and successfully acts on the calculation, he will violate the constraint against intentional harm.

The reason the pilot's conduct will violate the constraint against intentional harm is that the deliberative question "How?" is the mirror image of the question "Why?" that reveals an agent's intentions in acting (Section 4.3.3). Suppose the pilot successfully acts on the above calculation. In that case, what he does intentionally is also describable by the set of propositions D–A, except that in drawing out his further intentions we start at the bottom and read up: The pilot intentionally (A) drops his bombs on the residential districts of city X, and he does this with the further intentions of (B) killing and injuring noncombatants, (C) producing terror, and (D) weakening enemy morale – and all this for the sake of his end of advancing the war effort. The questions "How?" and "Why?" reveal one and the same order, looked at from two different perspectives: as an order of means to an end or an order of further ends or goals in acting. One therefore need not reflect explicitly on one's intentions when one deliberates about what to do with a view to acting permissibly. Following the deliberative rule "Do not kill or seriously harm innocent people" ensures that one's conduct will comply with the constraint against intentional harm.

[19] The practical syllogism could be further extended to specify how the pilot will go about bombing the residential districts of city X.

6.6 Responding to Agents with Bad Intentions

6.6.1 The Vengeful Doctor

Thomson also pioneered a different kind of objection to the PDE. This sort of objection purports to show that the PDE sometimes has absurd implications for how we should respond to others with bad intentions. One of Thomson's reductio arguments features a physician who administers a lethal injection in order to get revenge:

> *Vengeful Doctor*: A patient is suffering terribly from an incurable disease and the only available means of treatment involves injecting him with a drug that will both relieve his pain and hasten his death. The doctor who will give the injection hates the patient and will inject the drug intending his death only because his death will constitute revenge. Despite the doctor's bad intention, the patient desperately wants her to inject the drug (1999, 516).

Thomson writes:

> If we love [the patient], we too want [the doctor] to inject the drug. We can consistently believe it would be morally impermissible for her to act, while nevertheless wanting her to. But morality calls for us to feel ashamed of ourselves if we do. What is morally impermissible is, after all, exactly that: morality requires that the agent not do the thing, the agent must not do it. So if we really do believe it morally impermissible for the doctor to inject the drug, then it is a bad business in us to want her to, wanting this for the sake of the benefit to be got by the patient if she does. (Compare wanting Smith to murder your uncle, wanting this because of the estate you will inherit at your uncle's death.) I am certain, however, that no shame or guilt is called for in us if we want the doctor to inject the drug in this case. (1999, 516)

In other words, suppose for reductio that the PDE is true:

1. It is morally impermissible for the vengeful doctor to inject the drug.
2. If it is morally impermissible for the doctor to inject the drug, then we should feel ashamed for wanting her to inject it.
3. So, we should feel ashamed for wanting the doctor to inject the drug.
4. But (3) is absurd.
5. So, the PDE is false.

How should we evaluate this argument? First, we should highlight a potential confound (Liao 2012, 713). Some people believe that death is not a serious harm for the patient in the circumstances under consideration. But if death is not a serious harm, then the PDE does not apply, and if the PDE does not apply, then Thomson's argument cannot impugn it. In what follows, then, I will assume for argument's sake that death is a serious harm for the patient.

Let's remind ourselves what the PDE implies about *Vengeful Doctor*. It does not imply that it is morally impermissible for the doctor to inject the drug. There may be sufficient reasons for injecting the drug that are generated by the fact that the patient requests it and the fact that it is the only available way to end his suffering. What the PDE does imply is that it is wrong for her *to kill the patient intentionally*; she thus acts wrongly if she injects the drug in order to kill the patient and the patient dies as a result (see Section 6.4.2). With that in mind, we can distinguish two possible desires that you, the patient's loved one, might have:

(1) Wanting the doctor to inject the drug
(2) Wanting the doctor to inject the drug with the intention of killing the patient.

If the PDE is true and if we should feel ashamed for wanting someone to engage in impermissible conduct, then we should feel ashamed for having desire (2), not desire (1). However, it is not implausible that we should feel ashamed if we want the doctor to inject the drug with the intention of killing the patient. We are capable, after all, of having a complex set of attitudes toward the doctor's conduct. If we truly love the patient, then prospectively we can both want the doctor to inject him with the drug, since that will end his suffering, and we can want her not to inject it in order to kill him. And if we subsequently learn that the doctor injected the drug in order to kill our loved one, then we can be thankful that he is no longer suffering and that the doctor's conduct brought this result about, and yet feel indignant that she injected it for the reason she did. Not only is this set of attitudes possible, but it also seems to me that it is just the set we should have.

This analysis also reveals a flaw in the analogy that Thomson employs in the quoted passage. She compares wanting the doctor to inject the drug to wanting Smith to murder your uncle so that you can inherit his estate. The suggestion is that if the PDE is true, then it would be shameful to have the former desire just as it would be shameful to have the latter. But in the latter case, Smith's conduct is described in a way that categorizes it as wrongful. By contrast, it is not wrong by the lights of the PDE simply for the doctor to inject the drug.

6.6.2 *The Vicious Bomber Pilot*

A different reductio objection involves a vicious bomber pilot (McMahan 2009; FitzPatrick 2012). Suppose you are an air force commander and you have determined that destroying a certain munitions factory is an important military objective. Bombing the factory will also kill a number of noncombatants, but the incidental harm will not be disproportionate.[20] The twist is that the only available pilot is a vicious bomber pilot. He has revealed that if he is sent on the mission, he will drop his bombs on the factory with the intention of killing the noncombatants – he was brought up to have an irrational hatred of the adversary's population. However, he also promises that he will otherwise fly the mission exactly as a more well-motivated pilot would; e.g., he will not circle back for a second bombing run in the unlikely event his bombs destroy the factory but do not kill any noncombatants. To an outside observer, the pilot's conduct will look indistinguishable from a precision bombing run aimed solely at destroying the munitions factory. May you, as the vicious pilot's commander, send him on the mission?

Your options here are not restricted either to ordering the pilot to fly the mission or not ordering him to fly the mission. The pilot cannot simply delete the hatred he feels for the adversary's population, but provided he sees destroying the factory as desirable in some respect (e.g., destroying it will provide a military advantage, he was ordered to do it), he can choose whether to adopt as his end either the destruction of the factory or the deaths of the noncombatants. Since this is so, I think that what you should do is order him to drop his bombs in order to destroy the factory and not in order to kill or harm the noncombatants. If he obeys this order, any noncombatant casualties he brings about will not be intentional. In any remotely realistic scenario, the matter would end there – even if the pilot still planned to kill the noncombatants intentionally, he would surely conceal his bad intention. But let us consider a fantastic scenario, one in which the vicious bomber pilot retorts, "If you send me, I will drop my bombs in order to kill noncombatants." What should you do in this highly unrealistic scenario?

You should not *authorize* the pilot to fly the mission in order to kill noncombatants, for that would be to authorize the intentional killing of

[20] We will also assume that you are not in circumstances in which the constraint against intentional harm may be permissibly infringed.

the innocent.[21] Nonetheless, it is possible to send him without authorizing intentional killing: You can order him to fly the mission only in order to destroy the factory, even if you know or have good reason to believe that he will disobey your order. The question, then, is: May you send him on the mission knowing that he is going to kill noncombatants intentionally without being authorized to do so? Critics claim that proponents of the PDE are committed to the conclusion that you may not do so, a conclusion they find absurd. Assume for reductio that the PDE is true:

1. The vicious bomber pilot would act wrongly if he flew the mission.
2. If the vicious bomber pilot would act wrongly if he flew the mission, then you may not send him on the mission, with the consequence that it will have to be aborted.
3. So, you may not send him on the mission and it will have to be aborted.
4. But (3) is absurd.
5. So, the PDE is false.

The PDE implies that if the vicious bomber pilot flies the mission, his concrete action or conduct will be wrongful. Proponents of it are thus committed to (1). But even if we grant that (3) is absurd, the argument can be blocked by denying (2). This is McMahan's strategy. As the pilot's commander, you are in a position to prevent his wrongdoing, but McMahan denies that you are obligated to prevent it. Although morality demands of us that *we* not act wrongly, it does not demand that we prevent others from doing so. To be sure, morality does often demand that we prevent people from being harmed, and because many harms are caused by wrongdoing, preventing harm will often require preventing wrongdoing. But in McMahan's view, we have little reason to prevent wrongful conduct over and above the reason to prevent its harmful effects. In the case under consideration, he concludes, you are not required to prevent the harmful effects of the vicious pilot's actions given the proportionate military value of the factory's destruction (2009, 357).

I agree that there is no strong general moral obligation to prevent wrongdoing as such. For instance, suppose that a runaway trolley is about to hit five people and that a bystander is about to turn it onto a sidetrack where it will kill only one. Suppose that you also know that the individual on the sidetrack is the bystander's personal enemy and that the bystander is

[21] Recall that Anscombe's principal objection to awarding Truman an honorary degree was that he authorized the intentional killing of Japanese civilians (Introduction).

going to turn the trolley in order to kill him. In my view, the bystander will act wrongly if he intentionally kills the person on the sidetrack. Even so, I believe you have at most only a weak reason to push him out of the way and turn the trolley yourself (cf. Tadros 2011, 162). There is a feature of the vicious bomber case that makes it different in a significant respect from the trolley one, however. You are the pilot's commander and commanders bear a special responsibility for the conduct of their subordinates. McMahan denies that this fact about you gives you any strong reason against sending the pilot on the mission: "In general, military commanders and others in authority are responsible only for the *behavior* of their subordinates. Responsibility for the subordinates' motives and intentions lies with the subordinates themselves" (2009, 357).

I wonder whether a commander's responsibility for the conduct of his or her subordinates is really so narrow. The Rome Statute of the International Criminal Court (2011) states that commanders are criminally responsible for the war crimes committed by forces under their effective command and control when they knew or should have known the forces were committing or about to commit a war crime and failed to take reasonable measures to prevent or repress its commission (Article 28 (a)). This is a legal document, but it is plausible that its function is to provide a legal backing to a moral principle, namely, that commanders have a duty to prevent their subordinates from engaging in serious wrongdoing; this moral principle seems to me to be a compelling one. Now, according to the PDE, the intentional killing of noncombatants is ordinarily seriously wrong. Therefore, if we accept that commanders ought to prevent their subordinates from engaging in serious wrongdoing, it follows that if you, the pilot's commander, know that he will intentionally kill noncombatants and you can easily prevent him from doing so by not permitting him to fly the mission, then you ought not to send him, with the consequence that the mission will have to be aborted. This is, of course, the conclusion that the critics find absurd.

But why is it supposed to be absurd? It cannot be that your country will have to continue the war without the destruction of the factory. Anyone who accepts the existence of *in bello* constraints is committed to the possibility that circumstances may arise in which there are no legitimate means available for pursuing important military objectives. What critics find absurd about the vicious bomber case is not this point, however, but rather that the mission will have to be aborted simply because of the vicious bomber pilot's bad intention. Here is how FitzPatrick expresses the objection:

> [S]urely nothing that's going on inside any particular pilot's head can by itself make [the] mission impermissible. How could the permissibility of pursuing this bombing mission against the munitions plant be held hostage to a particular pilot's intentions, *independently* of what will actually be done in the world, such that the mission must be aborted unless another pilot turns up *who will not do anything differently apart from having better intentions* when he bombs the munitions plant? (2012, 100; italics in original)

This passage is intended to pump the intuition that what's absurd about the PDE is that, together with other plausible assumptions, it implies that the mission should be aborted simply because of what would be happening *inside the pilot's head*, independently of what happens in the world. I argued earlier, however, that it is false that whether an effect is brought about intentionally rather than incidentally is simply a matter of what is happening inside the agent's head (Section 6.2). It is true that due to the highly peculiar nature of the case the vicious pilot's bombing run would appear indistinguishable to an outside observer from a precision bombing run aimed at the destruction of the munitions factory. But the observation that it may be difficult, or even impossible, for an observer to *tell* whether the events he is witnessing are teleologically ordered to killing noncombatants or to destroying a military facility does not mean that no difference between them exists in reality.

Opponents of the PDE believe that the vicious bomber case provides strong reason to doubt the principle's truth. But I think we should instead conclude that the case is an outlier. It is an outlier because it is stipulated that the vicious bomber pilot is the only pilot available, that he shares with you that he will disobey your order to drop his bombs in order to destroy the factory, and that he would otherwise fly the mission just as a more well-motivated pilot would. It should not be all that surprising, though, if a true moral principle has implications that are interesting and unexpected in fantastical situations. We should also recall that the conclusion that you should not send the vicious pilot on the mission does not follow directly from the PDE. It also relies on the principle that military commanders have a responsibility to prevent their subordinates from engaging in serious wrongdoing. If a weaker principle, such as the one articulated by McMahan, is true then the conclusion does not follow.

6.7 Conclusion

The aim of this chapter was to critically examine objections to the PDE by philosophers who hold that intentions are irrelevant to moral permissibility.

In response to the objection that it is mysterious why something that happens "in the agent's head" should make a difference to the moral permissibility of her conduct, I argued that it is a mistake to think that whether a person brings about an effect intentionally, as opposed to incidentally, is merely a fact about her state of mind and not also a fact about what happens in the world (Section 6.2). In response to the objection that the PDE leads to judgments about cases that violate the rational norm of consistency, I argued that proponents of the PDE are not committed to making inconsistent judgments (Section 6.3). In Section 6.4, I then argued that Thomson's deliberative perspective objection fails to make contact with the PDE. I also argued that if it sounds queer to advise a bomber pilot that he may drop his bombs on a target area that contains both a military facility and civilian structures, but that he may not do so in order to kill noncombatants, the queerness of that advice is best explained not by its falsity but by features of the conversational context. Next, in Section 6.5, I showed why the existence of a constraint against intentional harm does not imply that agents who are concerned with acting permissibly must focus their attention inward on their own intentions when deliberating about what to do. Finally, I responded to two arguments for the claim that the PDE sometimes has absurd implications for how we should respond to agents with bad intentions (Section 6.6).

If the arguments of this chapter and the previous one are cogent, then the PDE is in much better shape than its critics make it out to be. In the final chapter, I will show how the solidarity rationale for the PDE from Chapter 3 also helps nonconsequentialists reply to an argument that empirical findings about the nature and origins of our moral intuitions call into doubt the existence of deontological constraints on causing harm.

CHAPTER 7

Has Cognitive Science Debunked Deontology? *Double Effect and Greene's Debunking Argument*

7.1 Introduction

Joshua D. Greene's dual-process theory of moral judgment is one of the leading theoretical frameworks for contemporary moral psychology. Greene claims that empirical psychology also has implications for normative ethics, insofar as it reveals the etiology of the processes that influence our moral judgments. In particular, Greene contends that understanding the nature and origins of our moral intuitions *debunks* deontology.[1] In this chapter, I argue that the PDE, when conjoined with the solidarity rationale from Chapter 3, provides a way of overcoming Greene's debunking argument in relation to deontological constraints on causing harm.

The debunking argument proceeds in two stages. Stage 1 aims to debunk the case-based intuitions that seem to support deontology over consequentialism, while Stage 2 aims to debunk deontological moral philosophy. It is important to make it clear at the outset that Greene does not attempt to undermine all uses of intuitions in normative ethics. He agrees that all moral theories, including consequentialism, depend at some point on intuitive judgments (2014, 724).[2] The target of the first stage of his debunking argument is a particular *class* of intuitions, namely, intuitions about cases that appear to support deontology over consequentialism.

Greene's argument is based on the dual-process theory of moral judgment, and I begin in Section 7.2 by reviewing the main elements of this theory. In Section 7.3, I reconstruct two arguments that Greene employs in Stage 1 of his debunking argument, which I call the Argument from

[1] Greene defines consequentialism as the view that the moral value of an action is a function of its consequences alone (2008, 37), and he thinks of deontology as encompassing any theory that denies consequentialism. He therefore counts both virtue ethics and Kantian moral theories as versions of deontology. "Nonconsequentialism" is a more accurate name for the target of Greene's debunking argument, but I will follow his terminology in this chapter.

[2] For instance, consequentialists rely on intuitive judgments about what sort of consequences are good and bad, and so worth pursuing and preventing.

Accidental Reliability and the Argument from Unfamiliarity. Section 7.4 is devoted to explaining Stage 2 of the argument, according to which deontological moral philosophy is an elaborate attempt to rationalize moral judgments initially held on the basis of the intuitions undermined by Stage 1. In Section 7.5, I argue that whatever we make of the Stage 1 arguments, Stage 2 is unsatisfactory, and I explain why it fails to undermine the solidarity rationale for the PDE. Finally, in Section 7.6, I outline two possible explanations of why our case-based intuitions should be sensitive (even if imperfectly) to a feature of conduct – intentional harm – that is morally significant.

Two qualifications are in order. First, the focus of this chapter is Greene's deontological debunking argument as it applies to constraints on causing harm. Greene intends the argument to apply to other regions of deontological moral philosophy as well, such as retributivist theories of punishment. I do not address these applications. Second, while it is possible that the empirical components of Greene's argument will require revision in the light of further experimental results, for our purposes I will simply assume they are correct. The question I want to address is whether Greene's debunking conclusions are well-supported by his empirical premises.

7.2 The Dual-Process Theory of Moral Judgment

The dual-process theory of cognition posits that human judgment and decision-making are influenced by the operation of two distinct cognitive systems (Stanovich and West 2000; Evans 2003; Kahneman 2011). In Greene's analogy, the human brain is like a dual-mode camera, equipped with both a "manual mode" and a variety of "automatic settings." Manual mode is a general-purpose reasoning system. It operates through the conscious application of decision rules, and its operations are typically experienced as voluntary and controlled, and often as effortful. On the other hand, our automatic settings consist in "reflexes and intuitions that guide our behavior, many of which are emotional" (Greene 2014, 696). Automatic responses are quick and effortless, and we are not ordinarily conscious of the processes that generate them. Some of our automatic settings are biologically endowed, but automatic responses can also be acquired and modified through cultural transmission and personal experience. Like the two modes of a camera, each of the two systems has different strengths and limitations. Manual mode reasoning is flexible but not very efficient; automatic settings are efficient, but at the price of decreased flexibility.

According to the dual-process theory of moral judgment, moral psychology is situated within this dual-process framework. In particular, our moral judgments are influenced both by conscious, controlled reasoning and by automatic emotional responses.[3] The most controversial element of Greene's version of the dual-process theory is what he calls the Central Tension Principle:

> *Central Tension Principle*: Characteristically deontological judgments are preferentially supported by automatic emotional responses, while characteristically consequentialist judgments are preferentially supported by conscious reasoning and allied processes of cognitive control (Greene 2014, 699).

The terms "characteristically deontological judgments" (henceforth, deontological* judgments) and "characteristically consequentialist judgments" (consequentialist* judgments) are terms of art and are defined functionally: Deontological* judgments are judgments that are more easily or more naturally justified in deontological terms, such as in terms of duties or rights, and more difficult to justify in consequentialist terms, while consequentialist* judgments are judgments that are more easily or more naturally justified by impartial cost–benefit reasoning and more difficult to justify in deontological terms. Making judgments of either type requires no commitment to deontological or consequentialist moral theory, and both ordinary people and moral philosophers make both sorts of moral judgment.

The Central Tension Principle is nicely illustrated by the trolley problem (Thomson 1985):

> *Switch*: A runaway trolley is headed toward five people who will be killed if it continues on its present course. You can hit a switch that will turn the trolley onto a sidetrack where it will no longer be a danger to the five. On the sidetrack, there is one person who will be killed by the trolley if you hit the switch.
>
> *Footbridge*: As before, a runaway trolley is headed toward five trapped people. You are standing on a footbridge that spans the tracks, and next to you is a large man. The only way to save the five is to push the man off the bridge and onto the tracks. The man's body will prevent the trolley from reaching the five, but he will be killed when he is struck by it.

[3] The dual-process theory of moral judgment is supported by an impressive body of empirical evidence, including fMRI imaging studies. For a summary of this evidence, see Greene (2014, 700–6).

Both dilemmas involve trading one life for five. Yet, in response to *Switch*, most people make the consequentialist* judgment that it is acceptable to hit the switch to save the five, whereas in *Footbridge*, many people make the deontological* judgment that it is wrong to push the bystander into the path of the trolley. The dual-process theory explains these different patterns of judgment as follows. In both dilemmas, manual mode reasoning typically favors the consequentialist* judgment that it is acceptable to trade one life for five.[4] In *Switch*, this conclusion is unopposed by our automatic settings, so it tends to prevail. However, certain features of *Footbridge* elicit an automatic "alarm-like" emotional response that opposes pushing the bystander onto the tracks in order to save the five. This automatic response tends to influence people to make the deontological* judgment that sacrificing the bystander is unacceptable.[5]

The dual-process theory also explains another salient feature of common responses to the trolley problem dilemmas. When in empirical studies subjects are asked to justify the consequentialist* judgment to *Switch*, they readily do so in terms of the costs and benefits of hitting the switch. But subjects who make the deontological* judgment about *Footbridge* are often unable to articulate a coherent justification for it (Cushman, Young, and Hauser 2006; Hauser et al. 2007). The dual-process explanation for this discrepancy is that the consequentialist* judgment to *Switch* follows the conclusion of manual mode reasoning, which consciously applies a cost–benefit decision rule. On the other hand, the deontological* judgment to *Footbridge* is typically based on an automatic emotional response rather than on the conscious application of a moral principle or theory.

What is it about *Footbridge* that elicits an automatic emotional response? Greene et al. (2009) identify two factors they argue have a reliable effect:

1. Our automatic responses are sensitive to harms that are *intended* rather than foreseen but nonintended side effects.
2. Our automatic responses are sensitive to harmful actions that involve *personal force*, where an agent applies personal force to a patient when the force that directly impacts the patient is generated by the agent's muscles.

[4] Greene notes that while manual mode reasoning typically favors a consequentialist solution to both dilemmas, this is not necessarily the case. A person might arrive at the judgment that the action in *Footbridge* is wrong by consciously applying a deontological principle or theory, such as the PDE or a version of Kant's categorical imperative.

[5] It does not determine that judgment, however. Some people do make a consequentialist* judgment about *Footbridge*, and on Greene's view, these people are using manual mode reasoning to override an automatic response.

More specifically, according to Greene et al., our automatic responses are sensitive to the interaction between these two factors in the following way. First, the personal force factor affects people's judgments only when harm is intended. Second, while the intentional harm factor has a weak effect in the absence of personal force, its effect is significantly enhanced in cases involving personal force.[6] In sum, our automatic settings seem especially sensitive to actions that actively bring about intentional harm through the application of personal force. Greene describes actions with this profile as *prototypically violent actions* (2013, 247). We can also say that such actions are paradigmatic cases of violent *attacks* on others (Section 3.5.2).

7.3 Debunking Deontological Intuitions

According to the PDE, there is a moral difference between *Switch* and *Footbridge*. The agent's conduct in *Switch* is morally permissible because the harm that comes to the person on the sidetrack is incidental, there is no other way to save the five, the harm suffered by the one is not disproportionate to the value of saving the five, and the action has no other wrong-making features. By contrast, the agent's conduct in *Footbridge* is wrong because she intentionally causes the large man to be hit by the trolley as a means to preventing it from killing the five (Section 5.3.2). Greene et al.'s findings are significant from the perspective of this book because they indicate that our automatic emotional responses to moral dilemmas like *Footbridge* roughly track a factor (intentional harm) that is morally relevant by the lights of the PDE. To be sure, our automatic responses may not be perfectly reliable. If Greene et al. are correct, then they are undersensitive, insofar as they are insufficiently sensitive to intentional harm in cases where personal force is not involved. But our automatic settings are not wildly off-track either.

Greene does not think we should take our case-based intuitions to support deontology, however. Rather, he argues that empirical findings about these intuitions debunk their epistemic significance. In his recent

[6] There is some reason for caution about Greene et al.'s conclusion. Liao (2017, 88) reports that in their study Liao et al. (2012) found that most of their subjects judged that the agent's conduct is impermissible in the *Push* scenario. In this scenario, the agent can stop a trolley from hitting five people by pushing a button that activates a moveable platform, which moves a bystander into the path of the trolley. As in *Footbridge*, in *Push* the bystander is harmed intentionally, but the action does not involve the application of personal force. Liao et al.'s study suggests that intentionally causing harm in the absence of personal force sometimes has a stronger effect than Greene et al. recognize.

work, Greene has developed two arguments that purport to cast doubt on the reliability of our automatic responses to moral dilemmas.[7] I will call these arguments the "Argument from Accidental Reliability" and the "Argument from Unfamiliarity."

7.3.1 *The Argument from Accidental Reliability*

The Argument from Accidental Reliability turns on the claim that it is unlikely that our automatic responses are adapted to tracking moral truths. Greene has proposed two different theoretical accounts of the mechanism that generates our automatic responses to cases like *Footbridge*. In Greene (2013), he hypothesizes that these responses result from the operation of an action plan inspection module (see also Cushman 2016, 770–1). The idea, roughly, is that we possess a cognitive module that inspects our "behavioral plans" – in my preferred language, our calculations – looking for violent harm, and if harm is found, it activates an automatic negative emotional response. Greene speculates that this module may have evolved as a means of self-regulation. It would have been fitness-enhancing at both the individual and group levels for our ancestors to be equipped with a mechanism that made them averse to employing violent means to achieve their ends. Since the module only inspects calculations, however, it only detects harms that are intentional. Expected incidental harm must be evaluated by manual mode conscious reasoning.

If this account is correct, then the action plan inspection module exists as part of a system of behavioral self-regulation. Why then do we also judge the actions of third parties to be wrongful in cases like *Footbridge*? A possible answer is provided by the evaluative simulation hypothesis (Cushman and Miller 2013). According to this hypothesis, we evaluate the conduct of others by simulating engaging in it ourselves. If we find

[7] In Greene (2008), the debunking argument took a different form from the ones I discuss below. This argument, which has been dubbed the "Argument from Morally Irrelevant Factors" (Berker 2009), was premised on Greene's early work, which hypothesized that our automatic settings are more responsive to harm that is "up close and personal" (e.g., pushing someone to his death) rather than "impersonal" (e.g., hitting a switch that redirects a threat). The argument was that since it seems evident that whether harm is brought about in a way that is "up close and personal" is not morally relevant, empirical psychology has shown that our automatic settings are responsive to factors that lack moral significance. The problem with the Argument from Morally Irrelevant Factors is that its empirical premise is false, or at least too imprecise. While our automatic responses are sensitive to a "personal force" factor, they are also sensitive to the distinction between intentional and incidental harm, and to assert that this distinction is not morally relevant would beg the question against proponents of the PDE.

engaging in the sort of conduct at issue to be personally aversive, then we condemn third parties for doing so.

Greene now favors a different theory of the origins of our automatic responses (Greene 2017). According to this theory, our tendency to have an automatic negative response to *Footbridge*-like cases is explained as a result of learning. We have learned, both from our own experience and from observing others, that paradigmatic violent attacks tend to have aversive consequences. Not only do violent attacks result in harm to their victims, which are associated with distress cues that people tend to find aversive (Blair 1995), but they are also typically lead to condemnation and punishment for the agent. When conduct of the type *violent attack* is repeatedly associated with aversive feedback, this conduct-type *itself* comes to take on a negative affective valence. The conduct-type then elicits a negative response whenever it is encountered in a new situation.[8] Once again, the evaluative simulation hypothesis may fill the gap between first-personal aversion and third-personal condemnation.

Greene believes that if either of these hypotheses is right, it casts doubt on whether our automatic settings are good moral guides in the relevant domain. After introducing the action plan inspection hypothesis, he writes, "Harms caused as a means push our moral-emotional buttons not because they are objectively worse but because the alarm system that keeps us from being casually violent lacks the cognitive capacity to keep track of side effects" (2013, 240). Prescinding from the details about the mechanism, I take it the point is that the explanation of our automatic response to *Footbridge*-like cases does not refer to facts about the wrongfulness of the agent's conduct. This suggests a possible epistemic debunking argument. The basic idea is that if the explanatory claim is correct, then if our automatic responses do happen generally to track the moral truth in *Footbridge*-like cases, their reliability would be an amazing stroke of good luck, a happy accident or coincidence. Coincidences of this sort are a priori unlikely.[9] Our realization that our automatic responses are unlikely to be reliable therefore undermines whatever justification we may have had for our deontological* judgments to the extent that those judgments are based

[8] According to one theory, the mechanism responsible for this process is a model-free learning and decision-making algorithm (Crockett 2013; Cushman 2013, 2016, 771–3). For criticisms, see Ayars (2016).

[9] This is suggested by Greene's remark, "[I]t is unlikely that inclinations that evolved as evolutionary by-products correspond to some independent, rationally discoverable moral truth" (Greene 2008, 72). The immediate target of this remark is our inclination to retributive punishment, but the point is supposed to apply more generally.

on automatic responses. Call this the Argument from Accidental Reliability.

The Argument from Accidental Reliability is similar in structure to an evolutionary debunking argument that has been widely discussed in the metaethical literature (Joyce 2006; Street 2006). The metaethical debunkers also argue that the casual explanations of our normative judgments (or our normative tendencies more broadly) do not appeal to any normative facts (described as such) and that it is therefore unlikely that they track mind-independent normative truths. There are also important differences, however. The target of the metaethical debunking argument is realism about the normative domain, and it appeals only to the highly general consideration that our normative attitudes have been shaped by evolutionary forces. The target of the Argument from Accidental Reliability is narrower: Its focus is a particular class of moral judgments – deontological* judgments to *Footbridge*-like cases – and it appeals to specific empirical hypotheses about the processes that influence people to make these judgments.[10]

Discussions of the metaethical counterpart of the Argument from Accidental Reliability suggest that this sort of argument has some force, though its precise strength is a matter of debate (Schafer 2017). I want to argue that even if the first stage of Greene's deontological debunking argument succeeds, it fails at the second stage. Before turning to Stage 2, however, I will briefly discuss a second intuition debunking argument that Greene employs.

7.3.2 *The Argument from Unfamiliarity*

The Argument from Unfamiliarity relies on the proposition that our automatic responses are adapted to be reliable only in certain environments. Greene observes that automatic responses function well only when they have been shaped by trial-and-error experience. This experience may be the agent's personal experience, as when one acquires good driving instincts as a result of practice. But automatic settings can also incorporate the experience of our genetic ancestors through evolutionary adaptations or our cultural ancestors through processes of cultural transmission (2014, 714). Automatic responses thus operate well only in situations that are

[10] Note, however, that insofar as the Argument from Accidental Reliability appeals to considerations about the probability of our deontological* judgments tracking moral truths, it is not immediately applicable to positions that combine deontology in normative ethics with metaethical antirealism.

"familiar," that is, situations where they have been shaped by adequate trial-and-error experience, whether it be personal, biological, or cultural. By contrast, it is a priori unlikely that automatic responses are reliable in unfamiliar* situations, or situations with which we have inadequate evolutionary, cultural, or personal experience. Greene dubs this the "No Cognitive Miracles Principle":

> *No Cognitive Miracles Principle (NCMP)*: When we are dealing with unfamiliar* moral problems, we ought to rely less on automatic settings (automatic emotional responses) and more on manual mode (conscious, controlled reasoning), lest we bank on cognitive miracles (Greene 2014, 715).

The argument's other premise is that *Footbridge* (and similar dilemmas) represents an unfamiliar* situation. Greene argues that while *Footbridge*-like cases represent a situation in which a paradigmatic violent attack on an innocent person is the action that produces the best overall outcome of any available option, in the vast majority of cases violent attacks on innocent people produce suboptimific outcomes (Greene 2014, 716; see also Greene 2013, 251; 2016, 180; 2017, 74–5). It follows from the NCMP that we ought to rely less on our automatic settings to *Footbridge*-like cases and more on manual mode reasoning. Since our automatic settings are responsible for the intuition that it is wrong to sacrifice the bystander, we should discount that intuition.

The Argument from Unfamiliarity can also be cast as an epistemic debunking argument for deontological* judgments about *Footbridge*-like cases. The argument is that our recognition that such cases are unfamiliar* together with our recognition that the prior probability that our automatic responses function well in unfamiliar* situations is low provides us with an undermining defeater for deontological* judgments about *Footbridge*-like cases, to the extent that those judgments are held on the basis of an automatic response.

The Argument from Unfamiliarity has an advantage over the Argument from Accidental Reliability, insofar as it does not turn on speculation about the details of the mechanism that generates our automatic responses to *Footbridge*-like dilemmas. It relies only on the proposition that automatic settings, however they are generated, are unlikely to be reliable in unfamiliar* situations. However, it does assume that *Footbridge*-like dilemmas are unfamiliar*, and this assumption is debatable. There is a difference between saying that a certain type of case is uncommon and saying that our experience with cases of this type is *inadequate*. Thus, even if cases in which a violent attack on innocent people produces a greater good are statistically uncommon, this does not license the inference that cases of this sort are unfamiliar*. Furthermore, it does not seem implausible that people – or at least some people – do have adequate experience with situations of this type. Cases where a greater good could be brought about through violent attacks on innocent persons are not uncommon in the history of armed conflict (e.g., the strategy of undermining enemy morale through killing civilians), and it might be argued that the automatic settings of some people have been shaped by cultural experiences of armed conflict through media such as books and films. A deontological moral philosopher might also contend that her own automatic responses to scenarios like *Footbridge* have been honed through years of experience considering moral dilemmas. For these reasons, it seems to me that the claim that *Footbridge*-like dilemmas are unfamiliar* requires more support to be persuasive.

7.4 Debunking Deontological Theory: The Rationalization Argument

Stage 1 of Greene's debunking argument purports to debunk the intuitions that support deontological* judgments to *Footbridge*-like dilemmas. On its own, this argument is of limited value, however, since many deontologists claim that it is also possible to reach deontological* judgments "on principle," that is, on this basis of applying more general moral principles or theories. Deontological moral theories, in turn, are not simple lists of case-based intuitions. They are sophisticated theories of the moral domain that are constructed utilizing manual mode reasoning and reflection. This is why Stage 2 is crucial to Greene's overall aim, for it purports to undermine deontological normative ethics.[11]

The Stage 2 argument draws on Jonathan Haidt's influential social intuitionist model of moral psychology (Haidt 2001). According to this model, moral judgment is not typically caused by reasoning. In most cases, moral judgments are caused by quick emotional intuitions. Reasoning is a post hoc affair and enters the picture when the subject is faced with a demand to provide reasons for her judgments. Moreover, the search for reasons is typically not an impartial search for the truth but is instead a biased attempt to find reasons that support one's prior moral judgments.

Greene believes that Haidt's model applies to deontological* judgments in particular. According to the Central Tension Principle, deontological*

[11] On the importance of Stage 2 to the larger debunking argument, see also Königs (2018).

judgments are the class of moral judgments that are preferentially supported by automatic emotional responses. People often make these judgments on the basis of their automatic responses, but they might afterward try to articulate some justification for them if faced with the demand for reasons. No philosophical expertise is required to engage in ex post facto rationalization, but Greene's claim is that deontological moral philosophy is the rationalizing process in its most sophisticated and systematic form:

> [W]hat deontological moral philosophy really is, what it is *essentially*, is an attempt to produce rational justifications for emotionally driven moral judgments, and not an attempt to reach moral conclusions on the basis of moral reasoning. (2008, 39)

In a slogan, "the psychological *essence* of deontology lies with the automatic settings" (2014, 700).

Greene intends this as an empirical claim, and there are three pieces of evidence that support it. The first is that people generally display a tendency to engage in post hoc reasoning to justify their prior judgments (Perkins, Faraday, and Bushey 1991). Second, there is evidence that professional moral philosophers are more likely than nonphilosophers to explicitly endorse a moral principle, such as the PDE, that fits their prior judgments made on the basis of intuitions about cases (Schwitzgebel and Cushman 2012). Finally, the rationalization hypothesis seems supported by one of the standard methods of ethical theorizing. This method proceeds on the basis of a model on which case-based intuitions play a role in moral theorizing that is analogous to the role that empirical observations play in scientific theorizing (Kagan 2001). Just as the task of scientific theory-construction is to construct a theory that fits the observational data and has other theoretical virtues, so too on this model the task of normative ethics is to construct a theory that mostly fits our case-based intuitions and possesses general theoretical virtues such as simplicity and internal coherence. Greene calls this *intuition-chasing*: conforming our general moral principles to specific judgments that mostly follow intuition (2014, 718).[12]

Here is how the two stages of Greene's deontological debunking argument fit together. Stage 1 concludes that our case-based deontological*

[12] Greene associates intuition-chasing with Rawls's method of reflective equilibrium. Greenspan (2015) points out, however, that for Rawls the inputs to reflective equilibrium are considered moral judgments, and that while our considered moral judgments are supposed to be pre-theoretical, their formation may still involve reflection and reasoning.

judgments are epistemically problematic to the extent that they are based on automatic emotional intuitions. Stage 2 then claims that deontological moral philosophy is the project of rationalizing deontological* judgments initially held on the basis of automatic responses. And insofar as deontological theorists engage in chasing their automatic emotional intuitions, their theories are also epistemically suspect.

7.5 Why the Rationalization Argument Fails

Greene's Stage 2 argument overlooks two important and related facts about deontological moral philosophy:

(1) Even if deontological moral theorizing is at bottom an attempt to provide reasons for deontological* judgments initially held on the basis of automatic responses, it does not follow that none of these attempts can succeed. That is, it does not follow that no deontological theories can provide us with justification for holding deontological* judgments.
(2) Even if intuition-chasing is a prominent part of the deontologist's methodology, Greene has not shown that it is impossible for deontological* judgments to have *independent* support, or support that is not derived from case-based intuitions.

Point (1) draws a distinction between deontological moral *theorizing* as an activity or practice and the *theories* that are the products of that activity. To see why this distinction matters, consider an analogy. Freud (1961b) notoriously claimed that belief that God exists is the product of wishful thinking, and it is undeniable that wishful thinking is epistemically problematic. But a question arises about how Freud's hypothesis fits with the fact that philosophically minded theists have offered theoretical justifications for belief in God, such as Aquinas's five ways. A Freudian psychologist might argue that these philosophically minded theists' belief that God exists is not caused by reasoning; their reasoning is rather an ex post (and biased) attempt to rationalize a belief that is already held on the basis of wishful thinking. If this psychologist had a flair for the dramatic, he might even claim that the psychological *essence* of philosophical theology is wishful thinking.

These claims provide one element of an atheistic worldview. But it is important to be clear about what work they do and do not do. They provide a possible naturalistic explanation for widespread belief in God. They do not, however, provide an argument for atheism, and they do not refute philosophical arguments for theism. A philosophically minded theist might therefore respond to our Freudian psychologist as follows:

> Perhaps you are right that my belief in God was initially produced by wishful thinking and that the discipline of philosophical theology exists because people like me are motivated to find reasons for our theistic beliefs. Perhaps you are also right that theists are subject to confirmation-bias – in fact, this would not be surprising, given that in general people's reasoning is biased toward confirming their prior convictions (and since atheists are people too, this applies to them as well). But even granting all that, it is still possible that I have found a philosophical argument for the existence of God, that I am justified in believing this argument's premises, and that this justification is transmitted to my belief in the argument's conclusion.

I am not here taking a stand on whether there are any good arguments for theism. I am rather explaining why the imagined Freudian psychologist's claims about what drives philosophical theology cannot undermine all theistic beliefs. It is indeed the case that theistic belief is unjustified to the extent that it is held on the basis of wishful thinking. But it is compatible with this that belief in God can come to be held on an independent basis, such as a philosophical argument, and that it is justified to the extent it is held on this basis. Similarly, if Greene is right, then deontological moral theory as a practice is motivated by the impulse to justify deontological* judgments initially formed on the basis of automatic emotional responses. However, this does not show that none of these theories are capable of providing justification for deontological* judgments.

Admittedly, there would still be a problem if the most that could be said for any deontological theory or principle is that it more or less summarizes our intuitions about cases, and this is why point (2) above is important. For even if intuition-chasing is prevalent in deontological moral theorizing, some deontologists do provide independent rationales for their principles – rationales that ground their principles "from above" in more abstract theoretical concepts rather than "from below" in intuitions about cases.

This is where the PDE comes in. Greene's empirical studies show that people's automatic responses are (imperfectly) sensitive to the distinction between intentional and incidental harm. Common deontological* judgments about causing harm would therefore be largely vindicated if the PDE could be provided with an independent rationale.[13] In Chapter 3, I provided just such a rationale, the core of which can be summarized as follows:

[13] See Lott (2016). When Greene considers this sort of move, he simply asserts, without argument, that there is no independent rationale for the PDE (2013, 223; 2014, 721).

1. There is a default standard of human solidarity (concern and goodwill) that measures one's conduct in relation to others. Conduct that deviates from this standard is morally wrong.
2. The existence of the standard of solidarity is grounded in the fact that human beings have an inherent value or dignity in virtue of which they are worthy of concern.
3. Intentional harm grossly deviates from the standard of solidarity, insofar as it successfully expresses a desire for a harm or evil for the victim.
4. Incidental harm does not have this wrong-making feature. Nevertheless, conduct that causes incidental harm that is excessive or gratuitous also deviates from the standard of solidarity toward those whom it negatively impacts.

To be sure, this rationale for the PDE does rely on certain intuitions, such as the intuition that human beings are inherently worthy of concern and the intuition that conduct is wrongful when it deviates from the standard of solidarity. Crucially, however, these intuitions do not belong to the class of intuitions that Stage 1 of Greene's debunking argument calls into question, for they are not automatic responses to particular moral dilemmas. In Sidgwick's (1907) terminology, they are high-level "philosophical" intuitions rather than "dogmatic" or "perceptual" intuitions. Greene acknowledges that even consequentialists must appeal to philosophical intuitions to ground their preferred theory, and it is not illegitimate to appeal to them in this context (2014, 724). This is just to say that the solidarity rationale must be judged on its own merits. If it is compelling, then nothing in Greene's deontological debunking argument undermines the justification it provides for holding the PDE.

7.6 A Miraculous Coincidence?

In this section, I address a remaining concern about my reply to Greene's deontological debunking argument. If the PDE is true, then our deontological* judgments to moral dilemmas like *Footbridge* are largely vindicated. But if, per the Argument from Accidental Reliability, our automatic responses are not adaptations that are designed to track moral truths, then it may still seem like an extremely fortunate coincidence – a cognitive miracle – that our automatic responses to moral dilemmas should turn out generally to track a feature of conduct (intentional harm) that is morally significant.

One thing to note in response to this worry is that even if inexplicable coincidences are a priori unlikely, they are not impossible. Moreover, it is often reasonable to accept the existence of coincidences when we have independent evidence that they obtain. Kieran Setiya gives the mundane example of meeting a friend at the DMV on a Saturday morning (2012, 72). If your choices are independent, then nothing explains your both being there at the same time: It is sheer coincidence. Yet, if you see your friend standing in line with your own eyes, it would be perverse to doubt the existence of this coincidence. This is important because the solidarity rationale provides a justification for the moral significance of the distinction between intentional and incidental harm that is independent of our case-based intuitions. Nonetheless, I think the deontologist's position would be further enhanced if he could provide some plausible explanation of why it should be the case that our automatic settings are generally reliable in the relevant domain. An explanation would provide us with some understanding or insight that would make it seem less surprising that a factor that makes (or tends to make) conduct wrong should also be a factor that engages our emotional responses.

I believe the solidarity rationale supplies the materials to construct the outlines of two possible explanations for the general reliability of our automatic responses to *Footbridge*-like dilemmas. These explanatory hypotheses are speculative, as any hypotheses in this area must be, but I think they are plausible. The explanations take their starting points from the two justifications for the standard of solidarity I discussed in Chapter 3 (Section 3.7).

The first justification centered on the value of relations of solidarity. To the extent that members of a group conform their conduct to the standard of solidarity, relations of reciprocal concern and goodwill obtain among them, and these relations are socially valuable. I argued that relations of human solidarity are valuable in their own right, but what I want to focus on here is their instrumental value. Relations of solidarity facilitate cooperation, are conducive to social trust, and mitigate faction, and in doing so, they enable group members to more effectively reap the benefits of social cooperation.

If conduct that conforms to the solidarity standard is thus "prosocial" in an obvious sense, then conduct that deviates from that standard deserves to be called antisocial. This seems especially true of attacks, which are the paradigm of unsolidarity with others (Section 3.5.2). Attacks constitute gross deviations from the standard of solidarity insofar as they seek to bring about an evil for their object rather than a good, and they tend to be followed by reprisals that lead to further social disruption. But the paradigmatic form of an attack is what Greene calls a prototypically violent action, that is, an action that uses personal force intentionally to bring about harm. Given that relations of solidarity are socially beneficial, and given that violent attacks on others are, *as a type or category* of conduct, egregiously contrary to solidarity, it is not so surprising that human beings have developed a mechanism that triggers an automatic negative response to violent attacks. For, as Greene notes, emotion provides a reliable, quick, and effective way of motivating a certain type of response to recurring types of situation (2008, 60). The emotional response at issue could be the result of an evolutionary adaptation that makes us averse to violently attacking others, or it could be that we learn through experience that violent attacks on others are especially likely to attract condemnation and punishment. The point is that, whatever the details about the mechanism, the explanation for why we are emotionally sensitive to intentional harm (especially in its paradigmatic form) is its inherently antisocial character.

On the other hand, conduct that causes incidental harm is not by its nature antisocial in the same way as conduct that brings about harm intentionally. Conduct that causes harm incidentally is not directed against the good of others and cannot accurately be described as an attack on those who are harmed. The agent in *Switch* who redirects the trolley away from the five is not attacking the bystander on the sidetrack, and a precision bomber who drops his bombs with the intention of destroying a military facility is not attacking nearby noncombatants. Of course, reckless actions that cause lots of incidental harm and relatively little benefit or which cause gratuitous harm might also be said to be antisocial insofar as they manifest indifference or a lack of sufficient concern for the good of those who are harmed. But whether such actions are reckless depends on facts about the wider circumstances, such as the value of the agent's end, the magnitude of the incidental harm, and the other possible ways of pursuing the end that are available (Section 3.6). It would be difficult for cognitively cheap and efficient automatic settings to keep track of these factors, and this in turn helps explain why there is no comparable automatic response to wrongful instances of incidental harm.

In Section 3.7, I argued that the utilitarian rationale for the standard of solidarity is not the whole story about the justification for it, and it may not be the whole story about why we feel an aversion to violent attacks either. I argued that the normative foundation for the standard of solidarity is the special value or worth – the dignity – of human beings. I also contended that an ordinary virtuous agent's knowledge of human dignity need not be explicit or theoretically articulate. It may rather take the form of a tacit sense that human beings matter and that human life is precious. Not everyone has this sense but many do, even if other factors sometimes prevent it from informing their conduct.

It is not difficult to understanding why someone who has a sense of the value of human life might experience aversion to the thought of attacking others. If something is precious, its value calls for caring for it and preserving it, but attacking something seeks not to care for it but to harm or destroy it. For this reason, a person might feel aversion to the thought of intentionally destroying a priceless heirloom or a unique and cherished photograph of a loved one. Such behavior is perverse given the kind of value that she ascribes to the object. Likewise, if an agent perceives certain persons as having dignity, then she may perceive paradigmatic attacks against them as inappropriate responses to them, and this may in turn help explain why she is averse to engaging in paradigmatic attacks on others herself and why she condemns it when third parties violently attack others.

An interesting feature of this second explanation is that if it is on the right track, then our negative emotional responses to prototypically violent actions are explainable in part as responses to the normative properties possessed by this sort of conduct after all, for the inappropriateness or incorrectness of a type of response is a normative property of it. This has an obvious bearing on the Argument from Accidental Reliability, and it is therefore worthy of further investigation.

7.7 Conclusion

The first stage of Greene's deontological debunking argument is aimed at undermining the case-based intuitions that support deontology over consequentialism, while the second is aimed at debunking deontological moral theories. The main focus of my critique in this chapter was Stage 2. I argued that Greene's claim that deontological moral philosophy is the project of providing ex post facto rationalizations for automatic emotional responses does not show it is not possible to provide a rationale for deontological moral principles that is based on more abstract "philosophical" intuitions rather than the sort of intuitions that are the target of the Stage 1 arguments. I also noted that the rationale I provided for the PDE in Chapter 3 is a rationale of just this sort. This is significant because if the PDE is true, then our automatic responses to moral dilemmas like *Footbridge* are generally reliable. Finally, I outlined two possible explanations why it is not a cognitive miracle that our automatic responses should be roughly sensitive to a factor – intentional harm – that is morally significant.

Conclusion

Normative ethics is concerned with the questions of how we should live, how we should act, and what sort of persons we should strive to become. One of its central aims is therefore to articulate and justify proposals about the moral standards that measure our conduct. According to one influential way of conceiving it, the execution of this task involves distinguishing the factors that have intrinsic moral significance, explaining why they have the significance they do and describing how they interact (Kagan 1998). The goal of this book has been to make a contribution to contemporary normative ethics by defending the claim that an agent's intentions in acting are among these morally significant factors. In particular, I have defended the *principle of double effect*:

> *PDE*: There is a strict moral constraint against bringing about serious evil (harm) to an innocent person intentionally, but it is permissible in a wider range of circumstances to act in a way that brings about serious evil incidentally, as a foreseen but nonintended side effect.

The PDE has been called one of the pillars of nonconsequentialist ethics. Yet, in recent years, it has been subjected to intense criticism, even by philosophers who are not otherwise friendly to consequentialism, and as a result, it is widely viewed with suspicion and hostility. This book has made the case that the principle deserves to be taken seriously and that it withstands the major objections that have been leveled against it.

The PDE is a principle that concerns the morality of human *conduct*. Recent normative ethics has tended to restrict its focus to what we do: to action or behavior understood narrowly as the instantiation of an act-type. The notion of conduct is richer than that of behavior, so understood. When human beings act, we perform actions of certain types, but we typically do so in a certain manner and for a certain reason (or reasons) and with a certain intention (or intentions), and the notion of conduct is intended to capture all three of these dimensions of human agency

(Audi 2016). This is important because in my view moral assessments are not limited merely to assessments of behavior. Morality sets standards for conduct, and the PDE relates to the intentional or motivational dimension of our conduct.

I will now review the main elements of my defense of double effect by summarizing each of the book's chapters. In Chapter 1, I discussed the key terms of *PDE* and I distinguished between an absolutist and nonabsolutist version of the principle. I also introduced two principles that provide partial guidance to agents who foresee their conduct will bring about incidental harm, the Principle of Proportionality and the Principle of Due Care, which serve to forbid incidental harm that is excessive or gratuitous. I then described the role of the PDE in the *jus in bello* principles of just war theory and in international humanitarian law, which forms a legal counterpart to just war theory's *jus in bello.*

In Chapter 2, I investigated the extent to which the PDE is supported by intuitions about cases. A number of cases suggest that we are intuitively more tolerant of incidental harm than intentional harm. However, I argued that it would be unwise for proponents of double effect to rest their case merely on case-based intuitions. In addition to the fact that the principle does not perfectly cohere with everyone's intuitions, it is possible that there are alternative principles that explain our intuitions at least as well as the PDE and there is evidence that human intuitions are not uniform or static. Finally, appeal to intuitions about cases does nothing to explain *why* the distinction between intentional and incidental harm is morally significant. For these reasons, it is incumbent on proponents of double effect to provide a rationale that explains why its central distinction is relevant to the moral permissibility of conduct. In the remainder of the chapter, I examined six proposals and I found that each is vulnerable to serious objections.

Chapter 3 was devoted to the constructive project of developing a novel grounding for double effect, the solidarity rationale. Taking a cue from Foot, I aimed to situate the PDE within a larger region of morality, one structured around the concept of solidarity. The central elements of the account were as follows. First, our conduct is measured by a standard of human solidarity toward each other person, that is, a standard of concern and goodwill that is based on our common humanity, and a person's conduct is wrong when it deviates from this standard. The solidarity standard is grounded ultimately in the dignity of the human being, in virtue of which human beings are worthy of concern and goodwill for their own sake. In addition, when people conform their conduct to the solidarity standard, relations of solidarity obtain among them, and these relations contribute to our flourishing as social animals. Some departure from the standard of solidarity is justified in responding to unjust aggression and for the punishment of wrongdoing, but it is fully in force in the case of the innocent.

Second, the standard of solidarity grounds more specific moral norms, including the precept of beneficence. Beneficence occupies a central place within the morality of solidarity because beneficent conduct expresses benevolent desire and a paradigmatic way in which we manifest concern for others is by acting in ways that express benevolence. Since the concern constitutive of solidarity is successfully expressed through beneficent conduct, a person who never acts beneficently toward others does not measure up to the solidarity standard. It is not the case, however, that we are morally required to act beneficently toward others whenever it is physically possible, for there may be considerations that countervail sufficiently against doing so. In particular, there is no privation of beneficence if a person omits to aid others when taking the only available means would involve wrongdoing. The duty of beneficence is circumscribed by other moral constraints, and this is important because intentionally harming an innocent person is a deviation from the solidarity standard in relation to the victim. Rather than aiming at procuring or securing a good for her victim, the agent of intentional harm successfully aims at bringing about a harm or evil for him, and in doing so, her conduct expresses a desire whose *valence* is contrary to benevolence. For this reason, it is (typically) wrong to harm a fewer number of innocent people as a means to procuring good or preventing evil to a greater number.[1]

Finally, I argued in Chapter 3 that the standard of solidarity also supplies a basis for the Principles of Proportionality and Due Care. Conduct that causes harm incidentally does not possess the wrong-making feature distinctive of intentional harm. Nonetheless, the agent of incidental harm that is excessive or gratuitous acts recklessly in the sense of running an unjustified risk of harming others (a risk which in some cases may be close to 1), and in doing so manifests a lack of sufficient concern for the people he harms. Conduct that causes excessive or gratuitous incidental harm therefore also deviates from the solidarity standard.

In Chapter 4, I elucidated an Anscombian account of intentional action. According to this account, when we conceptualize an action as "intentional," we are placing it within a distinctive sort of order, or as the sort of

[1] The qualification in parentheses makes room for the nonabsolutist version of the PDE.

thing which is fit to enter into such an order. The order at issue is *explanatory* and *teleological.* It is characteristic of intentional action that when an agent is acting intentionally she is doing something, A, *because* she is doing something else B and *in order to* do B, and she is doing B because she is doing C and in order to do C, and so on. The order of intentional action is also distinctive in that it is constituted in part by the agent's own understanding of it. If S is doing A in order to do B, then this is the case in virtue of the fact that S knows first-personally that she is doing A in order to do B. Since this is so, S will be in a position to answer the question "Why are you doing A?"

The teleological order of an agent's intentional action is determined by the calculation on the basis of which she acts. The agent's calculation can be represented by a practical syllogism, which lays out an ordered series of means for achieving an end and which concludes with a specification of an action that the agent knows how to perform immediately in her circumstances. Effects or aspects of the agent's conduct that fall outside this calculation are not intentional, and if the agent is aware of them, they are incidental.

The purpose of Chapters 5 and 6 was to respond to objections to the PDE. The focus of Chapter 5 was a problem that is often raised against double effect, the "closeness problem." Proponents of the problem claim that intentions are sufficiently fine-grained that an agent need not intend harm in nearly any situation. Since this is so, the PDE will fail to prohibit conduct that is morally objectionable in many cases unless it is supplemented with a criterion of excessive closeness, whose function is to identify things that are "too close" to harm to be considered incidental for purposes of double effect. However, the argument continues, attempts to specify a criterion of closeness have so far failed, and the failure of these attempts is grounds for pessimism that a satisfactory criterion exists.

In response, I argued that the magnitude of the closeness problem has been exaggerated. Proponents of double effect have resources for responding to the cases that have been supposed to demonstrate the need for a criterion of closeness. An important part of my argument was to emphasize, with other recent defenders of the PDE, that the principle does not constitute the whole of morality. The constraint against intentional harm, in particular, is best understood as one element of a pluralistic moral theory that allows for multiple grounds of wrongdoing. I also argued that in order to satisfactorily analyze certain cases, such as the *Craniotomy* case and Pruss's *Zookeeper* scenario, it is necessary to clarify the content of the constraint against intentional harm. The constraint can be understood either as a constraint against successfully executing an intention [to bring about serious harm for an innocent human being] (PDE_1) or as a constraint against successfully executing an intention to bring about what is, as a matter of fact, a serious harm for an innocent human being (PDE_2). If PDE_1 is correct, then for an agent's conduct to violate the constraint the concepts *harm*, *human being*, an *innocent* must figure in the *content* of her intentions in acting. By contrast, on PDE_2, an agent's conduct can violate the constraint without such concepts figuring in the content of her intentions so long as in the *context* what she intentionally brings about is a serious harm for an innocent human being. I argued that the constraint against intentional harm should be understood along the lines of PDE_2 rather than PDE_1.

In Chapter 6, I responded to five objections to double effect from proponents of the Irrelevance Theory, the theory that an agent's intentions and motivating reasons are not fundamentally relevant to assessments of moral permissibility. These objections were as follows: (i) It is mysterious why something in the agent's mind should matter for the moral permissibility of her bodily actions; (ii) the PDE leads to inconsistent judgments about cases; the PDE is objectionable from the perspective of the deliberating agent, either (iii) insofar as it makes the moral permissibility of doing things such as dropping bombs turn on the agent's intentions rather than objective features of her situation or (iv) insofar as it requires a deliberating agent to focus her attention on her own mental states rather than on the world; (v) the PDE sometimes has absurd implications for how we ought to respond to agents with bad intentions. I argued that, contrary to proponents of the Irrelevance Theory, none of these objections seriously damage the PDE.

In Chapter 7, I argued that an advantage of my rationale for the PDE is that it can help nonconsequentialists respond to Joshua Greene's argument that recent discoveries in empirical moral psychology undermine belief in deontological constraints on causing harm. The starting point of Greene's argument is the dual-process theory of moral judgment, according to which our moral judgments are influenced both by conscious, controlled reasoning and by automatic emotional responses. Greene cites empirical evidence that characteristically deontological judgments are preferentially supported by automatic emotional responses while characteristically consequentialist judgments are preferentially supported by conscious reasoning (The Central Tension Principle). His debunking argument then proceeds in two stages. The first stage aims to cast doubt on the notion that our automatic responses are good guides to moral dilemmas, such as

Footbridge, which involve causing harm to one person in order to prevent harm from befalling a greater number of others. The second stage adds that deontological moral philosophy is a sophisticated form of providing ex post rationalizations for moral judgments initially held on the basis of automatic emotional responses. I argued that, whatever we make of the first stage of Greene's debunking argument, the second stage fails. As Chapter 3 demonstrated, it is possible to provide a rationale for the PDE that is independent of intuitions about cases. I also argued that the solidarity rationale enables us to provide a plausible explanation of why our automatic responses should be sensitive to intentional harm. This enables us to understand why it is not a "cognitive miracle" that our automatic settings are generally reliable in response to moral dilemmas that involve sacrificing one person to save a greater number of others.

I have attempted to make my discussion of double effect as comprehensive as space would permit. I will conclude by mentioning three topics for further investigation.

First, the PDE is a moral principle that applies to conduct that brings about serious harm or evil. To apply the PDE, we therefore need to know what counts as harm in the circumstances of application, and different theories of harm sometimes yield divergent results. But other than briefly indicating my own preferred account (Section 1.2.2), I have bypassed debates about the nature of harm. The frame I used for introducing the PDE was just war theory, and it is not controversial that noncombatants are typically seriously harmed when they are killed, maimed, or otherwise injured in the course of armed conflict. Disagreement about the nature of harm is more prevalent in another area where the PDE is often applied, namely, biomedical ethics. One traditional use of the PDE is to distinguish morally between euthanasia, which essentially involves intentionally bringing about the death of a patient, and cases of palliative care where a foreseen side effect of administering pain-killing drugs is the hastening of the patient's death. The PDE only discriminates against euthanasia, however, if death is a serious harm for the patient whose life is ended, and there is controversy about whether death is a serious harm in circumstances in which euthanasia is typically requested. This controversy can only be settled by a theoretical account of harm and, I believe, of the human good more generally. For those of us who find euthanasia morally objectionable, this book provides a defense of some of the materials necessary to make the case for that conclusion.

Second, the PDE rests on a distinction between the effects of an action that are intentional and those that are incidental, and this distinction is not a moral distinction but an action-theoretical one. In Chapter 4, I articulated a theory for determining where the line between the intentional and incidental falls, one which is due to Anscombe's *Intention*. This is not the only extant account of intention and intentional action, however, and a more comprehensive discussion would need to defend it from its rivals. It would also need to say more about related topics, such as the nature of practical reasoning, the difference between practical reasoning and theoretical reasoning, and the evaluation of practical reasoning qua reasoning. These tasks are all on the agenda of contemporary philosophy of action.

The final topic for further investigation is the stringency of the constraint against intentional harm. *PDE* states that intentional harm is more difficult to justify than incidental harm, but it leaves open the question of whether inflicting serious harm on the innocent might ever be morally justified. Many contemporary philosophers who are sympathetic to the PDE will no doubt find the weaker, nonabsolutist version of the principle attractive. On the other hand, the starting point for this book was Anscombe's condemnation of the atomic bombings of Hiroshima and Nagasaki, and Anscombe would vigorously oppose the nonabsolutist position. In "Modern Moral Philosophy," she famously finds that the differences between the major English moral philosophers from Sidgwick to her day (the late 1950s) are of little importance. The reason is that despite the manifest differences between them each one "has put out a philosophy according to which, e.g., it is not possible to hold that it cannot be right to kill the innocent as a means to any end whatsoever and that someone who thinks otherwise is in error" (1981a, 33). This puts all the major English moral philosophers since Sidgwick in opposition to what Anscombe calls the "Hebrew-Christian ethic," which is characterized by the teaching that "there are certain things forbidden whatever *consequences* threaten" including "choosing to kill the innocent, for any purpose, however good" (1981a, 34).

I have not attempted to resolve the debate between moral absolutists and nonabsolutists in this book. But I think that in these pages I have put out a philosophy on which it is *possible* to hold that the intentional killing of the innocent can never be right. According to the solidarity rationale, it is not merely the case that there is a strong reason against intentionally killing the innocent (when death is a serious evil – which may be always), a reason which may however be outweighed by other reasons, such as ones that stem from considerations of utility. Rather, the proposal is that human conduct is wrongful when it deviates from the moral standards that measure it and intentionally killing innocent people grossly deviates from the standard of solidarity that measures one's conduct in relation to others. Moreover, this deviation is one that falls squarely within the extension of the concept *murder*. This is why it is wrong to kill one individual as a means to saving the lives of five others. And the absolutists' claim is that the moral logic remains the same if killing one person is the necessary means to saving 100, or 1,000, or even 1,000,000 others.

In reply, a nonabsolutist could contend that while it is true that in normal circumstances calculations of utility do not override the prohibition on intentionally killing the innocent, when the consequences of not doing so are truly catastrophic, ordinary moral standards – including the standard of solidarity – cease to apply. An example of this sort of position is familiar from the literature on just war theory. Michael Walzer (2015, ch. 16) and John Rawls (1999, 98–9) claim that the *jus in bello* Principle of Noncombatant Immunity is subject to a "supreme emergency exemption," which says that the leaders of a political community are allowed deliberately to kill noncombatants if doing so is the only way to save the community from extinction or enslavement.

If we were ever so unfortunate as to find ourselves in circumstances in which it seemed that the only options were either deliberately to kill innocent people or face the extinction or enslavement of our community, then of course we would experience a strong *temptation* to do whatever it takes to ward off catastrophe. Anscombe would not disagree. She would also point out, however, that in the real world, as opposed to the moral dilemmas concocted by philosophers, the options are seldom so stark and binary, and that a practically wise leader might well be able to discern some other way out of the dilemma (1981a, 40n6). In any case, the question the moral absolutist will press is what *justifies* the view that ordinary moral standards lapse when grave consequences threaten should we refuse to commit murder.[2]

[2] The absolutist can, and should, hold that there is room for the distinction between justifications and excuses to do work here. If a military or political leader were to authorize deliberately killing innocent people in a situation of supreme emergency, the extreme duress of avoiding catastrophe might mean that the amount of blame he or she deserves is substantially mitigated, or even that we should forego blame altogether. But this is very different from saying that the murderous conduct he or she authorizes is not wrong.

References

Adams, Robert Merrihew. 1999. *Finite and Infinite Goods: A Framework for Ethics*. Oxford: Oxford University Press.

Alexander, David E. 2012. *Goodness, God and Evil*. London: Continuum.

Alexander, Larry. 2000. "Insufficient Concern: A Unified Conception of Criminal Culpability." *California Law Review* 88 (3): 931–54.

Alvarez, Maria. 2010. *Kinds of Reasons: An Essay in the Philosophy of Action*. Oxford: Oxford University Press.

American Law Institute. 1985. Model Penal Code: Official Draft and Explanatory Notes: Complete Text of the Model Penal Code as Adopted at the 1962 Annual Meeting of the American Law Institute at Washington, DC, May 24, 1962. Philadelphia: The Institute.

Anderson, Elizabeth. 1993. *Value in Ethics and Economics*. Cambridge, MA: Harvard University Press.

Anscombe, G. E. M. 1963. *Intention*. 2nd ed. Oxford: Basil Blackwell.

1981a. "Modern Moral Philosophy." In *The Collected Philosophical Papers of G. E. M. Anscombe, Volume 3: Ethics, Religion and Politics*, 26–42. Oxford: Basil Blackwell.

1981b. "Mr. Truman's Degree." In *The Collected Philosophical Papers of G. E. M. Anscombe, Volume 3: Ethics, Religion and Politics*, 62–71. Oxford: Basil Blackwell.

1981c. "The Justice of the Present War Examined." In *The Collected Philosophical Papers of G. E. M. Anscombe, Volume 3: Ethics, Religion and Politics*, 72–81. Oxford: Basil Blackwell.

1981d. "The Two Kinds of Error in Action." In *The Collected Philosophical Papers of G. E. M. Anscombe, Volume 3: Ethics, Religion and Politics*, 3–9. Oxford: Basil Blackwell.

1981e. "War and Murder." In *The Collected Philosophical Papers of G. E. M. Anscombe, Volume 3: Ethics, Religion and Politics*, 51–61. Oxford: Basil Blackwell.

2005a. "Action, Intention and 'Double Effect'." In *Human Life, Action and Ethics: Essays by G. E. M. Anscombe*, edited by Mary Geach and Luke Gormally, 207–26. Exeter: Imprint Academic.

2005b. "Knowledge and Reverence for Human Life." In *Human Life, Action and Ethics: Essays by G. E. M. Anscombe*, edited by Mary Geach and Luke Gormally, 59–66. Exeter: Imprint Academic.

2005c. "Murder and the Morality of Euthanasia." In *Human Life, Action and Ethics: Essays by G. E. M. Anscombe*, edited by Mary Geach and Luke Gormally, 261–78. Exeter: Imprint Academic.

2005d. "Practical Inference." In *Human Life, Action and Ethics: Essays by G. E. M. Anscombe*, edited by Mary Geach and Luke Gormally, 109–48. Exeter: Imprint Academic.

2005e. "Practical Truth." In *Human Life, Action and Ethics: Essays by G. E. M. Anscombe*, edited by Mary Geach and Luke Gormally, 149–58. Exeter: Imprint Academic.

2005f. "The Dignity of the Human Being." In *Human Life, Action and Ethics: Essays by G. E. M. Anscombe*, edited by Mary Geach and Luke Gormally, 67–73. Exeter: Imprint Academic.

2008. "Contraception and Chastity." In *Faith in a Hard Ground: Essays on Religion, Philosophy and Ethics by G. E. M. Anscombe*, edited by Mary Geach and Luke Gormally, 170–91. Exeter: Imprint Academic.

Aquinas, Thomas. 1947. *Summa Theologica*. Translated by the Fathers of the English Dominican Province. 5 vols. New York: Benziger Brothers.

Aristotle. 1984. *The Complete Works of Aristotle*. Edited by Jonathan Barnes. 2 vols. Princeton: Princeton University Press.

Audi, Robert. 2016. *Means, Ends, and Persons: The Meaning and Psychological Dimensions of Kant's Humanity Formula*. Oxford: Oxford University Press.

Awad, Edmond, Sohan Dsouza, Azim Shariff, Iyad Rahwan, and Jean-François Bonnefon. 2020. "Universals and Variants in Moral Decisions Made in 42 Countries by 70,000 Participants." *Proceedings of the National Academy of Sciences of the United States of America* 117 (5): 2332–7.

Ayars, Alisabeth. 2016. "Can Model-Free Reinforcement Learning Explain Deontological Moral Judgments?" *Cognition* 150: 232–42.

Baron, Marcia. 2005. "Justifications and Excuses." *Ohio State Journal of Criminal Law* 2 (2): 387–406.

Bayertz, Kurt. 1999. "Four Uses of 'Solidarity'." In *Solidarity*, edited by Kurt Bayertz, 3–28. Dordrecht: Springer.

Bennett, Jonathan. 1995. *The Act Itself*. Oxford: Oxford University Press.

Berker, Selim. 2009. "The Normative Insignificance of Neuroscience." *Philosophy and Public Affairs* 37 (4): 293–329.

Biggar, Nigel. 2013. *In Defense of War*. Oxford: Oxford University Press.

Blair, R. J. 1995. "A Cognitive Developmental Approach to Morality: Investigating the Psychopath." *Cognition* 57 (1): 1–29.

Bland, Larry, ed. 1991. *George C. Marshall Interviews and Remembrances for Forrest C. Pogue*. Lexington, VA: George C. Marshall Research Foundation.

Blum, Lawrence A. 1980. *Friendship, Altruism and Morality*. London: Routledge & Kegan Paul.

Bommarito, Nicolas. 2016. "Private Solidarity." *Ethical Theory and Moral Practice* 19 (2): 445–55.

Boyle, Joseph. 1980. "Toward Understanding the Principle of Double Effect." *Ethics* 90 (4): 527–38.

2004. "Medical Ethics and Double Effect: The Case of Terminal Sedation." *Theoretical Medicine and Bioethics* 25 (1): 51–60.

Brewer, Talbot. 2011. *The Retrieval of Ethics*. Oxford: Oxford University Press.

Broome, John. 2013. *Rationality through Reasoning*. Oxford: Wiley Blackwell.

Cavanaugh, T. A. 2006. *Double-Effect Reasoning: Doing Good and Avoiding Evil*. Oxford: Oxford University Press.

Chang, Ruth. 2015. "Value Incomparability and Incommensurability." In *The Oxford Handbook of Value Theory*, edited by Iwao Hirose and Jonas Olson, 205–24. Oxford: Oxford University Press.

Chappell, Timothy. 2011. "The Action-Omission and Double Effect Distinctions." In *Bioethics with Liberty and Justice: Themes in the Work of Joseph M. Boyle*, edited by Christopher Tollefsen, 113–41. Dordrecht: Springer.

Coady, C. A. J. 2008. *Morality and Political Violence*. Cambridge: Cambridge University Press.

Coates, A. J. 2016. *The Ethics of War*. 2nd ed. Manchester: Manchester University Press.

Conway, Paul and Bertram Gawronski. 2013. "Deontological and Utilitarian Inclinations in Moral Decision Making: A Process Dissociation Approach." *Journal of Personality and Social Psychology* 104 (2): 216–35.

Cowan, Howard. 1945. "Terror Bombing Gets Allied Approval as Step to Speed Victory." *Washington Star*, February 18, 1945, 1.

Crockett, Molly. 2013. "Models of Morality." *Trends in Cognitive Science* 17 (8): 363–6.

Cullity, Garrett. 2004. *The Moral Demands of Affluence*. Oxford: Oxford University Press.

Cureton, Adam. 2012. "Solidarity and Social Moral Rules." *Ethical Theory and Moral Practice* 15 (5): 691–706.

Cushman, Fiery. 2013. "Action, Outcome and Value: A Dual-System Framework for Morality." *Personality and Social Psychology Review* 17 (3): 273–92.

2016. "The Psychological Origins of the Doctrine of Double Effect." *Criminal Law and Philosophy* 10 (4): 763–76.

Cushman, Fiery and Ryan Miller. 2013. "Aversive for Me, Wrong for You: First-person Behavioral Aversions Underlie the Moral Condemnation of Harm." *Social Personality Psychology Compass* 7 (10): 707–18.

Cushman, Fiery, Liane Young, and Marc Hauser. 2006. "The Role of Conscious Reasoning and Intuition in Moral Judgment: Testing Three Principles of Harm." *Psychological Science* 17 (12): 1082–9.

Dancy, Jonathan. 2018. *Practical Shape: A Theory of Practical Reasoning*. Oxford: Oxford University Press.

D'Arcy, Eric. 1963. *Human Acts: An Essay in Their Moral Evaluation.* Oxford: Oxford University Press.

Darwall, Stephen. 2002. *Welfare and Rational Care.* Princeton: Princeton University Press.

Das, Ramon. 2003. "Virtue Ethics and Right Action." *Australasian Journal of Philosophy* 81 (3): 324–39.

Davidson, Donald. 1963. "Actions, Reasons, and Causes." *The Journal of Philosophy* 60 (23): 685–700.

Delaney, Neil. 2015. "The Doctrine of Double Effect: Some Remarks on Intention and Evaluation." *American Catholic Philosophical Quarterly* 89 (3): 397–406.

Di Nucci, Ezio. 2014. *Ethics without Intention.* London: Bloomsbury.

Doestoevsky, Fyodor. 2002. *The Brothers Karamazov.* Translated by Richard Peaver and Larissa Volokhonsky. New York: Farrar, Straus and Giroux.

Dressler, Joshua. 2018. *Understanding Criminal Law.* 8th ed. Durham, NC: Carolina Academic Press.

Duff, R. A. 1996. *Criminal Attempts.* Oxford: Oxford University Press.

2007. *Answering for Crime.* Oxford: Hart.

Duffy, Shane. 2007. "Obstetric Haemorrhage in Gimbie, Ethiopia." *The Obstetrician and Gynecologist* 9 (2): 121–6.

Evans, Jonathan. 2003. "In Two Minds: Dual-Process Accounts of Reasoning." *Trends in Cognitive Science* 7 (10): 454–9.

Fernandez, Patricio A. 2016. "Practical Reasoning: Where the Action Is." *Ethics* 126 (4): 869–900.

Finnis, John. 1980. *Natural Law and Natural Rights.* Oxford: Oxford University Press.

1983. *Fundamentals of Ethics.* Washington, DC: Georgetown University Press.

1991. *Moral Absolutes: Tradition, Revision, and Truth.* Washington, DC: The Catholic University of America Press.

1995. "A Philosophical Case against Euthanasia." In *Euthanasia Examined*, edited by John Keown, 23–35. Cambridge: Cambridge University Press.

1998. *Aquinas: Moral, Political, and Legal Theory.* Oxford: Oxford University Press.

2011a. "Human Acts." In *Intention and Identity: Collected Essays.* Vol. 2, 133–51. Oxford: Oxford University Press.

2011b. "Intention and Side Effects." In *Intention and Identity: Collected Essays.* Vol. 2, 173–97. Oxford: Oxford University Press.

2011c. "Intention in Direct Discrimination." In *Intention and Identity: Collected Essays.* Vol. 2, 269–75. Oxford: Oxford University Press

2013. "Reflections and Responses." In *Reason, Morality, and Law: The Philosophy of John Finnis*, edited by John Keown and Robert P. George, 459–584. Oxford: Oxford University Press.

Finnis, John, Joseph Boyle, and Germain Grisez. 1987a. *Nuclear Deterrence, Morality and Realism.* Oxford: Oxford University Press.

1987b. "Practical Principles, Moral Truth, and Ultimate Ends." *American Journal of Jurisprudence* 32 (1): 99–151.

2001. "'Direct' and 'Indirect': A Reply to Critics of Our Action Theory." *The Thomist* 65 (1): 1–44.

FitzPatrick, William J. 2003. "Acts, Intentions, and Moral Permissibility: In Defense of the Doctrine of Double Effect." *Analysis* 63 (4): 317–21.

2006. "The Intend/Foresee Distinction and The Problem of 'Closeness'." *Philosophical Studies* 128 (3): 585–617.

2012. "Intention, Permissibility, and Double Effect." In *Oxford Studies in Normative Ethics*. Vol. 2, edited by Mark Timmons, 97–127. Oxford: Oxford University Press.

Foot, Philippa. 2002. "The Problem of Abortion and the Doctrine of Double Effect." In *Virtues and Vices and Other Essays in Moral Philosophy*, 19–32. Oxford: Oxford University Press.

2008a. "Morality, Action, and Outcome." In *Moral Dilemmas and Other Topics in Moral Philosophy*, 88–104. Oxford: Oxford University Press.

2008b. "Utilitarianism and the Virtues." In *Moral Dilemmas and Other Topics in Moral Philosophy*, 59–77. Oxford: Oxford University Press.

Ford, Anton. 2016. "On What Is in Front of Your Nose." *Philosophical Topics* 44 (1): 141–61.

2017. "The Representation of Action." *Royal Institute of Philosophy Supplement* 80: 217–33.

Ford, John C. 1944. "The Morality of Obliteration Bombing." *Theological Studies* 5 (3): 261–309.

Frank, Richard B. 1999. *Downfall: The End of the Imperial Japanese Empire*. New York: Random House.

Freud, Sigmund. 1961a. *Civilization and Its Discontents*. Translated and edited by James Strachey. New York: W. W. Norton.

1961b. *The Future of an Illusion*. Translated and edited by James Strachey. New York: W. W. Norton.

Fried, Charles. 1978. *Right and Wrong*. Cambridge, MA: Harvard University Press.

Garcia, Jorge L. A. 1993. "The New Critique of Anti-Consequentialist Moral Theory." *Philosophical Studies* 71 (1): 1–32.

Garrett, Stephen. 2007. "Airpower and Non-combatant Immunity: The Road to Dresden." In *Civilian Immunity in War*, edited by Igor Primoratz, 161–81. Oxford: Oxford University Press.

2014. "The Bombing Campaign: The RAF." In *Terror from the Skies: The Bombing of German Cities in World War II*, edited by Igor Primoratz, 19–38. New York: Berghahn Books.

George, Robert P. 1999. *In Defense of Natural Law*. Oxford: Oxford University Press.

Gleichgerrcht, Ezequiel and Liane Young. 2013. "Low Levels of Emphatic Concern Predict Utilitarian Moral Judgment." *PLoS One* 8 (4): e60418.

Goldman, Alvin I. 1970. *A Theory of Human Action.* Englewood Cliffs, NJ: Prentice-Hall.

Gómez-Lobo, Alfonso. 2002. *Morality and the Human Goods.* Washington, DC: Georgetown University Press.

Gómez-Lobo, Alfonso and John Keown. 2015. *Bioethics and the Human Goods.* Washington, DC: Georgetown University Press.

Gormally, Luke. 2013. "Intention and Side Effects: John Finnis and Elizabeth Anscombe." In *Reason, Morality, and Law: The Philosophy of John Finnis*, edited by John Keown and Robert P. George, 93–108. Oxford: Oxford University Press.

2016. "On Killing Human Beings." In *The Moral Philosophy of Elizabeth Anscombe*, edited by Luke Gormally, David Albert Jones, and Roger Teichmann, 133–53. Exeter: Imprint Academic.

Grayling, A. C. 2006. *Among the Dead Cities: Is the Targeting of Civilians in War Ever Justified?* London: Bloomsbury.

Greene, Joshua D. 2008. "The Secret Joke of Kant's Soul." In *Moral Psychology, Volume 3: The Neuroscience of Morality: Emotion, Disease, and Development*, edited by Walter Sinnott-Armstrong, 35–79. Cambridge, MA: MIT Press.

2013. *Moral Tribes: Emotion, Reason, and the Gap between Us and Them.* New York: Penguin Press.

2014. "Beyond Point-and-Shoot Morality: Why Cognitive (Neuro)Science Matters for Ethics." *Ethics* 124 (4): 695–726.

2016. "Reply to Driver and Darwall." In *Moral Brains: The Neuroscience of Morality*, edited by S. Matthew Liao, 170–81. Oxford: Oxford University Press.

2017. "The Rat-a-gorical Imperative: Moral Intuition and the Limits of Affective Learning." *Cognition* 167: 66–77.

Greene, Joshua D., Fiery A. Cushman, Lisa E. Stewart, Kelly Lowenberg, Leigh E. Nystrom, and Jonathan D. Cohen. 2009. "Pushing Moral Buttons: The Interaction between Personal Force and Intention in Moral Judgment." *Cognition* 111 (3): 364–71.

Greenspan, Patricia. 2015. "Confabulating the Truth: In Defense of 'Defensive' Moral Reasoning." *Journal of Ethics* 19 (2): 105–23.

Grice, H. P. 1975. "Logic and Conversation." In *Syntax and Semantics, Volume 3: Speech Acts*, edited by Peter Cole and Jerry L. Morgan, 41–58. New York: Academic Press.

Grisez, Germain. 1993. *The Way of the Lord Jesus, Volume 2: Living A Christian Life.* Quincy: Franciscan Press.

Grotius, Hugo. 1949. *The Laws of War and Peace.* Translated by Louise Ropes Loomis. Roslyn, NY: Walter J. Black.

Guglielmo, Steve and Bertram F. Malle. 2010. "Can Unintended Side Effects Be Intentional? Resolving a Controversy Over Intentionality and Morality." *Personality and Social Psychology Bulletin* 36 (12): 1635–47.

Gury, Joannes. 1874. *Compendium Theologiae Moralis.* Regensburg: Georgii Josephi Manz.

Haidt, Jonathan. 2001. "The Emotional Dog and Its Rational Tail." *Psychology Review* 108 (4): 814–34.
Hannikainen, Ivar R., Edouard Machery, and Fiery A. Cushman. 2018. "Is Utilitarian Sacrifice Becoming More Morally Permissible?" *Cognition* 170: 95–101.
Hanser, Matthew. 2005. "Permissibility and Practical Inference." *Ethics* 115 (3): 443–70.
Hart, H. L. A. 2008. "Intention and Punishment." In *Punishment and Responsibility: Essays in the Philosophy of Law*, 113–35. Oxford: Oxford University Press.
Hartle, Anthony. 2004. *Moral Issues in Military Decision Making*. 2nd ed. Lawrence, KS: University Press of Kansas.
Hauser, Marc, Fiery Cushman, Liane Young, R. Kang-Xing Jin, and John Mikhail. 2007. "A Dissociation between Moral Judgments and Justifications." *Mind & Language* 22 (1): 1–21.
Herring, Jonathan. 2018. *Criminal Law: Text, Cases, and Materials*. 8th ed. Oxford: Oxford University Press.
Heuer, Ulrike. 2015. "Intentions, Permissibility, and the Reasons for Which We Act." In *Reasons and Intentions in Law and Practical Agency*, edited by George Pavlakos, 11–30. Cambridge: Cambridge University Press.
Holmes, Robert L. 1989. *On War and Morality*. Princeton: Princeton University Press.
Hornsby, Jennifer. 1980. *Actions*. London: Routledge & Kegan Paul.
Hume, David. 2006. *An Enquiry Concerning the Principles of Morals*. In *Moral Philosophy*, edited by Geoffrey Sayre-McCord, 185–310. Indianapolis, IN: Hackett Publishing Company.
Hurka, Thomas. 2005. "Proportionality in the Morality of War." *Philosophy and Public Affairs* 33 (1): 34–66.
Husak, Douglas. 2009. "The Cost to Criminal Theory of Supposing that Intentions Are Irrelevant to Permissibility." *Criminal Law and Philosophy* 3 (1): 51–70.
Hyman, John. 2015. *Action, Knowledge, and Will*. Oxford: Oxford University Press.
International Committee of the Red Cross. 2010. Protocols Additional to the Geneva Conventions of 12 August 1949. Geneva: ICRC.
International Criminal Court. 2011. Rome Statute of the International Criminal Court. The Hague. www.icc-cpi.int/resource-library/documents/rs-eng.pdf (accessed January 25, 2020).
Jensen, Steven J. 2014. "Causal Constraints on Intention: A Critique of Tollefsen on the Phoenix Case." *National Catholic Bioethics Quarterly* 14 (2): 273–93.
Johnson, James Turner. 1999. *Morality and Contemporary Warfare*. New Haven, CT: Yale University Press.
Joyce, Richard. 2006. *The Evolution of Morality*. Cambridge, MA: MIT Press.
Kagan, Shelly. 1991. *The Limits of Morality*. Oxford: Oxford University Press.
1998. *Normative Ethics*. Boulder, CO: Westview Press.

2001. "Thinking about Cases." *Social Philosophy and Policy* 18 (2): 44–63.
Kahneman, Daniel. 2011. *Thinking, Fast and Slow*. New York: Farrar, Straus & Giroux.
Kamm, Frances M. 1991. "The Doctrine of Double Effect: Reflections on Theoretical and Practical Issues." *Journal of Medicine and Philosophy* 16 (5): 571–85.
2000. "The Doctrine of Triple Effect and Why a Rational Agent Need Not Intend the Means to His End." *Aristotelian Society Supplementary* 74 (1): 21–39.
2004. "Failures of Just War Theory: Terror, Harm, and Justice." *Ethics* 114 (4): 650–92.
Kant, Immanuel. 1996a. *Groundwork of the Metaphysics of Morals*. In *Practical Philosophy*, translated and edited by Mary J. Gregor, 37–108. Cambridge: Cambridge University Press.
1996b. *The Metaphysics of Morals*. In *Practical Philosophy*, translated and edited by Mary J. Gregor, 353–603. Cambridge: Cambridge University Press.
Kaufman, Whitley. 2009. *Justified Killing: The Paradox of Self-Defense*. Lanham: Lexington Books.
2016. "The Doctrine of Double Effect and the Trolley Problem." *Journal of Value Inquiry* 50 (1): 21–31.
Kenny, Anthony. 1995. "Philippa Foot on Double Effect." In *Virtues and Reasons: Philippa Foot and Moral Theory*, edited by Rosalind Hursthouse, Gavin Lawrence, and Warren Quinn, 77–88. Oxford: Oxford University Press.
Kindhäuser, Urs, Ulfrid Neumann, and Hans-Ulrich Paeffgen. 2010. *Nomon Kommentar Strafgesetzbuch, Volume 2*. 3rd ed. Baden-Baden: Nomos Verlagsgesellschaft.
Knobe, Joshua. 2003. "Intentional Action and Side Effects in Ordinary Language." *Analysis* 63 (3): 190–4.
Kolodny, Niko. 2011. "Scanlon's Investigation: The Relevance of Intent to Permissibility." *Analytic Philosophy* 52 (2): 100–23.
Königs, Peter. 2018. "Two Types of Debunking Arguments." *Philosophical Psychology* 31 (3): 383–402.
Konstan, David. 1997. *Friendship in the Classical World*. Cambridge: Cambridge University Press.
Lackey, Douglas. 2014. "The Bombing Campaign: The USAAF." In *Terror from the Skies: The Bombing of German Cities in World War II*, edited by Igor Primoratz, 39–59. New York: Berghahn Books.
Lavin, Douglas. 2016. "Action as a Form of Temporal Unity: On Anscombe's Intention." *Canadian Journal of Philosophy* 45 (4–5): 609–29.
Lee, Patrick. 2017. "Distinguishing between What Is Intended and Foreseen Side Effects." *American Journal of Jurisprudence* 62 (2): 231–51.
2019. "The New Natural Law Theory." In *The Cambridge Companion to Natural Law Ethics*, edited by Tom Angier, 73–91. Cambridge: Cambridge University Press.

Lee, Patrick and Robert George. 2008. "The Nature and Basis of Human Dignity." *Ratio Juris* 21 (2): 173–93.

Levine, Sydney, Alan M. Leslie, and John Mikhail. 2018. "The Mental Representation of Human Action." *Cognitive Science* 42 (4): 1229–64.

Liao, S. Matthew. 2012. "Intentions and Moral Permissibility: The Case of Acting Permissibly with Bad Intentions." *Law and Philosophy* 31 (6): 703–24.

2016. "The Closeness Problem and the Doctrine of Double Effect: A Way Forward." *Criminal Law and Philosophy* 10 (4): 849–63.

2017. "Neuroscience and Ethics: Assessing Greene's Debunking Argument against Deontology." *Experimental Pyschology* 64 (2): 82–92.

Liao, S. Matthew, Alex Wiegmann, Joshua Alexander, and Gerard Vong. 2012. "Putting the Trolley in Order: Experimental Philosophy and the Loop Case." *Philosophical Psychology* 25 (5): 661–71.

Lillehammer, Hallvard. 2010. "Scanlon on Intention and Permissibility." *Analysis* 70 (3): 578–85.

Lippert-Rasmussen, Kasper. 2014. "Just War Theory, Intentions, and the Deliberative Perspective Objection." In *How We Fight: Ethics in War*, edited by Helen Frowe and Gerald Lang, 138–54. Oxford: Oxford University Press.

Lott, Micah. 2016. "Moral Implications from Cognitive (Neuro)Science? No Clear Route." *Ethics* 127 (1): 241–56.

Lyons, Edward C. 2013. "Slaughter of the Innocent: Justification, Excuse, and the Principle of Double Effect." *Berkeley Journal of Criminal Law* 18 (2): 231–316.

Mangan, Joseph. 1949. "An Historical Analysis of the Principle of Double Effect." *Theological Studies* 10 (1): 41–61.

Marcus, Eric. 2019. "Reconciling Practical Knowledge with Self-Deception." *Mind* 128 (512): 1205–25.

Masek, Lawrence. 2018. *Intention, Character, and Double Effect*. Notre Dame, IN: University of Notre Dame Press.

Mason, Andrew. 2000. *Community, Solidarity and Belonging*. Cambridge: Cambridge University Press.

McCarthy, David. 2002. "Intending Harm, Foreseeing Harm, and Failures of the Will." *Noûs* 36 (4): 622–42.

McDowell, John. 2010. "What Is the Content of an Intention in Action?" *Ratio* 23 (4): 415–32.

McIntyre, Alison. 2001. "Doing Away with Double Effect." *Ethics* 111 (2): 219–55.

McMahan, Jeff. 2004. "The Ethics of Killing in War." *Ethics* 114 (4): 693–733.

2009. "Intention, Permissibility, Terrorism, and War." *Philosophical Perspectives* 23: 345–72.

Mikhail, John. 2011. *Elements of Moral Cognition: Rawls' Linguistic Analogy and the Cognitive Science of Moral and Legal Judgment*. Cambridge: Cambridge University Press.

Miscamble, Wilson D. 2011. *The Most Controversial Decision: Truman, the Atomic Bomb, and the Defeat of Japan.* Cambridge: Cambridge University Press.
Mourelatos, Alexander P. D. 1978. "Events, Processes, and States." *Linguistics and Philosophy* 2 (3): 415–34.
Murphy, Mark C. 2001. *Natural Law and Practical Rationality*. Cambridge: Cambridge University Press.
2004. "Intention, Foresight, and Success." In *Human Values: New Essays on Ethics and Natural Law*, edited by David S. Oderberg and Timothy Chappell, 252–68. New York: Palgrave Macmillian.
Nagel, Thomas. 1986. *The View from Nowhere.* Oxford: Oxford University Press.
Nathanson, Stephen. 2010. *Terrorism and the Ethics of War.* Cambridge: Cambridge University Press.
Nelkin, Dana Kay and Samuel C. Rickless. 2015. "So Close Yet So Far: Why Solutions to the Closeness Problem to the Doctrine of Double Effect Fall Short." *Noûs* 49 (2): 376–409.
Newman, Robert P. 1995. *Truman and the Hiroshima Cult.* East Lansing: Michigan State University Press.
Norcross, Alastair. 1999. "Intending and Foreseeing Death: Potholes on the Road to Hell." *Southwest Philosophy Review* 15 (1): 115–23.
Nye, Howard. 2013. "Objective Double Effect and the Avoidance of Narcissism." In *Oxford Studies in Normative Ethics*. Vol. 3, edited by Mark Timmons, 260–86. Oxford: Oxford University Press.
Orend, Brian. 2013. *The Morality of War*, 2nd ed. Petersborough: Broadview Press.
Otsuka, Michael. 2008. "Double Effect, Triple Effect and the Trolley Problem: Squaring the Circle in Looping Cases." *Utilitas* 20 (1): 92–110.
Øverland, Gerhard. 2014. "Moral Obstacles: An Alternative to the Principle of Double Effect." *Ethics* 124 (3): 481–506.
2016. "Why Kamm's Principle of Secondary Permissibility Cannot Save the Doctrine of Double Effect." *Journal of Applied Philosophy* 33 (3): 286–96.
Perkins, David N., Michael Faraday, and Barbara Bushey. 1991. "Everyday Reasoning and the Roots of Intelligence." In *Informal Reasoning and Education*, edited by James F. Voss, David N. Perkins, and Judith W. Segal, 83–105. Hillsdale, NJ: Erlbaum.
Perkins, Rollin M. 1934. "A Re-Examination of Malice Aforethought." *Yale Law Review* 43 (4): 537–70.
Plato. 1999. *Gorgias*. Translated by W. D. Woodhead. In *The Collected Dialogues of Plato*, edited by Edith Hamilton and Huntington Cairns, 229–307. Princeton: Princeton University Press.
Primoratz, Igor. 2007. "Civilian Immunity in War: Its Grounds, Scope, and Weight." In *Civilian Immunity in War*, edited by Igor Primoratz, 21–41. Oxford: Oxford University Press.
2013. *Terrorism: A Philosophical Investigation.* Cambridge: Polity Press.
Pruss, Alexander. 2013. "The Accomplishment of Plans: A New Version of the Principle of Double Effect." *Philosophical Studies* 165 (1): 49–69.

Quinn, Warren. 1993a. “Actions, Intentions, and Consequences: The Doctrine of Double Effect.” In *Morality and Action*, 175–93. Cambridge: Cambridge University Press.

1993b. “Reply to Boyle’s ‘Who Is Entitled to Double Effect?’” In *Morality and Action*, 194–7, Cambridge: Cambridge University Press.

Rachels, James. 1986. *The End of Life: Euthanasia and Morality*. Oxford: Oxford University Press.

Ramsey, Paul. 1968. *The Just War: Force and Political Responsibility*. New York: Scribner.

Rawls, John. 1999. *The Laws of Peoples*. Cambridge, MA: Harvard University Press.

Rich, Ben A. 2001. *Strange Bedfellows: How Medical Jurisprudence Has Influenced Medical Ethics and Medical Practice*. New York: Kluwer Academic.

Riisfeldt, Thomas David. 2019. “Weakening the Distinction between Euthanasia, Palliative Opiod Use and Palliative Sedation.” *Journal of Medical Ethics* 45 (2): 125–30.

Rorty, Richard. 1989. “Solidarity.” In *Contingency, Irony, and Solidarity*, 189–98. Cambridge: Cambridge University Press.

Rosen, Michael. 2012. *Dignity: Its History and Meaning*. Cambridge, MA: Harvard University Press.

Ross, W. D. 1930. *The Right and the Good*. Oxford: Oxford University Press.

Scanlon, T. M. 1998. *What We Owe to Each Other*. Cambridge, MA: Harvard University Press.

2008. *Moral Dimensions: Permissibility, Meaning, Blame*. Cambridge, MA: Harvard University Press.

Schafer, Karl. 2017. “Evolutionary Debunking Arguments, Explanatory Structure, and Anti-Realism.” In *Ethical Sentimentalism: New Perspectives*, edited by Remy Debes and Karsten R. Steuber, 66–85. Cambridge: Cambridge University Press.

Schwarzenbach, Sibyl A. 2015. “Fraternity, Solidarity, and Civic Friendship.” *Amity: The Journal of Friendship Studies* 3 (1): 3–18.

Schwenkler, John. 2019. *Anscombe’s* Intention*: A Guide*. Oxford: Oxford University Press.

Schwitzgebel, Eric, and Fiery A. Cushman. 2012. “Expertise in Moral Reasoning? Order Effects on Moral Judgment in Professional Philosophers and Nonphilosophers.” *Mind and Language* 27 (2): 135–53.

Setiya, Kieran. 2012. *Knowing Right from Wrong*. Oxford: Oxford University Press.

Shaw, Joseph. 2006a. “Intention in Ethics.” *Canadian Journal of Philosophy* 36 (2): 187–223.

2006b. “Intentions and Trolleys.” *The Philosophical Quarterly* 56 (222): 63–83.

Sidgwick, Henry. 1907. *The Methods of Ethics*. 7th ed. London: Macmillian.

Singer, Peter. 1972. “Famine, Affluence, and Morality.” *Philosophy and Public Affairs* 1 (3): 229–43.

Singer, Tania and Olga M. Klimecki. 2014. "Empathy and Compassion." *Current Biology* 24 (18): R875–8.

Slote, Michael. 2001. *Morals from Motives*. Oxford: Oxford University Press.

Smart, J. J. C. 1973. "An Outline of a System of Utilitarian Ethics." In *Utilitarianism: For and Against*, 3–74. Cambridge: Cambridge University Press.

Solomon, W. David. 2019. "Elizabeth Anscombe and the Late Twentieth-Century Revival of Virtue Ethics." In *Beyond the Self: Virtue Ethics and the Problem of Culture*, edited by Raymond Hain, 223–44. Waco: Baylor University Press.

Stanovich, Keith E., and Richard F. West. 2000. "Individual Differences in Reasoning: Implications for the Rationality Debate?" *Behavioral and Brain Sciences* 23 (5): 645–65.

Steinhoff, Uwe. 2018a. "Bennett, Intention and the DDE – The Sophisticated Bomber as Pseudo-Problem." *Analysis* 78 (1): 73–80.

2018b. "The Secret to the Success of the Doctrine of Double Effect (and Related Principles): Biased Framing, Inadequate Methodology, and Clever Distractions." *Journal of Ethics* 22 (3–4): 235–63.

2019. "Wild Goose Chase: Still No Rationales for the Doctrine of Double Effect and Related Principles." *Criminal Law and Philosophy* 13 (1): 1–25.

Stimson, Henry L. 1947. "The Decision to Use the Atomic Bomb." *Harper's Magazine* 194: 97–107.

Stjernø, Steinar. 2004. *Solidarity in Europe: The History of an Idea*. Cambridge: Cambridge University Press.

Strawson, P. F. 1974. "Freedom and Resentment." In *Freedom and Resentment and Other Essays*, 1–25. London: Methuen.

Street, Sharon 2006. "A Darwinian Dilemma for Realist Theories of Value." *Philosophical Studies* 127 (1): 109–66.

Stuchlik, Joshua. 2012. "A Critique of Scanlon on Double Effect." *Journal of Moral Philosophy* 9 (2): 178–99.

2017. "The Closeness Problem for Double Effect: A Reply to Nelkin and Rickless." *Journal of Value Inquiry* 51 (1): 69–83.

Suárez, Francisco. 1944. *A Work on the Three Theological Virtues, Disputation XIII: On Charity*. In *Three Works by Francisco Suárez, S.J*, edited by Gwladys L. Williams, Ammi Brown, and John Waldron, 799–865. Oxford: Oxford University Press.

Sullivan, Thomas D. and Atkinson, Gary. 1985. "Benevolence and Absolute Prohibitions." *International Philosophical Quarterly* 25 (3): 247–59.

Sverdlik, Steven. 2011. *Motive and Rightness*. Oxford: Oxford University Press.

Tadros, Victor. 2011. *The Ends of Harm: The Moral Foundations of Criminal Law*. Oxford: Oxford University Press.

2015. "Wrongful Intentions without Closeness." *Philosophy and Public Affairs* 43 (1): 52–74.

Thompson, Michael. 2008. *Life and Action*. Cambridge, MA: Harvard University Press.

Thomson, Judith Jarvis. 1976. "Killing, Letting Die, and the Trolley Problem." *The Monist* 59 (2): 204–17.

1985. "The Trolley Problem." *Yale Law Review* 94 (6): 1395–415.

1991. "Self-Defense." *Philosophy and Public Affairs* 20 (4): 283–310.

1999. "Physician-Assisted Suicide: Two Moral Arguments." *Ethics* 109 (3): 497–518.

2008. *Normativity*. Chicago: Open Court.

Tollefsen, Christopher. 2006. "Is a Purely First Person Account of Human Action Defensible?" *Ethical Theory and Moral Practice* 9 (4): 441–60.

Vitoria, Francisco de. 2001. *On the Law of War*. In *Francisco de Vitoria: Political Writings*, edited by Anthony Padgen and Jeremy Lawrence, 293–327. Cambridge: Cambridge University Press.

Vogler, Candace. 2002. *Reasonably Vicious*. Cambridge, MA: Harvard University Press.

Walzer, Michael. 2015. *Just and Unjust Wars*. 5th ed. New York: Basic Books.

Wedgwood, Ralph. 2009. "Intrinsic Values and Reasons for Action." *Philosophical Issues* 19: 321–42.

2011a. "Defending Double Effect." *Ratio* 24 (4): 384–401.

2011b. "Scanlon on Double Effect." *Philosophy and Phenomenological Research* 83 (2): 464–72.

Weir, Peter, director. 2005. *Master and Commander: The Far Side of the World*. Beverly Hills: 20th Century Fox Home Entertainment.

Wiggins, David. 1998. "*The Right and the Good* and W.D. Ross's Criticism of Consequentialism." *Utilitas* 10 (3): 261–80.

2009. *Ethics: Twelve Lectures on the Philosophy of Morality*. Cambridge, MA: Harvard University Press.

Wiseman, Rachael. 2016. *The Routledge Philosophy Guidebook to Anscombe's* Intention. London: Routledge.

Zamir, Eyal and Barak Medina. 2010. *Law, Economics, and Morality*. Oxford: Oxford University Press.

Zhao, Michael. 2019. "Solidarity, Fate-Sharing, and Community." *Philosophers' Imprint* 19 (46): 1–13.

Index

Milton Keynes UK
Ingram Content Group UK Ltd.
UKHW020303281023
431487UK00018B/90

9 781009 015738